MARGINALIZED PLACES AND POPULATIONS

Marginalized Places and Populations

A STRUCTURATIONIST AGENDA

EDITED BY

David Wilson and James O. Huff

PRAEGER

Westport, Connecticut
London

Library of Congress Cataloging-in-Publication Data

Marginalized places and populations : a structurationist agenda /
  edited by David Wilson and James O. Huff.
     p. cm.
   Includes bibliographical references and index.
   ISBN 0–275–94614–2 (alk. paper)
    1. Equality. 2. Geography, Economic. 3. Social structure.
  4. Income distribution. I. Wilson, David. II. Huff,
  James O.
  HM146.M37   1994
  305—dc20   93–32900

British Library Cataloguing in Publication Data is available.

Library of Congress Catalog Card Number: 93–32900
ISBN: 0–275–94614–2

First published in 1994

Praeger Publishers, 88 Post Road West, Westport, CT 06881
An imprint of Greenwood Publishing Group, Inc.

Printed in the United States of America

The paper used in this book complies with the
Permanent Paper Standard issued by the National
Information Standards Organization (Z39.48—1984).

10 9 8 7 6 5 4 3 2 1

Copyright Acknowledgment

An earlier version of Chapter 1 originally appeared in Adam Moos and Michael Dear,
Structuration theory in urban analysis: 1. Theoretical exegesis, *Environment and
Planning A* 8 (1986): 231–252. Reprinted by permission of Pion Press Limited.

This book is dedicated to Matthew and Andrew and to Betsy and David.

Contents

Illustrations

Preface

This book probes the empirical dimensions of Anthony Giddens's structuration theory for geographers and other concerned social scientists. We do not seek to persuade the reader of the value of structuration theory. Instead, we offer a wide-ranging glimpse into how this theory is currently being applied by geographers to understand contemporary societal inequalities. In this vein, we have asked a diverse group of geographers to employ structuration as a way of gaining insight into a specific issue that they have chosen to explore. We leave the decision up to you—the reader—to decide whether structuration theory has something to contribute to studies of social inequalities and how this theory might be fruitfully applied.

In the two years it has taken to compile this collection, a host of individuals have helped us. We would like to thank first and foremost the contributors to the book for their intellectual contributions, as well as their important commentary as the book evolved. Collectively, we would like to thank Mary Oberg for her diligence, patience, and forbearance as well as her high professional standards. Jim Huff also thanks Anne Huff, the ultimate in an editor's editor. David Wilson thanks Mary Anne and the boys for their patience and inspiration in the face of many late-night reading and writing sessions.

Introduction: Contemporary Human Geography—The Emergence of Structuration in Inequality Research

David Wilson and James O. Huff

I

Persistent inequalities in the well-being of peoples and places continue to characterize advanced capitalist societies. Here a complex web of entrenched forces— business cycle fluctuations, uneven development at diverse spatial scales, differential access to status and wealth across populations—have generated deeply rooted inequalities that continue to defy simple capitalist policy prescriptions. Indeed, their observable manifestations (inner-city neighborhood decay, growing poverty, a widening wealth gap, the sustained racial and gender discrimination in the workplace) suggest to some that many of these societies are now teetering on the brink of crisis. Whether this point is correct is certainly worthy of debate; it is sufficient to note in this introduction that in the face of this reality growing inequality has recently been put back on the mainstream agenda in the social sciences.

These social and geographical divisions materially affect the life chances of individuals who have been unjustly marginalized on the basis of their race, ethnicity, gender, or class. If we are to redress these inequalities effectively, it is essential that we first understand the mechanisms by which such inequalities are societally generated and maintained. A key premise of this book is that the social construction of inequality is intimately bound up with processes that divide, exclude, and subordinate people and places based on socially defined differences in race, place, gender, and class. What we propose to investigate is just *how* these social and spatial processes interact to create marginalized places and populations.

This book is about the forces and processes that continue to sustain pervasive inequalities in modern capitalist societies. What distinguishes the book from others on related topics is our focus on structurationist theory and methodology as a means of examining the geographic causes and consequences of subordination, isolation, and marginalization. Two themes are interwoven throughout the chapters that follow. The first deals with the diverse array of inequalities that currently afflict peoples and places. This focus involves empirically assessing issues ranging from gender discrimination to uneven state resource provision. The second theme centers around the rise of structuration theory in geography and how this approach may be applied to comprehend inequalities. Structuration theory, briefly stated, is an emergent and evolving body of theory originally expounded by Anthony Giddens (1979, 1981, 1984) that seeks to confront the relation between agency and structure in the social sciences. Many have argued that this ambitious project has paved the way for a bold restructuring of social research, taking the best principles from a range of perspectives and dramatically reworking them to create the rudiments of a new canon in social theory (cf. Bauman 1989; Cohen 1987).

Giddens's wide-ranging body of theory has recently been reviewed mainly for its theoretical coherence and consistency, but to date has been less critically scrutinized as a framework to guide empirical analysis (exceptions include Gregson 1986, 1989; Thrift 1986). This book contributes to the growing body of writing that is now addressing this shortcoming of structuration theory in a critical but constructive way. Our first focus is on the application of structuration theory—how it can be done, how it has been done, and whether it yields something different and important when compared with previous structural theories. The core of the book, therefore, is quite different from recent edited collections by Held and Thompson (1989) and Bryant and Jary (1991) that range across the vast theoretical terrain of structuration in an attempt to probe its theoretical robustness. We believe our agenda is important. To borrow from Gregson (1989, 237), "any form of critical social theory must engage with the concrete social world; and in a permanent rather than transitory, glancing manner." Or, as Giddens himself (1984, xxix) noted, "social theory has the task of providing conceptions of the nature of human social activity which can be placed in the service of empirical work" (from Gregson, 1989).

This book also examines the empirical dimensions of structuration for one specific discipline, geography. While this tack is less frequently taken in an age that often prefers to supersede "artificial" disciplinary boundaries, we felt a special need to offer something useful to geographers. The discipline of geography was one of the last social sciences to take critical social theory seriously; its prolonged preoccupation with cataloging regional differences and forging spatial analytic laws occurred at a time when most other disciplines had abandoned defensive quests to produce discipline-specific core concepts. While today geographers have actively jumped into the critical theory fray, this work has often been less probing and penetrating than work in other fields. In this context, geographers have frequently found structuration theory and the growing body of reviews about it daunting and obscure. We hope to narrow this chasm with this volume, by presenting a diverse body of empirical applications done by geographers for fellow practitioners to scrutinize. At issue in our exposition is the importance and applicability of structuration theory as it is increasingly being used to shed new light on issues of inequalities in capitalist societies.

II

The sources for persistent inequalities under capitalism may have deeply entrenched and far-flung roots, but it is at the scale of local places and settings that these forces are poignantly felt. Here, inequality collides with local tapestries of cultures and meanings to generate rich differences in how people live, work, think, and reflect on their condition. At this level, "people grow up, live, and die, interconnect with one another, and defend (or offend) the places in which they live" (Logan and Molotch 1987, 99). In the local context, inequalities reverberate across everyday life in multiple and unexpected ways. Daily life paths routinely mix with such things as occupational wage levels, opportunities for satisfying (and unsatisfying) employment, availability of safe and nurturing social fabrics, and qualities of social and educational institutions. It follows that the human production of inequality structures far more than the consumptive gratification of people; this process affects people's feelings about their daily round, their search for meaning in local settings, and their visions for future prospects and opportunities.

Despite the persistence of these forces, geographers have only recently made them a focus for research. With growing disillusionment about spatial analysis and its pursuit of frozen universal geometries after 1970, geographers became acutely aware of a nonequilibrated world. Further spurred to throw off the yoke of nonpolitical spatial analytics by the unpopular Vietnam War and the theatrics of Watergate, landscapes became increasingly seen as places of despoliation, racism, and poverty. The quasi revolution that restructured the subject matter of human geography quickly inserted into the disciplinary matrix a concern for praxis and everyday living. Kasperson (1971, 13) captured the intensity and excitement of this subject matter shift, noting that "this shift in the objects of study of geography from supermarkets and highways to poverty and racism has already begun, and we can expect it to continue, for the goals of geography are changing."

While the evolution of inequality studies in geography has demonstrated a growing theoretical sophistication, the initial flirtation proved superficial and theoretically problematic. Two lines of analysis were discernable. In the first,

scholars embraced neoclassical liberal tenets in examining the sources and solutions to problems like crime, poverty, and uneven development. Capitalist
societies tended to be seen as self-regulating systems that sporadically generated
negative consequences for select populations and places during periods of temporary disequilibrium. Such studies, moreover, frequently clung to a conception
of benevolent state apparatuses, where government interventions were believed
to be compelled by welfare state altruism. At the heart of this approach was the
assumption that governments were capable of enacting programs and policies
that could substantially eradicate social inequalities.

A second line of inquiry, emerging parallel to these neoclassical studies,
focused on the descriptive attributes of inequality. These studies sometimes
embraced variants of phenomenology, but mainly provided simple empirical
accounts of inequality—its magnitude, spatial dimensions, and impacts on the
psychological profiles of subjects. In this descriptive vein, geographers focused
on such projects as mapping differences in material well-being, charting intraur-
ban levels of residential discrimination, and cataloging personalized responses
to oppression and depravity. Here, geographers were projected as technical
experts who could generate information on which more equitable social planning
could be based. Once government was made aware of the magnitude and intensity
of deprivation, effective ameliorative efforts could purportedly follow.

By the late 1970s, geographers were ready for a change. Spurred by the small
core of Marxist and managerialist advocates who were calling for more rigorous
theorizing and a need to consider society as constrictive and penetratingly pol-
iticized, a brief period of Weberian-inspired research followed. This work, briefly
stated, emphasized the variables of supply and constraint in seeking to understand
the roots of societal inequalities. Managers and institutions were cast as key
entities of examination; they were seen to control scarce societal resources that
structured the life chances of people and places. Borrowing from Weber, two
key theoretical principles guided this work: that there is a weak relationship
between economic class and politics; and that government bureaucracies come
to dominate in modern societies. Unlike previous research approaches to inequality, power and politics became explicit dimensions of inquiry that moved
scholarly interest away from issues of choice and preference and toward notions
of resource distribution and control.

This research trend, however, was quickly muffled by the dramatic rise of
Marxist-inspired inquiry. David Harvey, more than anyone else, was responsible
for the simultaneous submergence of managerialism and the rise of Marxist
inquiry. Almost immediately, his blistering attack on managerialism as naively
reductionist and empiricist at the Conference on Urban Conflict and Change in
England in 1975 helped sway a coterie of progressive scholars to look elsewhere
at a pivotal time of competing research trends in human geography. His point,
simply put, was that "if one tries to abstract them [local managers] as autonomous
units, rather than relating them to a general conception of the political economy
of urbanization, then the whole point of studying these people is lost." Harvey

maintained that politics and economics in capitalist societies were ceaselessly interwoven. Since the materialist roots of society reverberated in every corner of social life, academic distinctions between politics and economics were superficial. To Harvey, a focus on local managers as autonomous agents naively ignored the larger structuring influence of economic forces whose power was rooted in the dialectics of capitalist development.

Harvey's provocative 1970s work further influenced the discipline to move in a relatively uncharted direction. He championed a structuralist approach to understanding capitalist society. His goal from the outset was to broaden a powerful Marxist tradition in the social sciences by addressing the neglected issue of how capitalism produces its own unique geographies. By placing concepts of spatial structure at the center of his analysis, his dramatic extensions of theory on the capitalist state (*Antipode* 1976) and rent extraction in the urban environment (*Regional Studies* 1974) demonstrated the power and persuasiveness of Marxist analysis. To a new generation of geographers, here was a body of theory capable of looking beneath the veneer of capitalist superficialities to expose the underlying mechanisms that generated inequality. The quest for deep-rooted mechanisms of deeply layered causalities struck a responsive epistemological chord among many who had been weaned on the pursuit of empirical regularities across a politically faceless globe.

Early Marxist work in geography could best be characterized as structuralist-functionalist and antiempiricist (cf. Hansis 1975; Hudson 1977). Works ranged in scope from neighborhood segregation to third world environmental degradation and drew on a concept of structures rooted in the functional wholes of capitalist systems to explain the production of inequality. These works, often opting to ignore the place-specific aspects of inequality, sought to uncover a science of capitalist societies. They searched for regularities in the trajectory of capitalism that made the system inherently exploitive and generative of inequality. Early works were not antiempiricist in the sense of not doing empirical work; rather, observable phenomena were cast as essentially reflective of underlying causal processes rather than generative of causal processes. Agents and localities tended to be seen as carriers of causation rather than as active participants in the creation of causation.

Gradually, as manifested in David Harvey's (1979, 1981) and Neal Smith's (1982, 1984) work on urban restructuring in the early 1980s, a more place-sensitive Marxist treatment of inequalities arose in geography. These works reflected a shifting structuralist form of analysis that was more attuned to the richness and diversity of places, a trend that culminated in the rise of the well-publicized locality studies debate in the late 1980s. Capitalist forces emanating from the logic of functional wholes were now seen as forces refracted through the complex lens of local cultures, places, and dominant biographies. Actors were increasingly portrayed as active constructors of inequality who were capable of reflexive action and engendering positive change. In this scheme, an array of actors—growth coalitions, housing advocacy agencies, tenant groups, local unions, and the like—became fruitful analytical subjects for their ability to restructure local conditions in unique and unpredictable ways.

This refashioned Marxist geography spawned a newfound appreciation for empiricism that recognized the need to mold theoretical categories to the specifics of place and locality. One research strand, for example, invoked a geological metaphor, conceiving of places as restructured in layers of capitalist processes that intersected with contingent historical specificities. A leading proponent of this approach, Doreen Massey (1983, 1984), presented places as repositories of past capitalist "deposits" that were ceaselessly restructured by successive "rounds of investment." In another research strand undertaken by geographers, preconfigured capitalist structures that "contextualized" everyday life were seen to fuse with local "interactionist" structures that represented active constructions of individuals. From this perspective people were critical mediators of broad-based processes by reflexively interpreting their local conditions and needs. The pioneer of this novel approach, Derek Layder (1981), asserted that places vary widely in their social and political cultures, but share the commonality of being conditioned by penetrative capitalist imperatives.

Issues of humanly constructed space and place found themselves increasingly on the Marxist research agenda after 1980. Places were no longer seen as simple passive creations of a powerful capitalist order, but were now complex store-houses for human idiosyncrasy whose active essence built and was built by capitalist structures. Space also became an object of intense scrutiny under the proposition that its complex structuring was rooted in a materialist logic that permeated capitalist society. This materialist interpretation of spatiality (Soja 1985, 1989) sought to extricate the interconnections between space, ideology, resources, and power in order to connect spatial fabrics with evolving capitalist processes. Space took on a distinctive form as a socially produced essence and as a set of relationships between groups and individuals. At the same time, the dictum that to be alive was to participate in the production and reproduction of everyday life now began to receive more serious attention from geographers after years of being submerged by structuralist analysis.

With the development of more place-sensitive Marxist inquiry, previous reliance on marcoscale structures to explain local inequalities was balanced by approaches that more rigorously incorporated the influence of local agents and less totalizing processes (see postmodern critiques by Curry 1991; Dear 1986). Critics of this "agency oriented Marxism," however, were not fully satisfied: they contended that even neo-Marxism failed to conceptualize the relativity of everyday life, failed to capture how actions and processes are set in a turbulent and disorderly world. The complexities of local life—the construction of symbolic worlds, the production of acts that have unintended consequences, and the quest for a whole host of nonmaterialist things in everyday life—generate unpredictable human acts that elude the theoretical categories of restructured Marxism. This serious criticism moved the paradigmatic debate beyond the longstanding charge that Marxism was crassly economistic. In response, a range of approaches have sought to sharpen the connections between conceptions of structure and complex local life. Anthony Giddens's structuration theory has, to date, attracted the most attention as a foundation for this new work.

III

The emergence of Anthony Giddens's structuration theory in the early 1980s touched off much critical debate in the social sciences. Giddens's project is ambitious; he seeks nothing less than to restructure the core of social theory by critically reassessing the structure-agency debate and articulating a new theoretical canon for theorists to follow. At the heart of his wide-ranging theoretical exposition is the elaboration of a hermeneutically informed social theory, a project that entails supplanting the traditional dualism of social life as being guided by either impersonal structures or free agency. Giddens is quick to reject the structuralist view that everyday life is a predictably patterned essence emerging from overarching figurations. He is equally dismissive of the generic hermeneutic perspectives that agents are unfettered voluntarists who deploy full knowledgeability in generating everyday life. Giddens's project thus strikes at the very foundation of current debate in social theory; it is deeply relevant in a world of turbulent theorizing that continues to dichotomize this artificially constructed dualism.

Giddens's project, briefly stated, is to generate coherent propositions that capture the importance of both agents and the broader society in producing everyday life. He relies on key theoretical insights from social theory while reworking some of its basic propositions. As Bauman (1989, 36) observes, structuration "promises to sift out valuable finds from the recent expedition and mark the tracks which proved blind; but it promises as well to salvage precious elements of the old tradition only too hastily abandoned and condemned in the universal stampede towards new-found fad idols." In borrowing the institutional emphasis in functionalism but discarding its numbing ontological linearity; in appropriating conceptions of boundedness and material reality from structuralism but rejecting its negation of human agency; in seizing on the importance of reflexive and active agents from hermeneutics but turning aside its marginalizing of social context Giddens cleverly patches together the rudiments of a theoretical framework that captures diverse elements of competing theories. He does not stop here, however.

Giddens adds substantial flesh to this skeletal outline by deeply rethinking the notions of structure and agency (see Thompson 1989). Out of this endeavor, he creates the centerpiece of structuration theory, the duality of structure, as the force that produces and reproduces the fabric of everyday social life. By the duality of structure, Giddens (1976, 121) means that "social structures are both constituted by human agency, and yet at the same time are the very medium of this constitution." The duality of structure, therefore, elucidates the recursive character of social life—that is, the power of situated practices to reproduce and rearrange the conditions that lead to the unbroken flow of new situated practices. Concepts of structure and agency now take on a very different meaning, one that runs contrary to past conventional theorizing, by being presented as mutually interpenetrated and transformative.

Giddens's casting of structure is arguably the most dramatic element of the duality of structure concept. As Thompson (1989) notes, few concepts in the social sciences are more basic and yet more ambiguous. The notion of macroscale informing impulses is supplanted by a notion of localized rules and resources that have only a virtual existence as they are tapped by individuals amid everyday living. Whereas structures were previously seen as something akin to skeletons of a system that girded the local from above, they now become resource fragments that permeate local life through the social positions of institutions. Structures now are characterized less as binding and defining than as penetrating social life; they are fleeting and instantiated elements that influence as much through the taken-for-granted world of the subconscious and unacknowledged custom as through the visible and corporeal. To Giddens, structural influences are not imperatives that hasten action; they are instantiated resources that people often unknowingly draw on in the everyday acts of signifying, dominating, and legitimizing local life.

Giddens has recently situated his structuration theory in a more sophisticated context by recognizing richly differentiated time-space intersections between and within places (see 1985, 283–289; 1989, 275–282). This work recognizes the superficiality of casting space and time as mere contexts for the unfolding of complex local life. Instead, he presents time-space as constantly implicated in the production of local life. All interactions purportedly reflect time-space distancing; they mix together sets of presences and absences that help mold the content of human interplay. Giddens has been particularly concerned with examining the ways in which time-space linkages connect with the production of power. He sees that modern life, marked by rapidity of communication, temporal conjoining of far-flung places, and increased political homogeneity across global ''villages,'' has increased opportunities for successful regulation and surveillance of places. To Giddens, time-space linkages must be a factor thrust to the forefront if scholars are to understand the current power of nation-states and the threat of totalitarian political rule.

We believe that, in the final analysis, structuration theory should be seen as a wide-ranging set of propositions whose purpose is to guide the scholarly dissection of local life in diverse settings. We agree with Gregory's (1989, 183) assessment that this theory ''appears as a loose-knit web of propositions, some more central than others, some spun more tightly than others.'' As Giddens has been quick to note, structuration is neither a concrete set of explanatory categories nor a body of theory to be used to generate lawlike principles. Instead, we have before us a diverse set of unevenly developed propositions, analogous to something like Lakatos's (1978) notion of a research program, that provides a base of principles on which we can draw to help inform analysis. Critics of structuration are right in pinpointing its silence about the empirically immediate, its failure to conceptualize in penetrating depth the production of space and time, its vagueness in delineating concepts like rules and resources, the difficulties of translating its concepts into practical realist analysis, and the like. We believe, however, that such commentaries will continue to fuel a reworked structurationist fabric that will render it, in the time ahead, still more substantial and profound.

IV

The central organizing theme of this book is the critical appraisal and application of structuration theory to the geographic causes and consequences of socially constructed inequality. All of the contributors are engaged in projects that are informed by Giddens's work on structuration theory. Although they agree that structuration theory is tremendously provocative in a positive sense, few if any are totally satisfied with Giddens's explication of the theory as a guide for empirical research. Each author confronts perceived inadequacies of Giddens's structuration theory and each finds a way around or through these deficiencies. Each author adapts and reinterprets structuration theory and, in so doing, creates new insights into the theory and into the processes producing and reproducing inequality.

The book is organized into two parts. Part I provides an overview and critical assessment of structuration theory with an emphasis on aspects of the theory that were first identified as relevant to geographic studies. Issues surrounding time-space distanciation figure prominently in the discussion, as do questions relating to the geographically situated individual's capacity to produce and reproduce social structure. Not surprisingly, the authors grapple with structuration as a set of theoretical principles that problematically reference a complex and ever-changing empirical world. Part II comprises empirical studies that contribute a structuration perspective to three important areas of more recent inquiry within geography: sense-of-place studies, local growth politics and coalitions, and gender and race inequalities. In the final chapter contribution, Eliza Husband provides a highly personal concluding commentary on the content and direction of the book as part of an ongoing conversation on social theory as it relates to the investigation of inequality.

The first chapter in Part I is a revised version of "Structuration Theory in Urban Analysis: A Theoretical Exegesis," the 1986 *Environment and Planning* paper by Adam Moos and Michael Dear. Most would agree that this paper has played a pivotal role in introducing geographers and urban theorists to structuration theory; the other contributions in the book are influenced by this paper and its companion (Moos and Dear, 1986), which use structuration theory as the theoretical basis for the critical analysis of the ghettoization of deinstitutionalized mental patients. The chapter begins with an explication of structuration theory that can be used as a common reference and point of departure for subsequent chapters. Dear and Moos follow their general review with a model of the structuration of urban space that provides a blueprint for empirical investigations of place-based marginalization. The proposed analysis of the strategic conduct of agents focuses on the power relationships among individuals, complemented by an institutional analysis elucidating the dominant structures embedded in power relationships.

The second chapter in Part I "The Limits to Human Constructiveness: Giddens and Structuration Theory in Geography," by David Wilson, provides a critical appraisal of structuration theory as it has been applied in geographic studies of social and economic inequality. This chapter follows logically from the Dear and Moos piece, in that one of the two empirical studies examined in detail is a later Dear and Moos study of the ghettoization of deinstitutionalized mental patients in Hamilton, Ontario (Dear and Moos, 1986). This work is paired in the chapter with Barney Warf's (1988) examination of the economic circumstances of lumberers in the Pacific Northwest. To Wilson, both studies are exemplars of empirical analysis informed by structuration theory. He argues, however, that both studies fail to demonstrate convincingly Giddens's duality of structure, because their analysis is restricted by the problematic application of Giddens's brittle theoretic categories. He suggests that the structurationist ontology of system-structure-agency needs more specificity if the power of agency is to be captured in empirical analysis.

Barney Warf's chapter, "Structuration Theory and Electronic Communications," begins with a discussion and critique of time-space distanciation, a key construct in Giddens's theory of structuration and a construct of primary importance to geographers working with structuration. Warf objects to Giddens's uncritical adoption of time-geography, with its primary emphasis on face-to-face communication and presence availability. He argues that information flows and communications are fundamental aspects of any social system; but electronic communication is fast replacing face-to-face communication, resulting in time-space convergence and compression that dwarfs the effects of time-space distanciation articulated by Giddens. Warf thereby casts Giddens's concept as technology specific and in need of analytical revision.

Part II is built around a series of case studies of communities in which the quality of life and the life chances of the residents studied are declining as a consequence of structural changes largely outside the immediate control of the local community. The members of these communities are portrayed as active agents engaged in efforts to gain greater control of their circumstances. While structuration is the theoretical centerpiece for each of the chapters, it is not the only theory brought to bear on the empirical issues examined. To these analysts, structuration is an ontologically informing set of propositions that needs a grounding theoretical core.

Chapter 4, John Jakle initiates one of three examinations of sense of place in the North American context. Jakle's chapter, "Small Towns as Historical Places: A Symbolic Interactionist Approach to Structuration Theory through the Study of Landscapes,'' explores the changing character of four small towns as members of the community work to shore up or transform marginal local economies. The towns are represented as historical landscapes that are more or less consciously manipulated and constructed to achieve different social and economic agendas. Jakle argues that historical place making as a survival strategy involves the creation of a landscape that evokes a strong positive response on one of three evaluative dimensions: integrity, authenticity, and/or aesthetics. In each of the four towns, knowledgeable actors were actively renegotiating the meaning of the historical place through the manipulation of important icons in the landscape.

In Chapter 5, ''Context Is Everywhere: Structuration, Community, and Social Order,'' John Eyles examines the connections between structuration theory and a person's sense of place, home, and community. The theoretical discussion is grounded in two empirical studies of marginalized families trying to maintain a sense of place under adverse, socially coercive conditions. The first case study involves the social practices of Italian-Canadians. Eyles argues that the home and the family are central to the process of obtaining and retaining ethnic identity, and they create islands of meaning and understanding within an otherwise confusing world. The second study looks at the disruption to daily routines and subsequent coping responses following the occurrence of an unforeseen, potentially health threatening environmental disaster that stigmatized a small rural community.

The final sense-of-place study is Jefferson Rogers's ''Taking Control in the American West: An Application of Pred's Theory of Place.'' This chapter focuses on an all too familiar story of a former mining community caught up in a boom and bust cycle largely outside the control of local inhabitants. The main theme of the study is how people in the community cope with the aftermath of the bust. The analysis focuses on efforts to gain community support for tourism-related projects and the mobilization of community resources in the development of a regional Exposition Center. Rogers uses Pred's theory of place to analyze the process by which local people try to regain control of their community. This theoretical package, as a variant of Giddens's structuration theory, offers a meaningful conceptualization of the historically contingent actions of local agents.

Chapter 7 by Lynn Staeheli and Chapter 8 by Joshua Van Lieu and John Paul Jones examine local growth politics and the structuration of local institutions when community viability is threatened by structural changes largely outside the control of the community and by internal struggles for control within the community.

Lynn Staeheli's perspective on local growth control initiatives comes from a study of women who became actively involved in the political debate over local growth controls in Boulder, Colorado during the 1960s and 1970s. Her chapter, ''Gender Relations in Urban Growth Politics,'' demonstrates that ongoing power relations between women and men in their homes, offices, political organizations, and communities influence the values and interests that individual women and men bring into and away from the growth control project. The analysis is based on the feminist and structurationist premise that politics is situated. In particular, the contexts within which these people operate condition their values, intentions, and actions.

The Van Lieu and Jones study, "Discursive Limits to Agency," considers the changing relationship between a local growth coalition and unionized workers in an externally controlled manufacturing plant slated for closure. In the negotiations leading up to and following the plant closure, Van Lieu and Jones find that workers are rendered powerless as much by the discourse of economic development and community employed by the growth coalition as by the material context—the restructuring of the American economy. This analysis teases out the complexities of locals contesting increasingly globalized capital decisions, a situation where global mobility of capital allows for the control of local discourses. This discourse, moreover, is convincingly described as a complex human construction crafted to meet the contingencies of a specific place but driven in its raison d'être by the imperatives of capital accumulation.

Chapters 9 and 10 examine the social construction of gender and race inequalities. Jeremy Browning's study, "The Reproduction of Racial Differences in Educational Achievement: A Structurationist Analysis," looks at the processes by which school officials continue to reproduce educational programs that fail to meet the needs of Latino and African American students in the San Diego school system. Programs ostensibly designed to redress the chronic underachievement of minority students are found to be ineffective; and yet they continue to be praised as solutions, thereby preempting and deflecting alternative courses of action and silencing dissenting voices from the Latino and African American communities. At the heart of Browning's study is an analysis of the "culture of deprivation" as a social construction used by school officials to justify a Magnet Schools program.

The final empirical study by Cherub Antwi-Nsiah and James O. Huff, "A Critical Analysis of Gender-based Property Relations in Ghana," explores the marginalization of women as an ongoing process within Ghanaian society. This study focuses on gender-based property relations that contribute to male-dominated patterns of property acquisition, inheritance, and control, thereby reproducing traditional social structures. Interviews with a sample of Ghanaian women and men indicate that male-dominated property relations are breaking down. Ghanaian women are becoming active agents in the acquisition and exchange of private property. These actions are undermining traditional inheritance rules and are transforming the very fabric of traditional social structures that have subordinated women in Ghana.

V

Structuration is a novel and bold attempt to resolve the persistent structure versus agency causal quandary that has plagued studies of social inequalities in the social sciences. Its codifier, Anthony Giddens, fashions an analytic framework that seeks to recognize both societal structures and active human agents as joint producers of everyday life. He provides a guide for sensitizing researchers to the notion that the production of inequalities is both a skilled human accomplishment and a societally influenced outcome. Its basic tenets—the duality of structure, the double hermeneutic, structural constraints/enablements, time-space distanciation—present an everyday life that is ceaselessly fashioned by conscious action and constraining or enabling structures. Giddens poignantly recognizes that people, places, and society interconnect recursively to forge differentiated social and spatial landscapes.

This framework is important to social theorists for a number of reasons. First, Giddens offers us a more lucid and profound skepticism about previous social theoretic work. His unique and powerful dismemberment of past structure-based and agency-based perspectives illuminates their theoretical shortcomings. He targets the limitations of these perspectives—their assumptions and preconceptions—and raises the issue of their practical utility to new heights. Second, Giddens places at center stage a profoundly new ontology for social theorists to ponder. The everyday world is no longer a visual plane for the unproblematic segmentation of structure and agency. Instead, the everyday is now seen as a blurred and dynamically conjoined set of relations and objects. The everyday is ontologically messy and turbulent; the world is forever in a state of becoming even as forces and processes interconnect to generate recursively what is observable. As Giddens observes, simple empirical taxonomies of the world are simplistic and frozen academic representations; their construction as much obfuscates the world as it clarifies it.

Geographers have unabashedly jumped on the structuration bandwagon. In these applications, it becomes obvious that the framework's open-endedness allows for diverse interpretations and applications. As this book demonstrates, its concepts may be applied at different spatial scales, to different forces and processes, and to different temporal frameworks. To some, this open-endedness smacks of eclectic degeneracy; to others, it reflects the power of a far-reaching ontology. Many complex issues about this framework's empirical utility are only now coming to the forefront of contemporary academic debate. It is in the spirit of this debate that we offer this preliminary forum for structuration's empirical utility in geography.

Part I

Issues in Structuration Theory
and Application

1

Structuration Theory in Urban Analysis

Michael J. Dear and Adam I. Moos

The production and reproduction of social life is the accomplishment of skilled, knowledgeable actors living in society. This statement reflects the core of Anthony Giddens's theory of structuration. This societal view holds that both the social system and the individual actor are equally important in explaining social phenomena. Structure and agency are interconnected things—dualities that recursively produce one another in a ceaseless interplay. Structuration theory is a bold and new attempt at resolving a great conflict in social theory. It considers the interconnections between agents and structures as everyday social life is generated. The goal is to overcome this pervasive dualism in social theory by providing an explanatory framework that transcends the limitations of both views without dispensing with the beneficial aspects of each.

The solution to the structure and agency dualism is being sought at a time when researchers are examining the role of social theory in human geography. The questions being asked concern not only structure and agency but also a reconsideration of space in geographic thought. These two areas of study have led some geographers, notably Gregory, Pred, and Thrift, to explore Giddens's structuration theory in an attempt to reconstitute the geographic research agenda within a social theoretic perspective. However, the development of the new agenda has so far focused primarily on theoretical and philosophical issues surrounding structuration theory; with the exception of a handful of papers in the early and mid-1990s (cf. Gregory 1982a; Thrift 1981; Warf 1988), there has been little exploration into the empirical viability of structuration theory for geographic research.

The lack of empirical research is understandable given the complexity and novelty of the theoretical issues involved in structuration theory. However, if structuration theory is to realize its promise it must also show its power to inform practice. With this in mind, we dissect structuration theory and outline a framework for its practical application. This project carries with it two implications. First, the empirical application of structuration theory aids its continuing theoretical development, since the many complex theoretical issues that structuration theory addresses may be augmented through practice. Second, the conceptual view of structure and agency in structuration theory enables a very different perspective in the study of social phenomena. It provides promise of a comprehensive explanation that considers how agency and structure come together in the production, reproduction, and transformation of society.

Some important caveats must be offered before we continue. First, it will become obvious that structuration theory operates somewhat uncomfortably on several theoretical interfaces (most notably, Marxian and Weberian sociology). This we take to be a positive asset (cf. Giddens 1984, xxii; Sayer 1984, 60, 71–72). The confrontations prompted by this deliberate eclecticism have been a major force in the current convergence in the social sciences, compelling theorists of many persuasions to sharpen their ideas and to recognize commonalities. (Giddens [1984, 286] makes an explicit plea for a disciplinary "coming together"; see also Sayer [1984, 234] and various issues of *Society and Space*.) Second, in recent commentaries, Giddens (1983, 77; 1989, 295) has warned against the haphazard use of structuration theory as the "magical key that unlocks the mysteries of empirical research." He argues instead that structuration theory is best employed as a means of sensitizing social analysis by paying particular attention to three analytic themes: the hermeneutic nature of social investigation, stressing the importance of "mutual knowledge"; the need to treat the individual as knowledgeable in the reproduction of social practices; and understanding the major role of the unintended outcomes that result from intentional human activity. This chapter outlines a framework for the application of structuration theory. We believe that the probing of this framework's empirical viability is crucial at a time when geography searches to modify the extremes of structuralist and human-centered theoretical perspectives.

Our investigation into the empirical dynamics of structuration theory involves an exposition of structuration theory and the proposing of a model for its application. The study has three research objectives. First, we present an exegesis of Giddens's theory of structuration. It is necessary to clarify the main concepts of structuration theory before they may be applied in practice. Second, we assess current structurationist work in geography. This outline brings out weaknesses of prevailing empirical applications. Third, we seek to develop this theory by placing its main concepts into both a general conceptual framework for analysis and a more focused model of the structuration of the urban built environment. We believe this exploration to be important: explicating the essence of structuration and probing its empirical dimensions will help lead to a more robust analytic framework.

STRUCTURATION THEORY[1]

The theory of structuration (Giddens 1976, 1979, 1981, 1982b, 1984) is an attempt to overcome a serious problem in social theory by transcending, without dispensing with, two social analytic perspectives. The first perspective concerns itself with objective structural relationships in society. This perspective includes social theories as diverse as functionalism, Marxism (in some forms), and structuralism. The common ground in these explanations is a disavowal of the importance of individuals, concentrating instead on the conditions that determine social outcomes. The second perspective concerns itself with individuals and pays primary attention to subjective societal interpretations. This type of analysis reflects the work of phenomenologist and existentialist authors who accord primacy to how individuals attach meaning to the life world; explanations tend to lack a theoretical understanding of institutions and societal totalities. The division between these two perspectives cannot be resolved through a simple marriage. Theories that focus on the structures that determine social outcomes (e.g., Parsonian functionalism; Althusserian Marxism) fail to consider the individual as active, knowledgeable, and reflexively contemplative (Giddens 1979, 54). Agent-oriented philosophies, on the other hand, treat structures as mere background "to which action is negotiated and its meaning formed" (p. 50). Furthermore, these philosophies marginalize the importance of power relations and societal conflict in focusing "almost exclusively upon the nature of reasons or intention in human activity" (p. 50). Giddens overcomes this dualism by developing a position where "the notions of action and structure presuppose one another; [the] recognition of this dependence, which is a dialectical relation, necessitates a reworking both of a series of concepts linked to each of these terms, and of these terms themselves" (1979, 53).

Structure, System, and Structuration

The theory of structuration differs from other structurally inclusive theories of society by separating the concepts of structure and system (Giddens 1982a, 32–36). In this separation, a *system* embodies the reproduced relations between actors or collectivities that are organized as regular social practices. These social practices reflect everyday social norms and are situated in particular time-space contexts. *Structures* exist as recursively organized rules and resources that individuals draw on and reconstitute in their day-to-day activities. Structures, unlike systems, do not exist in time-space, but have only a virtual existence in being drawn on and ceaselessly reconstituted. Thus, structures are both the

medium and the outcome of the situated practices that make up the system.[2]
They embody three influences—signification, domination, and legitimation—
that are present in all social interaction (Giddens 1976, 118–126). Structures of
signification become manifest in interaction through the communication of meaning. Structures of *domination* refer to the use of power in interaction. *Legitimation*
refers to the moral constitution of interaction through "the application of norms"
(Giddens 1976, 123). In all three cases, structures enable interactions to occur
(the medium of interaction), while interactions act to reconstitute those structures
(the outcome of interaction).

The condition governing the reproduction or transformation of structures—
the sustaining or rearrangement of systems—is structuration. The connection
between structure, system, and structuration is that "social systems are not
structures; they have structure or, more accurately, exhibit structural properties.
Structures are, in a logical sense, properties of the social systems or collectivities,
not of the situated activities of subjects. Social systems only exist in and through
structuration, as the outcome of the contingent acts of a multiplicity of human
beings" (Giddens 1982b, 35). This quotation brings out why the separation of
structure and system is fundamental. This partitioning allows one to understand
the interplay of individuals and social systems. Structure is the medium whereby
the social system affects individual action and the medium whereby individual
action affects the social system. The outcome of these individual-system interactions always (in varying degrees) affects the structural rules governing the next
interaction. Thus, the theoretical separation of structure and system enables
Giddens to capture both agency and structure in the production and reproduction
of social life without according primacy to either.

The system, structure, and structuration tripartite produces a view of society
where structures both enable and constrain human action. Giddens (1979, 69–
73) notes that previous attempts to incorporate structural analysis into subjectivist
social theories included structure merely as constraint. The enabling aspect of
social action rested solely with agent intentions and motives. These motives and
intentions unfolded within boundaries imposed by the social structure. The social
structure was not an active part of the structuration of social relations; rather,
social relations result solely from the activities of individuals. Conversely, in
much functionalist, Marxist, and structuralist social theories it is argued that
individual action is determined by the needs of the totality. This position poses
two problems. First, the activities of individuals are determined without regard
to the agent's motives or intentions. Second, the functionalist characterization
of the needs of a system is false. Giddens asserts that people, not social systems,
have needs and that it is misguided to attempt social analysis concerned with
the needs of a particular society (Giddens 1979, Chapter 2; 1982b, Chapter 1).
Thus, Giddens (1982b, 6) maintains that the concept of function has no place
in social theory.

This conception of structure forms the basis for Giddens's understanding of
institutions. He defines institutions as "practices which are deeply sedimented

in time-space: that is, which are enduring and inclusive 'laterally' in the sense
that they are widespread among the members of a community of society'' (1979,
80). These practices are akin to the structural properties of social systems, and
a classification of institutions follows a similar logic to the analytically separable
properties of structures (Giddens 1981, 46–48):

Structural sequence	Institution
S-D-L	Symbolic orders or modes of discourse
D(authoritative)-S-L	Political
D(allocative)-S-L	Economic
L-D-S	Legal or modes of sanction

where S is signification, D is domination, and L is legitimation (adapted from
Giddens 1981, 47).

In this schema, domination takes two forms depending on whether the institution is engaged in power over individuals (authoritative domination) or maintains power over the material environment (allocative domination). The four
structural sequences are not a functional classification schema, but indicate the
possible directions for institutional analysis. The structure listed first provides
the focus for the analysis, but the additional structures in each sequence are
present because structures exist interdependently in institutions.

Agency

The individual in structuration theory is seen to be active, knowledgeable,
and reasoning. The social system consists of conditions that bound the action
of the agent, yet do not determine the agent's activities. This is brought to light
by Giddens's "stratification model of action" (1979, 55–59; 1982b, 28–32):

Unacknowledged conditions of action	Reflexive monitoring of action	Unintended consequences of action
	Rationalization of action	
	Motivation of action	

(adapted from Giddens 1982b, 30)

The individual reflexively monitors her or his own actions. Actor self-contem-
plation follows two paths. The first is the accounts of reasons provided by an
actor for a given action. The rationalization of action is an attempt by an actor
to "form discrete accounts in the context of queries, whether initiated by others,
or as elements of a process of self-examination by the actor" (Giddens 1979,
55). The second is the intentions or purposes the agent employs for the actions.

Purposeful conduct does not refer solely to goal-oriented behavior; it includes such mundane practices as salting food. The motivation for action results from the self-examination by the agent as to possible outcomes.

The reflexive monitoring of action occurs at three levels of consciousness: unconscious, practical consciousness, and discursive consciousness. *Unconscious motives* for action operate outside the range of the agent's self-understanding. *Practical consciousness* refers to knowledge that the individual uses but cannot verbalize. Giddens cites as an example the idea of language use. Actors know and communicate via language without necessarily being able to formulate the rules that govern their speaking. Practical knowledge concerns the stocks of knowledge that result from the social system within which the actor lives. The resulting acts are not unconscious but instead reflect how the structural properties of the social system are embedded in practical consciousness. *Discursive consciousness* refers to that which the agent can verbalize. In the giving of reasons or intentions the actor may supply accounts, yet these are themselves incomplete explanations because areas of practical knowledge may enter into the act.

All social action is bounded by the unacknowledged conditions and unintended consequences of action. Much activity escapes the intention of the agent and is bounded on one side as an unacknowledged condition of action and on the other as an unintended outcome. Since history is not an intentional product, it becomes important to situate the intentional activities of agents within history. The concepts regarding conditions and outcome of action enable Giddens to accomplish this historical specificity by connecting intentional human activity to the social system.

The Duality of Structure and Social Reproduction

Structuration theory seeks to overcome the problems of both objectivist and subjectivist social theories by elucidating theoretical connections between social systems and individuals. The treatment of each—without relegating the social system to becoming a mere backdrop upon which human action occurs and without relegating the individual to becoming the mere carrier of structural logic—is achieved via the duality of structure. The structuration of society occurs via the duality of structure, which Giddens defines as connecting "the production of social interaction, as always and everywhere a contingent accomplishment of knowledgeable social actors, to the reproduction of social systems across time-space" (1981, 27). This can be illustrated through the dialectic of control. Individuals engaging in power relations draw on structures of domination that characterize the relationship of autonomy and dependence in interaction and, in doing so, reconstitute these rules. The structural rules become the medium where the power relation is generated, and in the production of the interaction the agents contribute to the reproduction of the system.

The dialectic of control is important, for it enters into every area of social interaction via structures of domination. Power relations are always relations of autonomy and dependence and are necessarily reciprocal. The distribution of power in a relationship may be asymmetrical, but an agent always maintains some control in the relationship and may avoid complete subjugation. As Giddens (1979, 149) notes, "in a social system, the most seemingly 'powerless' individuals are able to mobilize resources whereby they carve out 'spaces of control' in respect of their day-to-day lives and in respect of the activities of the more powerful" (Giddens 1982b, 197–198). This conception is fundamental, for it removes any notion of determinism from an understanding of power relations.

The duality of structure is directly involved with questions of societal reproduction, transformation, and determination. Giddens's view stresses the nonfunctionalist nature of societal change. Theories that examine this issue on the basis of the needs of the social system incorrectly impart teleology on the social system. Thus, Parsonian sociology or Marxism (following Althusser or Poulantzas) view the reproduction of society as occurring behind the backs of the agents whose conduct constitutes that society (Giddens 1979, 112). Giddens (1979, 112–113) offers an example of the industrial reserve army in capitalism to illustrate how Marxist explanations of the phenomenon tend to follow functionalism. Thus, according to Giddens, "all social reproduction occurs in the context of 'mixes' of intended and unintended consequences of action; every feature of whatever continuity a society has over time derives from such 'mixes,' against a backdrop of bounded conditions of rationalization of conduct" (1979, 112).

This reasoning by Giddens is also applied to the analysis of institutions. He rejects a functionalist line of reasoning to understand institutions, stating that "not even the most deeply sedimented institutional features of societies come about because societies need them to do so. They come about historically, as a result of concrete conditions that have in every case to be directly analyzed; the same holds for their persistence" (1979, 113). This conception of social reproduction does not exclude questions about "what has to happen for given features of a social system to come about or persist or be altered." Thus, the proposition that "in order to persist in a relatively stable form, the capitalist economy has to maintain a certain overall level of profit" is valid if the "has to" is seen as identifying conditions that must be met for a certain outcome to be obtained. "The 'has to' is not a property of 'need' of the system, and has no explanatory force—unless actors within the system get to know about the conditions in question and actively incorporate them in a process of reflexive self-regulation of system reproduction" (Giddens 1979, 114).

Structuration theory considers the social reproduction of people and society at two levels. First, this process is presented as a form of change. Reproduction is not simply replication, but is rather a process whereby "any and every change in a social system logically implicates the totality and thus implies structural modification, however minor or trivial this may be" (Giddens 1979, 114). This change occurs through the structuration of social systems across time-space. Second, social reproduction is seen to be embedded in the remarkable continuity that exists in society amid the routinization of day-to-day activities. Routinization refers to the taken-for-granted character of day-to-day interaction. Giddens (1979, 216–222) develops this concept through an analysis of tradition, yet avoids any notion of functionalist explanation in understanding the daily round of common activities. Thus, "the most deeply sedimented elements of social conduct are cognitively (not necessarily consciously, in the sense of 'discursive ability') established, rather than founded on definite 'motives' prompting action; *their continuity is assured through social reproduction itself*" (Giddens 1979, 218). In this way, social reproduction encompasses both the evolutionary and continuous nature of society.

Time-Space Relations

Giddens (1979, 1981, 1984) demonstrates the importance of time-space relations in the structuration of society. To Giddens, time unfolds at three levels as it recursively connects to spatial locales. The *durée* refers to "the immediate nexus of interaction as contingently 'brought off' by social actors, the most elemental form of social reproduction" (Giddens 1981, 28). The second layer of temporality is the *dasein*. This layer of time refers to the biologic life of the living human organism, "the contingency of life in the face of death" (1981, 28). The third conception of time is the *longue durée*. This concept refers to "the long-term reproduction of institutions across the generations, the contingency of the transformation/mediation relations embedded in structural principles of system organization" (1981, 28). The duality of structure weaves together these analytically different categories, allowing the binding of day-to-day reproduction (the durée) to institutions (the dasein) and structural principles (the longue durée).

Giddens also asserts that space is an important determinant of social interaction. For him, the concept of the locale refers to the "physical settings associated with the 'typical interactions' composing . . . collectivities as social systems. . . . The locales of collectivities are integrally involved with the structural constitution of social systems, since common awareness of properties of the setting of interaction is a vital element in the sustaining of meaningful communication between actors" (Giddens 1981, 39). The scales of the locale range from the dwelling to the small community to nation-states. Locale is very closely tied to the idea of presence availability.

The 'small' community can be defined as one in which there is characteristically only a short distance in the time-space 'meshing' of interaction. The interactions constituting the social system are 'close' in both time and space: the present of others is readily available on a direct face to face basis. Locales are regionalized on a time-space basis. By 'regions' within locales I mean aspects of the settings which are normatively implicated in systems of interaction, such that they are in some way 'set apart', for certain individuals, or types of individuals, or for certain activities or types of activities. (Giddens 1981, 39–40)

The regionalization of locales is closely associated with the durée of interaction as the most elemental form of social reproduction. Additionally, "the regionalization of locales is important in the concealing of social practices, a phenomenon of no small significance for the analysis of power relations" (Giddens 1981, 41). Space, then, "is not an empty dimension along which social groupings become structured, but has to be considered in terms of its *involvement in the constitution of system of interaction*" (Giddens 1984, 368, emphasis added).

GEOGRAPHY AND STRUCTURATION

From a geographical view, one of the important implications of structuration theory is that social theory must become more contextual, that is, situated in space and time (cf. Thrift 1986). For Giddens, society consists of a "regionalization" of resources that intersect with a mosaic of places to construct everyday social reality (1984, Chapter 3). Hence, illuminating the concrete practices of social reproduction *requires* a contextual theory of social life. This concern finds clear echoes in much recent human geographical research. For example, a concern over structure and agency is evident in many recent works in geography addressing such diverse topics as economic geography (Barnes 1984; Sayer 1982) and Marxist analysis (Eyles 1981b; Williams 1981). The debate in the geographic literature concerns whether the social formation or the individual should be the ultimate basis of explanation (cf. Chouinard and Fincher 1983; Duncan and Ley 1982; 1983; Gregory 1981; Ley 1980). Structuration theory has been proffered as a possible resolution to this debate. It does not seek to join these two opposing camps at some middle ground, but rather to transcend the dualistic nature of this debate to lend greater understanding to the complex relationship between social-cultural reproduction and the practice of everyday life.

Another reason for the increasing interest in structuration, particularly as developed by Giddens, involves the centrality it accords to time and space in the constitution of social systems (cf. Giddens 1979, Chapter 6; 1981). For example, an early structurationist application by Gregory demonstrates the failings of both the humanist tradition (1981) and systems theory (1980) to theorize spatial structure effectively. Structuration theory provides Gregory with a means of transcending the structure and agency dualism while recapturing spatial structure through social theory (1978, 168–172; 1982b). Similarly, Pred employs structuration theory to demonstrate that time-geography is more than "an extremely effective device for describing both behavior and biography in time and space" (1982, 151). This is accomplished by integrating the concepts of structuration to the movement of individuals through time and space to the social formation via the external-internal and daily-path-life-path dialectics (Pred 1981b, 1982). This blending of structuration and time-geography is developed further by Pred (1983) to reformulate the concept of a sense of place. It has also led him (1981b) to theorize power relations as a dialectical relation of the individual's "power to" with the institution's "power over." However, this formulation is not fully satisfactory, for although it portrays effectively the daily effects of the power dialectic (that is, path and project changes), the limitations of the time-geography framework leave an explanation of the long-term reproduction of the social system wanting.

This problem reflects one main area of current debate concerning Giddens's theory of structuration—the *concept of determination*. For Pred, determination occurs in the time-space path that individuals trace out in their daily existence (cf. Pred 1982, 163–166; 1984, 282–284). For Gregory (1982b) and Thrift (1983a), determination rests with the conjoining of structuration theory to a nonfunctionalist historical materialism that avoids the structure and agency dualism and explicates "the material grounding of practical life which is at the root of both the genre de vie and the mode of production" (Gregory 1981, 16). However, both of these schemas of determination are problematic since Giddens never addresses the question of determination. The notion of determination is crucial and must be reformulated in light of the implications of the duality of structure.

A MODEL OF STRUCTURATION

With a critical reading of Giddens, a structurationist model of societal interconnections may be forged (Figure 1.1). At the base of such a model, Giddens's three-tiered ontology of system, structure, and agency must be maintained. In the model that we propose, agency embodies the dialectic of control and the stratification model of action. Following Giddens, power is presented as a central aspect of all human interaction. The dialectic of control is the primary force mediating the interaction between individual agents (represented by the bidirectional arrows in Figure 1.1). Control in social interaction is not simply unidirectional in nature.

All actors maintain some degree of control within social interaction, although the power relations may be extremely asymmetrical. This is important when considering direct forms of domination. Political and economic domination involves exercising power via the rules and resources of authoritative and allocative institutions to influence the actions of agents. The ability of agents to understand social relations as discursive knowledge plays an important role in the dialectic of control. The greater the knowledge the agent has about the reproduction of society and the relations within that society, the greater is his or her ability to engage effectively in interaction. In other words, the greater the ability of the agent to understand in a discursive way continuing social reproduction, the more power he or she will be able to exercise within the dialectic of control. Thus, some agents may be able to combine political or economic power and discursive knowledge to create an even greater asymmetry in relations, or the effective use of discursive knowledge by an individual with less power may have the effect of reducing those asymmetries.

Figure 1.1
A Model of Structuration

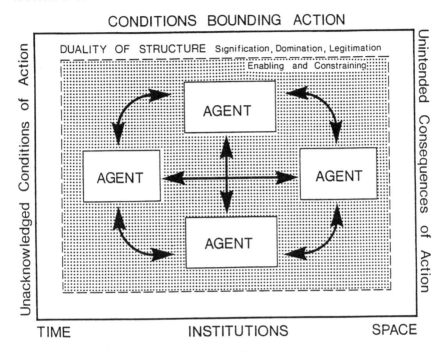

We cast the social system as a nexus of acknowledged/unacknowledged constraints and enablements that bound action. Actions that generate unintended consequences for future actions are conducted through the filter of the stratification model of action. Institutions at the level of system embody the structural principles of the system. This is not to argue that institutions directly correspond to these principles; rather, these structural principles achieve their enduring and inclusive nature through various societal institutions whose actions spatially and temporally manifest these structural principles. Time bounds action in three ways following the concepts of dasein, durée, and longue durée. Space bounds action through physical settings (locales) that are associated with typical interactions. As social interaction occurs in space, the locale generates constraints and enablements for action.

Structures are represented in our model as the medium and outcome of social interaction. This portrayal of structure in the model is meant to emphasize that the duality of structure binds social system to agency. Structural properties are embedded in the social system through the recursive interplay of institutions and agents. Structures in this model reflect the medium and outcome of interaction by being posited as an *infrastructure* situated between social system and agency. This is not to claim that these structures have a phenomenal form; they most certainly do not. Rather, structures have an instantiated essence that provides the rules that characterize the social system and thereby enable various forms of action. In performing acts, agents reproduce these structures and the social system (recall that reproduction also implies change).

The intrastructure conception that we employ seeks to discard the implicit granting of determination to structure that has characterized much previous work. To Sayer (1983, 109), one benefit of Giddens's theory is that it resolves the structure and agency problem "and the unsatisfactory poles of determinism and voluntarism." The determination scheme implicit in Pred's work is similarly open ended because it accords primacy to the time-space paths of individuals. This tenet implies that social interaction in the last instance is explained by the desires of the individual to trace out a particular path. A similar line of reasoning demonstrates how Thrift's attempt to attach structuration theory to a historical materialist framework, and Gregory's conjoining of Giddens to Bhaskar's transcendental realism, are ultimately determinist. Here, determination is accorded to structure, and in the last instance it is these structures that determine social outcomes. Thrift (1983b) is sensitive to this problem in his concern for the "contextual dimension" as well as compositional questions, but his papers (1983a, 1983b) treat these questions separately and point toward a dualism rather than to an integration of structure and agency. (See Figure 1.2.)

This dualism and the problem of the last instance are avoided in this model by reconstituting the concept of determination through an extension of the duality of structure. Determination in structurationist explanation may only be understood through the outcome of agent-structure-system interaction, and the importance of any of these three attributes cannot be specified a priori. This removal of determination from structurationist explanation follows Smith's (1983) understanding of the relationship between human agency (intentionality), social structure (practices), and socially defined context, where "in the complex interplay of intentions, context and practices there exists *no set pattern of dominance*: the intentionality of actors may dominate, the socially defined context may dominate or established practices may dominate" (Smith 1983, 6; emphasis added). This tenet implies that individuals simultaneously retain the characteristics that enable them to alter the social system and are socialized individuals that live in a constituted and reconstituted social system. Furthermore, structures, although ontologically real, are not accorded primacy since they reflect the structural properties that are embedded in the longue durée of social reproduction. Structures have an instantiated essence and are drawn on and reproduced/rearranged in interaction.

The reconstruction of determination also carries consequences for empirical research. This conception of determination leads to less tidy packages with which to study society; structurationist explanations must balance system, structure, and agency in practice and not accord a priori primacy to one or the other. This is well demonstrated by Thrift (1981) in a study in which he considers the

Figure 1.2
Different Diagrammatic Representations of Structuration from (a) Thrift (1983a);
(b) Gregory (1982a); and (c) the Outline Discussed in This Chapter

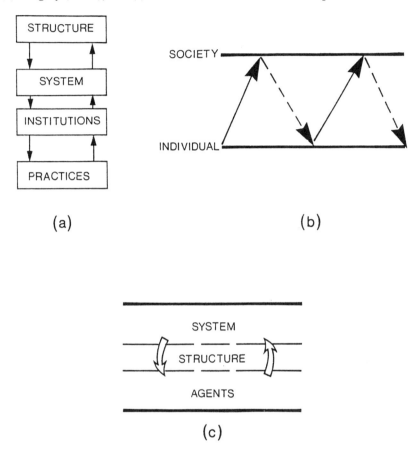

Diagrammatic representation of structuration (a) from Thrift (1983a) views structure as supra to both
   the system and agency; (b) from Gregory (1981) portrays society and individual but there is no
   indication of structure; (c) follows my conception of an intra-structure which characterizes the
   relationship between agency and system.

changing social relations surrounding the development of capitalist time consciousness over a 580-year span. This study captures the richness and complexity
of the problem by examining both the changing social conditions of the period
and the role of human agency in the development of a capitalist time consciousness. Thrift's study successfully demonstrates the utility of employing the unique
interpretative schema of structuration theory in social research.

STRUCTURATION THEORY IN EMPIRICAL ANALYSIS

While structurationist analysis must separate agent and system for analytical purposes, a danger is to impose the dualism that Giddens so strenuously seeks to avoid. In this context, such an analysis must avoid two main pitfalls. First, the analysis must remain true to the theory and not accord a priori primacy in explanation either to system or to agent. The goal is to avoid making one component the passive receptor of the actions of the other. Agency and system should be accorded equal ontological importance in the production and reproduction of society. Second, the analysis must pay attention to the interaction of agent and system. This means that a structurationist account is not simply the blending together of two separate analyses, one at the level of the system and the other at the level of the individual. The integration of these categories would capture the essence of the duality of structure.

The obvious problem is the tendency to separate system and agency analysis in application. Giddens (1979, 80–81) introduces the notion of *bracketing* to overcome this dilemma. Bracketing permits a focus on one level of analysis without forsaking the other. In other words, bracketing provides a way of applying structuration theory without succumbing to either of the problems just outlined. First, the notion of bracketing in no way places agent or system in a superior causal position. Second, this method of studying either the social system or human agency necessarily integrates both areas of concern even though the focus may be on one or the other.

An analysis at the level of the social system seeks to understand how institutions affect society. The way to achieve this is to focus on institutions as repositories for recursively produced rules and resources. This focus does not mean that agents are unimportant. Agents are a key to the analysis; institutions are directly affected by the actions of individuals who reproduce/rearrange them. As an example of this, consider the state. An analysis of the actions of the state cannot ignore the individuals who make up the state apparatus. The intentions, motives, reasonings, and other aspects of agency have a distinct impact on how the state affects society. Such an institutional inquiry does not consider the agency aspect incorrectly; it portrays institutions as autonomous wholes outside the grasp of human influence. It is granted here that institutions, by definition, exist in a time-space that is greater than the lives of those who constitute them, yet this fact alone does not provide criteria for employing an institutional analysis in which the necessary and important role of agency in the reproduction of the social system is ignored.

These same concerns exist when conducting an analysis of agency. An analysis of strategic conduct is concerned with how individuals draw on the structural elements (reproduced rules and resources) in social interaction. The modalities here are the "stocks of knowledge and resources employed by actors in the constitution of interaction as a skilled and knowledgeable accomplishment within the bounded conditions of the rationalization of action" (Giddens 1979, 81). In

Figure 1.3
Levels of Analysis in Structuration Theory

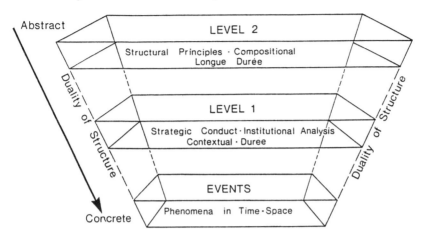

this way, the components of the social system are seen as integral to explaining the actions of individuals. This view separates structurationist explanation from phenomenological analysis. Institutions are not the focal point of analysis, but become relevant in the explanatory framework since individual action is contextually influenced. The rules and resources of the social system both enable and constrain action and for this reason cannot be dismissed as unimportant in the explanation. Returning to the example of the state helps to illustrate this point. The state as an institution embodies specific rules and resources that the individual agent can draw on when engaging in ongoing interaction. The dialectic of control present in the interaction of these agents reflects the conditions that bound the state. An analysis in which this is not considered fails to provide a comprehensive picture of agency.

Levels of Analysis in Structuration Theory

Structurationist studies need to understand the relationship between various levels of explanation in an empirical project.[3] The schema that guides our application is depicted in Figure 1.3. This separation of levels indicates the various ways in which structuration theory may be applied in analysis. The lowest level is events. These are the actual empirical occurrences that are the focus for action by agents and institutions. Magnitude is unimportant, for an event is equally the act of salting food as it is the response by financial institutions to economic crisis. The event is the actual empirical happening that results from the production and reproduction of social life through the interplay of agents and institutions.

These events may be analyzed in two ways, each representing a different level of analytical abstraction. First, events may be considered by examining the relationship between agents and institutions in the production of social reality (level 1). These are contextual questions and involve a concern with identifying the agents involved in a particular event and the interaction these agents engage in among themselves and their interaction with institutions. At this level, events may also be analyzed by considering how various institutions are involved in the structuring of social reality. In either case, the analysis should not become polarized into a dualistic representation of agency and institutions, but instead draw out the dialectical relation that characterizes agency-institutional interaction.

Second, events may be analyzed at a higher level by considering the structural properties that affect agency and institutions in interaction (level 2). These are compositional questions that may be considered through examining the structural properties of the social system embedded in the longue durée of social reproduction. At this level, the focus is the abstract structural properties that both enable and constrain human actions. Thus, the concern is not with particular agents or institutions, but with those characteristics embedded within the longue durée that are drawn on and reconstituted in everyday practice.

Structure enters into this schema through the duality of structure. The structures of signification, domination (authoritative and allocative), and legitimation are the basis for interaction at both levels of analysis. The duality of structure enables a binding of both contextual (level 1) and of compositional (level 2) analyses. The duality of structure enables a transcending of both the agency-institution dualism and the context-composition dualism. As the medium and outcome of all interaction, these structures are necessarily implicated in a dialectical understanding of the relationship between levels 1 and 2, and between the agent-institution characterization at levels 1 and 2. In other words, the duality of structure binds not just institutions and agency (at levels 1 and 2), but also context and composition of everyday life.

A MODEL OF THE STRUCTURATION OF URBAN SPACE

We propose a structurationist model of urban space that seeks to comprehend the complexities of urban life and physical patterning (Figure 1.4). The focus on urban phenomena is not an attempt to treat urban as a theoretical category; rather, the inclusion of urban is a recognition that the many social problems and the myriad of actors and institutions involved in the structuring of society may differ between rural and urban locales. This does not involve setting up a mutually exclusive distinction between urban and rural; there may indeed be overlap between a model for understanding the structuration of rural space and urban space. This model seeks to provide insight into understanding problems in urban space. The conditions preceding action in this context may be either acknowledged or unacknowledged by the actors involved. In either case, these preconditions to action constrain and enable human agency. The interactions between the various agents are characterized by the dialectic of control. Agents relate to

Figure 1.4
A Model of the Structuration of Urban Space

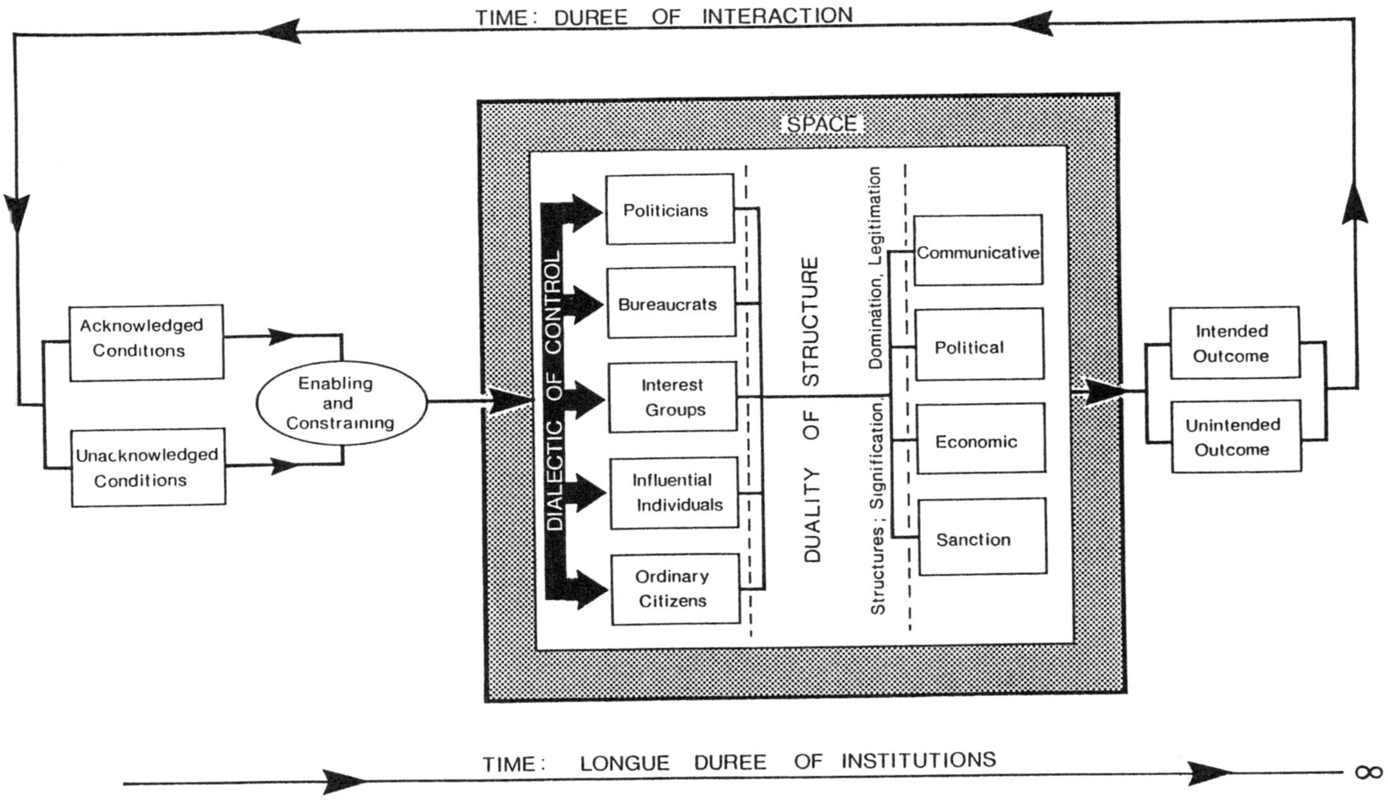

TIME: DUREE OF INTERACTION

SPACE

Communicative

Political

Economic

Sanction

Structures: Signification
Domination, Legitimation

DUALITY OF STRUCTURE

DIALECTIC OF CONTROL

Politicians

Bureaucrats

Interest Groups

Influential Individuals

Ordinary Citizens

Intended Outcome

Unintended Outcome

Enabling and Constraining

Acknowledged Conditions

Unacknowledged Conditions

TIME: LONGUE DUREE OF INSTITUTIONS

institutions via the duality of structure that captures agency effects on institutions and also institutional effects on agents. The constant interaction between agents and institutions yields outcomes that may either be intended, unintended, or some combination. These outcomes of interaction structure processes within the longue durée of social reproduction; they form the preconditions for action in the next durée of interaction.

Agents and institutions represented in the model are deliberately urban based and are seen to exert influence on forces and processes within this setting. The categories of agents and institutions in this model follow the Weberian conception of ideal types (see Giddens 1971, 141–144; Saunders 1981, 25–35). These categories reflect both existing empirical knowledge of the urban arena and the theory of structuration. In this manner, the categories "involve the logical extension of certain aspects of reality [and structuration theory] into a pure, artificial yet logically possible type against which existing phenomena can be measured and compared" (Saunders 1981, 28). Thus, the agent categories in the model are ideal types based on the relations of actors in the urban built environment and on the dialectic of control.[4] A similar argument also guides the unearthing of institutional categories. These institutions are examined because of their physical presence in cities and because of their correspondence to Giddens's institutional categories. In both cases—agents and institutions—these ideal types are only a means to analysis and not an end in themselves. In the following subsections we detail ideal type conceptions of agents and institutions in the urban built environment. The discussion of agency prior to institutions follows Figure 1.4, which has agents on the left and institutions on the right; the presentation does not imply that the analysis of agent strategic conduct is of greater importance than institutional analysis.

Strategic Conduct

The analysis of the strategic conduct of agents requires an understanding of the *power* relationships between individuals. In its current stage of development, structuration does not provide a theoretical understanding of power akin to the relation of capital and power in Marxian analysis. However, structuration provides the dialectic of control as a mechanism for realizing the exercise of power in agent interaction. The emphasis is on how power is employed by various actors in the reproduction of society.

There are five types of agents in the model. The first group is those individuals who are elected to public office (politicians). The second group consists of those in the government bureaucracy or quasi-governmental organizations (bureaucrats). The third, interest groups, may be considered to be an agent because, in the structuration of urban space, a common concern tends to bond individuals together and they speak with one voice. The fourth group, influential individuals, characterizes those whose status in the community—wealthy individuals, entertainers, former politicians, athletes, and the like—gives them a greater degree of power than more typical individuals. The final category of agent is the ordinary citizen. This refers to the remainder of individuals who are not affiliated with an interest group and lack the status of the influential individual, but are a part of the structuration of urban space. It must be emphasized, however, that the distinction between influential individual and ordinary citizen is not a permanent one and that individuals do indeed move between these categories.

For each category of agent, the dialectic of control mediates the relations within these groups as well as between the five groups. For the present, however, this discussion focuses on the dialectic of control in intergroup relations. The first group of agents involves elected officials (politicians). This group is very powerful within the dialectic of control in two ways. First, these agents have the ability to control resources and laws in the urban built environment. This status as the ultimate decision maker in the urban arena puts these agents as the dominant force in political relations. Second, these agents generally have far greater knowledge of the situation in the urban arena than most other actors simply by the nature of their jobs. This does not mean that in all areas of concern politicians have superior discursive knowledge; only in a general sense is this so.

Bureaucrats have less power than politicians but still retain a high degree of control. This power is realized in three ways. First, bureaucrats generally have higher technical expertise than politicians. This enables the bureaucrats to have a definite input into the decision-making process. In some cases, this technical expertise can give the bureaucrat the upper hand in a relationship with a politician. This technical superiority suggests a second area where the bureaucrat exercises influence in the dialectic of control; this is in the writing of legislation. A committee of politicians makes recommendations for a bylaw, yet the actual writing of the bylaw rests not with the politicians, but with the bureaucrats. Thus, the way in which the bureaucrat deals with the politician's recommendations can affect the way in which the policy affects the urban built environment. The third area of control concerns the differing mandates for politicians and bureaucrats. The mandate for the politician comes from the electorate, whereas the bureaucrat is shielded from any such review. This is at once a source of both weakness and strength. The lack of a popular mandate hinders the bureaucrat since he or she cannot employ it to alter the power relations between politicians and himself or herself. It is a source of strength, however, since bureaucrats may pursue a course of action that is deemed necessary although not popular with the electorate, and they are shielded, in most cases, from any reactions.

A third group in the dialectic of control is interest groups. A set of common concerns shared by members of an interest group serves as a means of mobilizing a great number of people around a specific cause. This gives the interest group a good deal of power in the dialectic of control. It means that within the dialectic of control politicians, bureaucrats, and interest groups come together in an attempt to arrive at a mutually agreeable solution. However, the power of the interest group is limited, and the possibility always exists that the politicians and bureaucrats can ignore the demands of the interest group and continue along the path they choose to follow. This could lead to two outcomes. First, the use of power may lead to future difficulties as the politician may become the target of a negative campaign run by an interest group to keep him or her from being reelected. Second, the courts exist as another venue where the interest group may try to exercise its strength. Thus, decisions made by politicians and bureaucrats do not have a carte blanche because the interest group commands some degree of power within the dialectic of control.

A fourth group of agents is the influential individual. The basis of power for the influential individual may vary—the charismatic athlete or entertainer with a highly recognizable name, the retired politician with easier access to government, or the wealthy person with vast amounts of money. In each case, the status of the influential individual often legitimizes his or her actions and enables the agent to mobilize a great number of people and/or resources. The way in which this mobilization occurs may take several different forms. An influential individual may use power for social activism or personal gain, and this cannot be specified a priori. The point is not which way these individuals will attempt to influence decisions, but that their status gives them greater power and legitimacy in the dialect of control than individuals who lack these qualities.

The final category of agent is the ordinary citizen. The amount of power commanded by these agents within the dialectic of control varies and in most cases is not very significant. For this set of agents, the ability to understand society discursively is their main source of power within the dialectic of control. The ordinary citizen lacks the additional sources of power available to the other agents in the model, but this does not make him or her powerless; all agents possess some degree of power in a relationship. Concerned individuals can become very involved in urban questions through their discursive understanding of urban issues. In this way, these individuals can attract the attention of politicians, bureaucrats, interest groups, influential individuals, and other agents to various problems and concerns.

Institutional Analysis

Four aspects of institutional analysis are incorporated into the model that are nonmutually exclusive categories for elucidating institutions as modalities of interaction (Figure 1.4). These modalities of interaction reflect directly the structural features inherent in all human interaction: signification, domination (authoritative and allocative), and legitimation. The first category concerns institutions influencing the built environment through communicative actions. These institutions affect the change through a communicative modality of interaction. The second institutional category concerns political domination; these institutions engage in authoritative domination. The third category for institutional analysis involves economic domination. Institutions control economic resources that induce change. Finally, the last category encompasses institutions that control through social sanctions. Such institutions legitimate practices and acts that make up everyday life.

There are two ways in which the communicative modality of interaction affects the built urban environment. First, institutions may be considered an interpretive community, providing a single relatively stable code that actors employ when engaging in interaction (Clark and Dear 1984, 87). This may be considered within the context of the specific languages of various institutions such as government, professional organizations, or academia, where the language employed affects the interaction of agents. For example, a community-based movement consists of agents all speaking a similar language concerning a governmental action that will affect their neighborhood. Yet the entrance of the community movement into the governmental arena brings a new language into play that represents the government as an interpretive community. The effectiveness of the community movement depends in part on the ability of the agents in the movement to engage effectively in interaction characterized by the language of the government. The style of language employed in these contexts forms the second way in which institutions as a communicative modality of interaction affect urban space. Clark and Dear (1984, 90–91) identify four styles of political language. These styles consider how language is used to engender support (hortatory language); to resolve conflicts, yet remain flexible for subsequent interpretations (legal language); to serve a particular group and exclude others through the use of jargon (administrative language); and to offer a deal as well as an appeal (bargaining language). Although these styles of language bring forward the way in which economic or political power and sanction are implicated in the communicative modality of interaction, the goal in this area of analysis is to understand how institutions, via communicative modalities, affect interaction.

A second form of institutional action concerns political domination. The authoritative control of individuals may be understood specifically in cases where some aspect of authoritative control is identifiable (e.g., the medical profession and its control over members and dependent groups). In a more general context, the state as an institution is powerful through its ability to legislate the rules of society. In this way the state provides the power for politicians and bureaucrats to achieve desired goals. This is important in the structuration of urban space since the state can enact policies that may be considered unpopular. The authoritative power of the state enables it to withstand opposition to its actions. This authoritative power over society is limited, however, for at the same time the populace the state controls also contains its mandate for existence. Through political parties or interest groups the populace can exercise some degree of authoritative control over the state. There is another arena where authoritative control enters into the production and reproduction of the urban built environment. The control over certain programs realized at the local level (but administered at either the provincial, state, or federal levels of government) affects the local-level bureaucracy since the directions of a given program may not correspond to how the officials at the local level want to handle the situation.

The third area for institutional analysis involves the control of economic resources. This affects the urban built environment in four main ways: taxation, finance, land speculation, and intragovernmental transfer payments. The power to tax rests with the state. The state may use this power to encourage or discourage various actions in urban space. Tax incentives are used by the state to encourage investment into a particular area (e.g., urban renewal). Conversely, excessive taxes may be imposed to dissuade investment that the state considers to have an overall negative impact. Financial institutions, banks, and insurance companies affect the built environment in the way in which they allocate capital. This is important since redlining can affect how investment takes place in urban areas. Land speculation can affect the urban area by creating artificially high land values. This may lead to urban renewal schemes that are outside the direct control and monitoring of the state. Finally, many programs are executed at the urban level but are funded at either the provincial, state, or federal level. In this situation the money available for a given program is provided by an agency not directly connected to the urban arena.

The final area of institutional analysis involves the legitimation of institutional action through the sanction modality. There are three avenues through which institutions may take action to demonstrate that various activities fall within legitimate social practices. First, institutional action may occur outside legal bounds. Sanction of institutional action in this sense occurs through the criminal justice apparatus where the action in question will be determined legal within existing legal definitions, legal through a reinterpretation of the law, or illegal. Second, institutional action, although legal, may result in a dispute between other institutions or individuals. Sanction in this situation involves the legal or arbitration apparatus of civil law to determine whether the institutional action infringed on the rights of another party. The sanctioning apparatus may let the action stand or may force a repeal of the action; and in either case, this may occur with or without an award for damages. Finally, institutions may seek sanction through ideology. This involves demonstrating how controversial actions (both progressive and conservative) fall within socially defined norms. The appeal to various ideological components of society may fail if society is undergoing a structural change with respect to that aspect of ideology. Conversely, the ideology may prevail and thus sanction the action. In each of these modes of sanction, the other modalities of institutional action—communicative, political, and economic—are important, but are not the preponderant modality involved in explaining the sanctions of institutional action.

Time and Space

The two final components of the model are time and space. Both concepts are important for understanding the structuration of urban form, since both position the urban built environment in its geohistorical context. The two concepts of the durée and longue durée are maintained in the model. The durée of interaction is manifest in the feedback loop in the model. This model depicts in essence the durée of immediate interaction. Yet this model does not erroneously distinguish between statics and dynamics, for it also incorporates the longue durée of interaction. This is accomplished through the recognition of this process as just one interaction in the continuing evolution of the urban built environment through time. Thus, although the model graphically illustrates the durée of interaction, it also binds this process to the longue durée.

Space as the setting for interaction bears certain affinities of Soja's (1980) concept of the sociospatial dialectic, but it is articulated within the language and concepts of structuration theory and can be developed along two lines of thought. First, urban space contains the built environment, which is continually evolving yet at the same remarkably stable. If viewed from the joint ideas of reproduction and routinization of social life, the stability of the urban form lends stability to the social form. As the urban form evolves, it not only reflects the changing social form, but also affects it by changing the setting for interaction. Second, urban space reflects the idea of regionalized locales. Within an urban system, several settings of interaction (such as communities) occur throughout. This affects interaction via the idea of time-space distanciation and presence availability. The combination of these two aspects of space assists in the effort to understand the relationship between social relations and spatial form.

NOTES

1. We do not intend to provide a critique or a formal extension of structuration theory in this section. Rather, we intend to lay out sufficient details about the theory to enable us to demonstrate a rational and logical process to empirical analysis. Those interested in a critique may consult, *inter alia*, Gregory (1982b), Layder (1981), Thrift (1983a), and Wright (1983).

2. Layder (1981), working from early texts by Giddens (e.g., 1976), is highly critical of the system-structure dichotomy.

3. The focus on levels of abstraction and analysis is a manifestation of one major methodological convergence currently recognizable in many social theories. For example, see Duncan (1981) and Gibson and Horvath (1983) on levels of abstraction in Marxist analysis; Layder (1981) on the structure-interaction dualism; Sayer (1984) on realist method in social science; and the collection of essays on postmodernism by Foster (1985).

4. We are aware that the conventional approach to ideal types is open to charges of arbitrariness in selection of analytical categories (for instance, see Sayer 1984, 216). It might be preferable to devise a series of empirical categories with a more substantive theoretical pedigree, deriving, for example, from class. Some thoughts in this direction are offered by Gregory (1981), Layder (1981), and Thrift (1983a). We are unable to offer a satisfactory resolution of this problem at this stage; it must suffice to indicate that the identification of appropriate categories is one of the major unresolved difficulties in moving from the abstract to concrete in structuration analysis.

2

The Limits to Human Constructiveness: Giddens and Structuration Theory in Geography

David Wilson

In this chapter, I appraise the structurationist work in geography that has examined inequality of peoples and places. At the risk of alienating two of the volume's contributors, I critique two seminal works on this topic—Moos and Dear (1986) and Warf (1988)—with specific attention to what Giddens calls the duality of structure. I use these works to illuminate perceived weaknesses in structuration theory as illustrated in even the best attempts to apply this framework empirically. I focus on the duality of structure because it lies at the heart of Giddens's theoretical enterprise: it attempts to collapse the traditional structure-agency dualism in social theory by presenting everyday social life as an ongoing human production involving complex interconnections between active beings and bounding circumstances. Three forces—agency, structure, and social system—are seen as ceaselessly penetrating and mutually constructing to generate everyday life and social inequality (Table 2.1).

The duality of structure has been seen as an advance over Althusserian-inspired structuralist accounts of social life, whose casting of structure, agency, and social system have posited essentially frozen and discontinuous dualisms (Bryant and Jary 1991; Cohen 1989). Unlike Althusserian-inspired work that tended to present structures as invariant and uniformly influential impulses coursing across landscapes, Giddens presents structures as place-specific rules and resources whose

Table 2.1
Duality of Structure Conceptions

I.   GIDDENS

SYSTEM: Patterns of local relationships recursively reproduced (sets of regular social practices).

STRUCTURE: Rules and resources instantiated in social reproduction/rearrangement that individuals and collectivities draw upon amid signifying, dominating, and legitimating in everyday life.

AGENCY: Contemplative and reflexive acts of individuals and collectivities that tap structures to reproduce/rearrange social systems over time.

II.   MOOS AND DEAR

SYSTEM: Recurring social practices in Hamilton (capitalist system).

Production of Ghetto: quest for accumulation among housing marker actors and institutions; quest for revenues and political legitimacy among government fractions; quest to protect home equity and neighborhood fabric among households; quest to improve psychiatric patient quality of life among social workers.

Reproduction of Ghetto: quest to upgrade social fabric among residents nearby and within ghetto; quest to improve psychiatric patient quality of life among social workers and Social Planning and Research Council; quest to maintain political legitimacy by Councilperson Brian Hinckley.

STRUCTURES:

Housing Market Actors:
    signification - communicative symbols in English language
    domination - control of housing vacancy information; control of housing capital
    legitimation - invoking prestige of entrepreneurial spirit and ethic

Local Government:
    signification - communicative symbols in English language
    domination - local property assessment powers; eminent domain powers; right to zone districts
    legitimation - invoking value-free bureaucratic ethic

AGENCY: Individual and institutional acts that collectively create psychiatric patient ghetto space.

III.   WARF

SYSTEM: Recurring social practices in Pacific Northwest (capitalist system).

Production of Everyday Life: quest for accumulation among lumber company owners; quest for suitable standards of living among lumber workers; quest for revenues and political legitimacy among government actors and institutions.

Table 2.1 (continued)

STRUCTURES:

<u>Lumber Workers</u>:
signification -	communicative symbolism in English language
domination -	appeal to familial sense-of-place ethic; draw upon organized union actions
legitimation -	invoke exploitation of labor ideology

<u>Lumber Owners</u>:
signification -	communicative symbols in English language
domination -	control of jobs; control of wages
legitimation -	invoke economically benevolent ideology

AGENCY: Individual and institutional acts that collectively shape a uniquely textured everyday life and transformation of region.

instantiated presence gives form and shape to social life (but is not itself that shape). Structures emerge as recursive entities: they are a product of human actions even as their ongoing construction imposes a presence that shapes human actions. In this context, human actions and structures become blurred and ceaselessly interpenetrating influences. Structures are no longer distant translocal impulses that unproblematically direct human actions; they are now locally evolving human constructs whose acknowledged and unacknowledged influences affect everyday life.

Giddens's attempt to collapse these polarities takes on special significance in the area of inequality studies. Before Giddens, the tendency to ascribe social causality to the extremes of structure or agency frequently left scholarship in the peculiarly polarized position of advancing the power and influence of either impersonal structures or contextless agents (see reviews in Cloke et al. 1991; Johnston 1991). Whereas structuralist and functionalist studies accorded preeminence to the role of society over individuals, the alternative view emphasized the properties of individuals as collective builders of their social circumstance. Under structuration, such politically charged categories as "society" and "individual" become interconnected and mutually constructive elements rather than discrete and nominally connected. A more complex presentation of causation potentially emerges that considers the melding of micro and macro, agent and society, and system and place.

THE FOCUS

My focus in this chapter is on the ability of these analyses credibly to cast structure, agency, and social system as mutually transformative elements. Moos and Dear seek the causes for sustained segregation of the mentally ill in Hamilton, Ontario; Warf explores the production of everyday life among lumberers in the U.S. Pacific Northwest. Both studies address a persistent form of societal inequality that has defied simple policy prescriptions. Their objective is admirable: to demonstrate a mutually constructive essence among agency, system, and structure that would substantially advance our understanding of these issues and permit theory to move beyond the analytic quagmire of individual versus society, action versus context, and person versus system.

I argue in this chapter that these studies are provocative social theoretic analyses in their innovative restructuring of Marxian concepts; but they fail to demonstrate convincingly a recursive structure-agency-system link. My argument is similar to the seminal structurationist critiques of Sheppard (1988) and Cadwallader (1988); however, my focus on two recent applications permits a deeper penetration into the issues raised. Unlike structurationist critics like Nicky Gregson (1987, 1989), I do not believe that this set of propositions collapses analysis into an amorphous "relativism" (1989, 237) and has little to offer empirical work. Rather, I think this theory has important informing value in the empirical realm but cannot aptly demonstrate a mutual constructiveness between its constituent elements. I believe that the empirical grounding of the agency, structure, and system concepts grants a priori causal primacy to the forces of structure and social system in the analysis of things like inequality. I argue that this ascription of unequal power to these elements renders agency as something bounded and less important in the production of inequality. With social system and structure granted the capacity to inform the motivations and compulsions behind the patterning of everyday life, agency emerges as reflexive and contemplative but ultimately less causally significant.

At the heart of this problem, I believe, are the difficulties implicit in applying this ontological model. When the hollow core of the structurationist ontology is theorized and the apparatus is empirically grounded, its three-tiered layering of everyday life—agency, structure, and system—take on very different causal roles. Dear and Moos and Warf follow closely Giddens's ontological model, and end up according causal primacy to structure and system. While agency can construct a wide range of rules and resources that help to structure diverse everyday actions, the power of pregiven capitalist imperatives embedded within the social system defines the limits for this human construction. The limits to human constructiveness are set by powerful preconfigured forces in the social system that are persistent and defy local restructuring. In the end, segregation of the mentally infirm and lumberer qualities of life emerge as contextually driven processes.

These two studies are selected for review because I think each has been and will continue to be enormously influential in shaping the agenda of social geography. In my estimation, these studies are important illustrations of what I would call agency-oriented Marxism, a type of analysis that modifies the extremes of structuralist analysis by melding individualist and institutionalist influences with totalizing forces. Despite aforementioned disclaimers, these studies demonstrate that human agency can matter in determining local sociospatial patterns and processes. These studies, however, follow Giddens's ontological model and thereby fail to demonstrate the full potency of human agency. I submit that this shortcoming in these works stems from the difficulties of adding concrete theory to this ontological model. Analysts seeking to theorize extralocal societal forces must implant them within the local social system. This necessary stage in implementing structuration is crucial, because local social systems become carriers of forces whose power to define the essence of structures gives them a determinative status.

I must add two brief caveats. First, I do not wish to suggest that individuals and collectivities cannot transform their local lives and the broader forces that come to imprint their existences. Indeed, multiple social transformations across the globe within the last three years—in the former Soviet Union, former Yugoslavia, Romania, and elsewhere—attest to the potential transformative capabilities of agents. My point, rather, is that these two studies illustrate the problems associated with using structuration theory to unearth this complex process. I do not believe that this weakness is a flaw of these two works in terms of undertheorized concepts or superficial applications of this framework. Rather, I believe that Giddens's brittle ontological categories of agency, structure, and system do not, at the moment, provide us with sufficient robustness to capture the complexities of local social life.

My critique also flows out of a belief in the ability to take apart these blurred conceptions of everyday life (evolving social "messiness") and to assign them points of origin. I am saying, in other words, that the complex social forces seen to permeate social life have conceptual roots that may be assigned to Giddens's three-layered ontological categories: system, structure, and agency. Some critics may find this point contentious, suggesting that these three categories were never meant to represent directly the everyday world. These critics rightly recognize, moreover, that structuration theory seeks to transcend the dualistic nature of the structure-agency debate in focusing on the complex relationship between the evolving social formation and everyday social practices. I agree with these points, but suggest that disentangling the complexities of local life is possible and that each force has a source in the categories of Giddens, regardless of how these categories are precisely defined and empiricized. I treat the categories that Giddens gives us, therefore, as a priori starting points for the initiation of concrete theorization.

THE LITERATURE

Adam Moos and Michael Dear (1986) present a provocative two-part investigation of the utility of structuration theory in an analysis of the Hamilton, Ontario, built environment (for background, see Dear and Moos, Chapter 1). They use structuration to explain the production and reproduction of a psychiatric patient ghetto in Hamilton's inner city between 1975 and 1986 (Table 2.1). In the first part, the deinstitutionalization and spatial isolation of patients are examined as base stages that lead to ghetto creation. These stages are dissected through an institutional assessment that emphasizes the acts of strategic conduct and the production of intended and unintended consequences for local restructuring. In the second part, the ghetto's reproduction is examined by exploring the interrelations of diverse actors in the context of a public outcry against its existence. Moos and Dear present the ghetto as a complex and fluid social construction that involves the interplay of diverse scales, institutions, agents, and processes.

Structuration theory informs the study throughout the various analytical stages. Following Giddens, an institutional examination constitutes the crux of the study (Giddens 1981, 46–48). Institutions are treated as repositories of local rules and resources (structures) that shape the ghetto in multiple ways through four modalities of interaction: communicative, political, economic, and sanction. The study, moreover, adheres to the structurationist plea for a consideration of outcomes as unintended unfoldings (Giddens 1981, 64–65). For instance, benevolently intentional social workers monopolize the communication modality in the patient discharge process that inadvertently helps produce this unintended ghetto. Further, the study demonstrates that uneven power characterizes the diverse actors involved in this process whose routinized procedures generate limits to individual actions (see Giddens 1989, 253–267).

Moos and Dear center their analysis in the duality of structure notion that seeks to bridge the traditional structure and agency chasm. These dualisms are connected by presenting structure and agency as mutually constructive. Through the use of bracketing, human actions are presented as structurally penetrated while structural properties are presented as humanly created. The various forces that spawn this contingent ghetto—core property devaluation, deinstitutionalization, residential steering of psychiatric patients, and others—are seen as produced by contemplative people who negotiate the constraints and enablements of local structures. A rich and varied set of human responses is identified whose effect is to create a locality-specific ghetto space, one constructed by the interplay of a diverse constellation of reflexive actors. These actors—politicians, social workers, realtors, and developers—draw on structural rules and resources amid their active creation of everyday structural properties.

Moos and Dear go far in demonstrating the important role of human agents in constructing the psychiatric patient ghetto. This space is now cast as an active human production, a response to contemplative individuals who negotiate the rules and resources of structures as they circulate through a localized web of institutions. This patient ghetto emerges as spatially, temporally, and physically contingent and reflective of the interventions of multiple actors. Further, these actions are set in a sophisticated theoretical context that considers interactions of unequally powerful actors and institutions, the constraining and enabling influences of structures, and the hermeneutic capabilities of individuals. At the heart of this presentation, structural properties are simultaneously shaped by and shapers of local actors who draw on these rules and resources to generate actions that have intended and unintended outcomes.

Moos and Dear, however, never demonstrate a recursive relationship between agency, structure, and system. While agents are capable of generating diverse local rules and resources, these emerge as diverse shades of gray whose color appears to have a logic steeped in the social system.

On the one hand, agents actively generate local spatial forms. Local government draws on the resources of local zoning powers and local property tax assessment rights (in domination) that inadvertently create a decaying core. Likewise, social workers tap the resources of welfare state altruism and housing referral information (in domination and legitimation) that steer patients to the core. Similarly, builders and developers tap local state political links, planners tap technocratic legitimation ideologies, and suburban block clubs tap local exclusionary zoning codes whose collective outcome is to generate the downtown psychiatric ghetto. Individuals are accorded the capacity to produce a range of rules and resources whose existence comes to circumscribe them and their institutions. On the other hand, individuals are ostensibly unable to get to the core of the forces that structure *the logic* of rules and resources that are actively produced. Agents become doomed to create structures reflexively within limits that are imposed by preconfigured capitalist forces embedded in the social system.

This disproportionate granting of causality is evident from the beginning of their exposition. Moos and Dear rightfully note the profound influence of extralocal structural features like post-World War II suburbanization and the fiscal crisis of the state on the psychiatric ghetto's emergence. They bring out how these forces intersected with the richness of place—its culture, dominant biographies, and economic circumstances—to create a spatially and temporally distinct psychiatric ghetto. In this context, structuralist features (not of the type identified in structuration theory) come to influence profoundly the unfolding of this local form. With these forces being impervious to either intended or unintended local transformations, agents produce local structures (the type identified in structuration theory) that reflect the boundedness of their circumstances. It appears that humans in this locality can determine the timing, location, and physical features of this ghetto construction but cannot deter its emergence. To do this would require the restructuring of capitalist imperatives that lie deeply embedded within Moos and Dear's social system and society.

The power of preconfigured capitalist forces in Moos and Dear's study is also evidenced by the failure of government intervention to break down the ghetto amid pockets of community opposition to its existence. Set against the logic of forces embedded within the social system that created and sustained this entity, public outcries against it and government ameliorative efforts proved fruitless. In this process, community opposition to the ghetto directed at the city council set the stage for a dialogue of several parties. The formalizing and institutionalizing of this dialogue within city council debate resulted in the writing of a counter ghetto bylaw that mandated psychiatric patient facility registration and safeguards against facility clustering. In the end, the bylaw was gotten around and had little impact. Facility operators, motivated by a force—the search for

Figure 2.1
Selected Depictions of Multilayered Social Life

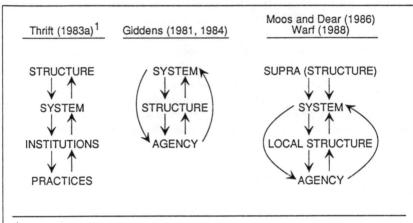

¹Thrift does not advocate the use of this analytical construct but merely outlines it as a theoretical base adopted by numerous social theorists.

profits and cheap buildings—that was impervious to local regulation, continued to locate downtown.

Local opposition therefore facilitated the enacting of regulations that could have affected the size and location of the ghetto. They could not regulate, however, the forces that accounted for its emergence. Opposition was thus potentially important in shaping the ghetto's spatial and temporal dimensions, but in being unable to restructure the sedimented forces that led to its creation was unable to blunt its rise. One suspects that even if local regulations could have banned the acts that collectively led to the ghetto's reproduction, its re-emergence would have been inevitable. While the legal acts of agents could be locally regulated, the forces that generated the logic of its unfolding remained intact. Whether through illicit acts or repealing legislation, the ghetto would have again arisen.

Moos and Dear follow Giddens's duality of structure proposal to its finest nuance. They conceptually situate structures as mediaries between agency and social system, producing the structurationist skeleton of agency-structure-system that is supposed to collapse the traditional structure-agency dualism and powerfully implicate each in the shaping of everyday life. However, when they fill the ontological model with deeper theory to explain concrete local conditions, things change (Figure 2.1). Needing to incorporate the influence of broad social and economic forces on the local, structures emerge as local rules and resources that embody the logic of extralocal functions and imperatives. Interestingly enough, the impulses that drive the reflexive construction of rules and resources go unmentioned in the text, but are glaringly apparent in the discussion of strategic conduct that guides actors and institutions. Structures *exist* as local rules and resources, but have a *logic* ingrained within the local social system that appears to be part of a pregiven universe of capitalist objects.

Barney Warf (1988) has recently used structuration to examine the social and economic transformation of the U.S. Pacific Northwest lumber industry (Table 2.1). Structuration is used as a lens to capture this region's contingent but ordered economic transformation and to unearth its consequences for local capital and labor. His two bodies of theory—structuration as envisaged by Giddens and business cycle spatial division of labor theory as put forth by Massey (1983, 1984)—are used to illuminate the complexities of regional change. Warf has a twofold motivation for conducting this study: to begin fashioning a regional geography that is sensitive to political-economic concerns and to unearth the complexities of capital-labor relations within contemporary U.S. society.

At the most basic level, local places are seen to be profoundly affected by the broader societal process of production and uneven development. Under changing conditions of comparative economic advantage that characterize capitalist production, layers of investment incrementally fashion the specifics of place: "The associated layers of investment decisively come to shape the history, geography, and social life of local places. Each 'wave' of production alters the local form of the labor process, levels of prices, profits, wage and standards of living . . . and more subtly, patterns of state intervention and local ideological and cultural climates" (1988, 329). Through actors like firms, workers, and the state, each round of production becomes etched into a local social and physical fabric. Places are thus ceaselessly being penetrated by the unfolding of broader economic circumstances, a process that defines the economic and social grist for human negotiation and the construction of everyday life.

While capitalist production defines the broader parameters of everyday life, individuals and institutions creatively process and act on these stimulants to create distinctive places. Humans create their own localized worlds as reflexive beings that inherit preconditions to action. While everyday life cannot be divorced from the production process because work is a central determinant of income and socioeconomic status, the perceptions and ideologies that people actively manufacture come to order common affairs. Stocks of internalized knowledge derived from the repetitious and ceaseless tapping of existent cultures and ideologies mediate the broader process of uneven development at the ground level. Everyday life, therefore, does not passively reflect regional structures, but actively contributes to their creation: "Processes such as regional growth and decay do not simply 'occur' without reference to the way in which people experience and interpret their world. . . . As 'common sense,' therefore, ideology is thus not incidental to the functioning of society but [is] a necessary condition for its operation: knowledge is not simply descriptive of social reality, but constitutive as well" (1988, 329).

Warf begins by tracing changes in rounds of production that have reverberated powerfully across the Pacific Northwest since 1840. Lumber production, long dominant in the region's economy, was continually altered in its output, needs and fiscal health by business cycle fluctuations. The most important wave, the Kuznets, altered local labor needs and production requirements and thereby set the stage for various changes in levels of wage rates, union resistance, and appeals to the state for intervention. Having demonstrated that each regime of production defined the parameters for capital-labor relations, Warf then brings out the specifics of how cultural and ideological diversity negotiated local conflicts. Four waves of production are correlated with the specifics of local social conditions from 1860 to 1969. While the actions of capital and labor never unfolded independently of the labor process, it was continually being informed by an evolving matrix of taken-for-granted knowledge and ideology. This knowledge and ideology was a humanly configured set of constructions. Individuals become carriers of both class relations and the localized circumstances of the Pacific Northwest in their confrontation with changing economic conditions.

I believe that Warf goes similarly far in demonstrating the utility of structuration theory. As in Moos and Dear's study, everyday life is salvaged as a humanly constructed thing, a contingently unfolding flow of events that creatively builds while it mirrors evolving society. At the center of Warf's exposition are the imperatives of broader economy, a humanly produced apparatus whose inner law of uneven development penetrates the fabric of far-flung local places. This casting of these two interactive dualities permits Warf to connect the capitalist economy and local everyday life along a mutually presupposing continuum. The broader economy is constitutive of human action; everyday life is impregnated with economic forces. In the process, the once frozen and discrete categories of structure and agency meld together in a fluid interconnectedness that collapses conceptions of mutually exclusive domains.

I believe that similar to Moos and Dear, Warf falls prey to the implicit granting of causal primacy to structures and the social system. Structures are seen as local rules and resources that, in being constructed by reflexive individuals, bear the dominating imprint of forces embedded within the capitalist social system. Steeped in the logic of the social system, structures are accorded the capacity to produce "boundedness of individual action and thought" (p. 327), "new preconditions to action of the laborers" (p. 327), and "the matrix of available resources and constraints" (p. 342). In the final analysis, structures emerge as creatively generated rules and resources that are produced under the local circumstance of guiding capitalist impulses and imperatives. While the production of structural rules and resources is a skilled accomplishment of reflexive actors, structures bear the imprint of forces that define the limits for creative human construction.

Human agency emerges as a rich, open-ended set of potentialities that take a different form across time-space. The commodity production system itself, for example, varies widely across space, for "it has no predetermined form: it is contingent, arising from and given its shape by the people who live and create it daily" (p. 328). Active agents may thereby substantially rearrange structures (i.e., virtually existent local rules and resources) that alter the texture and flavor of local social life. The problem here, however, is a failure to address explicitly *the degree* to which local life can be restructured under conditions infused with capitalist prerogatives. Once again, the range of possible structures that can arise (as carriers of nonlocal capitalist forces with a local "flavor") appears to be limited.

Agency's circumscribed capacity to create is revealed in the study's most crucial proposition: boom and bust fluctuations in lumber production affect and are affected by agency-induced wage conflicts. This proposition is key because it advances a mutually constructive relationship between economic waves and human actions that is at the heart of Warf's theoretical agenda. In the first half of this constructiveness, Warf demonstrates how the four waves generate levels of capital-labor conflict. For example, where economic slumps and declining output necessitated wage cuts, conflict frequently ensued. On the other hand, the affective role of conflict in the structuring of and logic behind these waves was not demonstrated. Nowhere in the analysis does the power of repetitious human actions have the potential to restructure the temporal rhythms and the constitution of these waves. In the end, Kuznets and Kondratieff waves appear as inexorable capitalist outgrowths. While their effects can be modified somewhat through localized human interpretation and response, their existence and essence appear inalterable.

In this unbalanced granting of causation to structure, lumberers tapped everyday rules and resources while their limits to constructing everyday life were bounded by extralocal forces. The limits to human constructiveness were defined by the overarching social system that guided humans to build structures consistent with an entrenched commodity production system. In the final analysis, local life was actively shaped but circumscribed in its range of unfoldings by structures that absorbed nonlocal capitalist forces. Individuals were important creators of their worlds, but did so as they operated within bounded circumstances. Once again, the pregiven universe of capitalist configurations provided the power to define the dynamics of the local.

THE BRITTLE ONTOLOGY OF STRUCTURATION

Structuration is an ontological model of everyday social life that establishes a lens for the filtering of concrete theory. It is not a set of causal propositions about social reality, but is rather a scheme that informs research about how actors both create and are created by social systems. With its emergence, two areas of criticism have dominated. First, critics have questioned the utility of a framework that does not attempt to promulgate concrete theories of social action. Second (the one that this chapter addresses), many have been skeptical of Giddens's ability to forge a ceaselessly interconnecting duality out of the dualisms of structure and agency that have so bedeviled the social sciences.

Giddens (1989, 1991) has recently defended his framework in a series of articles. First, he suggests that structuration was never meant to be a stand-alone theory, but rather was designed to sensitize social theoretic investigations to the belief that actors are both creators of social systems and are created by them (Giddens 1991, 204). Second, Giddens deems the structure-agency causal issue irrelevant in relation to the debate around structuration's utility. To Giddens structuration "is not a series of generalizations about how far 'free action' is possible in respect of social constraint," but is rather "an attempt to provide the conceptual means of analyzing the often delicate and subtle interlacings of reflexively organized action and institutional constraint" (Giddens 1991, 204).

At the heart of my thesis is the belief that Giddens's defense on this last point is misguided. While he is correct that structuration is a scheme for understanding the general interplay between agents and society, I believe his writings specify the reach of these respective entities. When social systems are accorded the capacity to catch and disseminate the influence of broad-based economic and political imperatives, their capacity to influence situated practices is a priori potent. In this context, knowledgeable and reflexive agents build local structures and social systems but are ostensibly less able to define their essence. Giddens, in other words, gives us an informing apparatus at a fairly general level and, in the process, alerts us to the capabilities of structure and agency in crafting the other. By exposition, his informing theory has implications for how far human creativity is possible in respect to social constraint and social enablement. His explicit goal may not be to address this important issue; he nevertheless does so as an unintended consequence of his theorizing.

This chapter builds on those who have scrutinized structuration theory on this point by probing the ability of structurationist studies to demonstrate a true system-structure-agency recursiveness. My point throughout has been that with Giddens's theoretical tools, this recursiveness cannot be demonstrated. While a connectiveness between free action and structural influence can be shown with deft theorizing, such work in the end cannot show a mutual constructiveness among these elements. When neo-Marxism or other grand modes of theorization are used to fill the ontology's hollow core, these bodies of theory conflict with the goal of demonstrating this recursiveness. How agents tap structures to produce and rearrange the penetrative influence of things like accumulation functions, commodity consumptionist imperatives, and the like is problematic. In the end, plugging in broad processes and illustrating that local agents and institutions are important constructors of these forces renders this enterprise most difficult.

Local social systems, or sets of localized social practices, are the points for inserting these extralocal influences. It is here that the potency of regional economic forces, nationalist political ideologies, far-flung cultural mores, and a wealth of other nonlocal forces are brought to bear on local conditions. These forces, refracted through a complex local lens of cultures, biographies, and institutions to influence local life, are rightfully cast in Marxian, Weberian, or other terms that lend a sophistication to a place-based examination. Once in place, however, these pervasive forces appear to take on a deterministic status that makes it enormously difficult (if not impossible) to demonstrate that active agents can rearrange their guiding influence. While agents may be portrayed as complex and contemplative, the degree to which they can reflexively rearrange local life is an issue that plagues the duality of structure concept.

Moos and Dear and Warf wrestle with the aforementioned quandary and inadvertently present two types of structures that circulate through daily life (Figure 2.1). The first type, similar to Thrift's (1983a) depiction of the "compositional structure" concept, represents broad-based materialist impulses that transcend local places. These impulses exert influence in the fabric of local life, in what Bourdieu (1977) calls the taken-for-granted preconditions to routinized acts. The second type, what Giddens identifies as local instantiated structures, represents the everyday rules and resources that individuals draw on in daily life. These structures are the constraints and enablements embedded in the everyday acts of signification, domination, and legitimation that constitute the heart of the duality of structure concept.

In the end, Thrift's (1983a) and Giddens's (1979, 1981, 1984) divergent conceptions of structure appear in the same studies. While compositional structures define the broad parameters within which everyday life is constructed, instantiated structures define the rich complexities of place. Compositional structures bound daily life in defining possible options for emergence; localized structures shade daily life with the array of human possibilities that reflexive agents can produce. In these studies, a connectedness between these structures exists with the compositional structures being determinative. Its far-flung and penetrative essence configures the roots of localized structures; it penetrates every corner of local life whose mediation by active agents embeds place-specific values and assumptions in local social fabrics. The problem, of course, is that structures are now not only locally instantiated rules and resources, but also far-flung logics and imperatives.

There is another interesting twist to these authors' insertion of two operative structural types. These studies, with no explicit recognition of having done so, resuscitate Derek Layder's (1981) well-known distinction between two simultaneously existing structures, contextual and interactional structures. On the one hand, interactional structures, defined as the "situation-specific elements or indexical features of interaction" (p. 101), are the localized and humanly created constraints and enablements that are variable and easily modified across places. Humans are purposive beings and are the crucible for understanding localized interactions. On the other hand, contextual structures, defined as "the relatively autonomous and impersonal set of preconstituted constraints which govern conduct quite independently of the creative and constituting capacities of actors" (p. 94), are the objective and prior inheritance of constraints coursing through everyday life. I believe that, in the end, the works of Moos and Dear and Warf are forced into this layering of social life by the limited ontological categories that Giddens provides for them.

CONCLUSION

Geographers have made increased use of structuration theory in their quest to unravel the intricacies of people and place inequalities across the globe. With growing disillusionment about the insights that could be yielded from rigidifying structuralist analysis and contextless hermeneutic perspectives, increased experimentation with this new model has ensued. As the chapters in this book suggest, rich and suggestive structurationist studies are emerging in geography that are building on a corpus of seminal studies (see early studies by Evans 1987; Gregory 1982a; Kellerman 1987; Pred 1984, 1985; Smith 1983). Whereas much of this work is continuing to use neo-Marxist theory to ground structuration, a growing number of studies have looked to the writings of Bhaskar, Bourdieu, Layder, Habermas, and others in interesting ways.

Upon reflection, these rudimentary structurationist studies appear to offer the same strengths and weaknesses that structurationist studies in parallel disciplines reflect (see Giddens 1989, 1991). On the one hand, these studies exhibit a growing theoretical sophistication in recognizing the important roles of individuals and institutions in generating local inequalities. In the process, previously human-decentered objects like uneven metropolitan development, regional restructuring, economic profit cycles, and patterns of residential investment become seen as humanly constructed and institutionally crafted things. Agents no longer act out preconfigured social scripts, but instead reflexively generate unique social and spatial imprints in local settings.

On the other hand, these works fail to demonstrate the mutually constructive role of agents and society in generating inequality. The duality of structure ontology that Giddens provides is at the center of this shortcoming. Even with agents presented as reflexive and capable of generating unintended consequences from actions that can reverberate across local settings, they appear as bounded. My point throughout this chapter has been that Giddens's ontology offers us a set of categories that is not up to the task of demonstrating the full power and influence of agents. When these categories are empirically grounded, a determinative status is ascribed to concepts of structure and social system that is somewhat reminiscent of Althusserian-inspired structuralism. While there is a danger of carrying the parallel between these two immensely different theorists too far, their frameworks share one important commonality: their ontologies accord causal primacy to preconfigured capitalist forces.

It is obvious that a great deal of difference divides the work of Althusser and Giddens. While Althusser sought to offer a science of Marxism that relegated empirical differences across places (and, for that matter, empricism) to an epiphenomenal status, Giddens aspired to just the opposite. Giddens rejected unequivocally the structural-functionalism of Althusser and his marginalizing of local richness to the power of totalizing wholes; he sought to cast local actors and social settings as vital constructors of everyday life. In this vein, Giddens has clung to only certain key principles of Marxism, noting that "there is much in Marx that is mistaken, ambiguous or inconsistent; and in many respects Marx's writings exemplify features of nineteenth century thought which are plainly defective when looked at from the perspective of our century" (Giddens 1981, 1). The ontologies of Althusser and Giddens, however, are similar in their granting of causal dominance to preconfigured capitalist forces.

Giddens provides us with more theoretical sophistication, presenting structures as a conduit for agency and social system that captures the human-constructed essence of local rules and resources and how they simultaneously reflect and shape local life. Althusser (1965), in contrast, presents structures as overarching compulsions and forces that flow out of the needs of capitalist economic systems to reproduce and flourish. Structures are outgrowths of totalizing wholes, constitutive of forces that bind and regulate local settings. In the final analysis, however, the social systems of Giddens become somewhat like Althusser's structures—embodying translocal forces and preconfigured at their core to define the parameters for human constructiveness. The inheritance of such imperatives and functions embedded in social systems becomes enormously influential, serving to define the conditions under which active agency operates.

I conclude that there is an enigmatic quality to structuration. On the one hand, its ability to elucidate the power of agents in constructing the nature of local life adds much to our comprehension of the social sphere. The work of Moos and Dear and Warf illustrate this, casting agents as reflexive beings capable of generating diverse local structures and conditions. On the other hand, structuration's difficulties in demonstrating a mutual constructiveness between its essential ingredients—agency, system, and structure—undermine a central theoretical objective. It is enormously difficult, if not impossible, to show the transformative capabilities of these entities when concrete theorization (e.g., Marxism) is employed. The irony, therefore, is that structuration advances our ability to implicate agents and structures in the production of social inequalities but fails to offer a way to supersede the persistent individual-society distinction.

Studies of societal inequalities appear to have come full circle in geography. Early attention focused on the capacity of autonomous agents and institutions to generate things like segregation, poverty, and inner-city decay. Under the sway of structuralist Marxism, an emphasis on the power of totalizing wholes soon supplanted this. The logic of systemwide functions and imperatives was thrust to the forefront. Over recent years, geographers have sought a middle ground between these extremes, one that recognizes the influence of agents but also the power of bounding circumstances. Structuration is the most recent novel attempt to excavate this middle ground, and it offers the prospect of reconciling notions of structural influence with potent human action. While this framework helps to dissect the categories that make up everyday life, its ability to demonstrate structure-agency recursiveness remains problematic. It is on this important issue, I believe, that the basis for a revisionist structuration must soon be fashioned.

3

Structuration Theory and Electronic Communications

Barney Warf

By emphasizing how social practices are situated historically and geographically, critical social theory has rescued conceptions of time and space from their sterile Kantian reputations as static, uniform, objectively given entities. On the contrary, history and geography are socially produced phenomena that cannot be comprehended except through the structured, contingent actions of people. The relatively of time and space is derived from the specific structures of production and reproduction found in every society (i.e., via praxis). However, although space and time are socially defined and vary historically, they generally assume the qualities of objective (i.e., naturally given) facts that condition the everyday lives of individuals (Harvey 1990).

With these comments in mind, it is worth pondering the profound changes of the late twentieth century, including unprecedented technological innovation, an explosion of services, the internationalization of production, and rapid increases in global trade. A significant aspect of the recent sea change in the global economy, and with it the patterns of everyday life, is the widespread introduction of electronic communications systems, which have had profound effects on the geography of the world system and the locales that comprise it. So extensive has been the deployment of electric communications that they are often celebrated as a principal harbinger of the "Fifth Kondratieff" wave (Hall and Preston 1988). Unfortunately, mainstream accounts of electronic communications generally lack a grounding in social theory and political economy. Because geographers have, until very recently, largely shied away from this topic, the understanding of the spatial repercussions of electronic communications remains poorly developed.

This chapter offers a discussion of the role of electronic communications within structuration theory. It begins with an overview of Giddens's presentation of time-space distanciation, arguing that his emphasis on time-geography led to an incomplete understanding of spatial relations that exaggerates the importance of face-to-face communications. Second, it turns to the role of information flows and communications as fundamental dimensions of the structuration of any social system. Third, it points to the profound transformation in the time-space distanciation inaugurated by electronic communications, particularly the elimination of the need for what Giddens calls presence availability. Fourth, it dramatizes how electronic communications have played a key role in the global transition to a post-Fordist regime of production. Fifth, it stresses the emphatically political nature of these technologies, intertwined as they are with existing and potential power relations. The conclusion offers some comments on the theoretical implications of these observations, calling for an understanding of electronically mediated spaces in which the semiotics of image and language play a central role.

TIME-SPACE DISTANCIATION: FIELD NOTES AND A CRITICAL READING

The reassertion of time and space to the forefront of social theory is a critical task of contemporary analysis. Structuration theory has contributed mightily to this project through its portrayal of social systems as chronically repeated forms of social conduct situated in particular locales. Much analytical attention has been devoted to the problem of how societies differentially bind time and space (i.e., the ways in which agents utilize and are simultaneously constrained by their histories and geographies in the course of daily life). Temporal relations (i.e., the daily round, life span, the longue durée) and the geographical environment (i.e., the landscape, architecture, the body) thus simultaneously constitute a set of resources and constraints that heavily condition the circumstances in which social reproduction occurs. Giddens (1984) defines the multiple ways in which societies are differentially "stretched" over time and space as distanciation (i.e., the temporal and spatial patterns of existence that people draw on daily and in turn reproduce unknowingly).

Like many other European contributors to social theory (notably, Foucault 1972b, 1979, but see also Lefebvre 1974), Giddens's analysis of time and space places a heavy emphasis on the individual human body. In large part, this focus derives from his extensive reliance on time-geographers, particularly Hagerstrand (1970), who depicted the structures of everyday life in terms of coupling and capability constraints. Pred (1990b) continues this tradition admirably, portraying societies and geographies as "weaving dances" of individuals unintentionally reproducing and changing social and spatial relations through their everyday actions. The exercise of human agency, therefore, was confined to the time-space prisms in which individuals physically exist. Cohen (1989, 100) notes that "the human body, in effect, serves as the vehicle that connects one set of face to face encounters with others during the course of system reproduction." Consequently, Giddens argues that social integration (agents' self and mutual monitoring of behavior) occurs largely through face-to-face communication in small locales (e.g., the workplace, conversations, the household, etc.). What Giddens calls "presence availability"—the location of two or more bodies in the same place at the same time—therefore becomes a necessary precondition for social integration to occur. Spatially, the "packing" of interactions in particular locations was instrumental to the formation of "locales," which range in spatial scale from the household to the nation-state (Giddens 1984, 118).

Time-geography provided an important avenue to ground structuration theory geographically (Pred 1984) and productively emphasized the temporal nature of locales; its precepts continue to exert a strong influence on Giddens's perspective. However, there were inevitably heavy analytical costs to be paid by borrowing so heavily from this approach. Time-geography has always lacked a coherent account of structural context and is even more deficient in its account of human consciousness and the living subject. Without appropriating for itself these necessary conceptual foundations, time-geography is doomed to recapitulate the obvious. By relying on Hagerstrand so extensively, therefore, structuration theory suffered from an unnecessarily narrow depiction of how social relations are mediated territorially.

Consequently, as Gregory (1989) notes, structuration theory is theoretically compromised in its understanding of both the social production of space (i.e., the spatial division of labor) and the symbolic meaning of place (i.e., the hermeneutics of lived experience), both of which comprise essential dimensions woven into the fabric of everyday life. What structuration theory desperately needs, therefore, is to take political economy as seriously as scholars of political economy have taken Giddens's arguments. In particular, structuration theory must emphasize that social interaction and integration occur differentially over time and across a variety of spatial scales; as will be seen shortly, presence availability is only one way in which interaction occurs. In the context of the capitalist innovative juggernaut, time-space distanciation is subject to profound and continuous technological change, about which Giddens says relatively little. Although he acknowledges the roles of such events within the context of emerging capitalism (Giddens 1987), structuration theory still exhibits a persistent bias that focuses on presence availability and the human body. With electronic communications and the increasingly nonlocal ways in which consciousness is constructed, this emphasis is largely unwarranted. Before a deeper explication of this process is offered, however, the role of communications in binding agents together must be addressed.

INFORMATION, COMMUNICATIONS, AND STRUCTURATION

The Wittgensteinian revolution in social science forced an irreversible recognition of the importance of language in social reproduction. Language and related notions of culture, consciousness, and ideology have taken a place next to labor as a central feature of human life. The ways in which information is made available or restricted over time and space, therefore, have enormous impacts on the particular form of any society and the reproduction of ideologies and social knowledge across time and space.

Nonstructural Marxists, notably the Frankfurt School (e.g., Horkheimer and Adorno 1972), were among the first to link these issues to wider concepts of power, ideology, and the social production of discourse (however, see Smythe 1977). Habermas (1979), the intellectual heir to the Frankfurt School, developed a sweeping perspective on social life and epistemology centered around language. In his view, social emancipation comes with the elimination of barriers to discourse, or the movement toward an "ideal speech situation," a perspective that substantially retains the Enlightenment notion of reason. Habermas's project, however, holds important lessons for structuration theory. In particular, Habermas's concern is largely epistemological, while Giddens's is primarily ontological, leading Giddens (1982a) to accuse Habermas of a "hollow core," the lack of an explicit concept of social relations. It follows that an effective interpretation of communications must originate from a social critique grounded in historical and ontological, rather than philosophical, origins.

In structuration theory, communications play a central role in the negotiation of everyday life and in the reproduction of social relations. Social reproduction is held to occur (albeit not unproblematically) through the recurrent rhythms of everyday life, which is a skilled accomplishment. To live in a society, people must know a great deal about how it is structured and how it operates. For social relations to exist, therefore, people must possess considerable amounts of common sense (i.e., the living subject is epistemologically significant, even if this body of knowledge is largely taken for granted). Giddens has succeeded in arguing that the route between the Scylla of structural determinism and the Charybdis of ahistorical voluntarism is by portraying social relations as the unintended outcomes of conscious individual actors conducting their everyday lives. Agents' acquisition of information and its transmission to others in time and space, which is central to their mutual monitoring of behavior, occurs only through the act of communication; it is through participation in language acts that the human subject is socially constituted. The ways in which information is acquired, represented, stored, processed, and transmitted, therefore, are fundamental to how social relations unfold over time and space.

Because all acts of communication necessarily draw on, reproduce, and transform ideologies (subjects must know about the world in order to communicate), they necessarily reflect and affect power relations deeply embedded in everyday life (Warf 1986). Thus, communication is an inherently political act inseparable from wider structures of political economy (Garnham 1990). For these reasons, Giddens argues that the control and storage of information and knowledge are fundamental authoritative resources. The importance of the structure of communications clearly transcends Marxism's casual dismissal of the media as part of an epiphenomenal superstructure.

In preliterate societies, communication occurs almost entirely through oral tradition (i.e., speech), in which presence availability was a prerequisite for communication. The time-space structure of most tribal societies, therefore, conforms to the simplest time-geography model. Speech as a critical form of social interaction has remained critical long after oral language was supplemented by other forms of communication.

With the emergence of class divided society, however, writing radically changed how information was disseminated over time and space, allowing for the first time communications without presence availability. As part of a complex series of intertwined socioeconomic and technological changes, writing had significant political and spatial repercussions. Geographically and historically, the invention of writing coincided with the emergence of the city within early slave-based empires. Within these, writing emerged as the first method by which information could be stored, largely to allow early state bureaucracies to tally the surplus extracted from their populations (Mann 1986).

Similarly, the invention of the printing press and mass literacy coincided, not accidentally, with the shift in the "container" of power relations from the city to the nation-state during the emergence of capitalism (Giddens 1981). Indeed, as Giddens (1987, 124) argues, the formation of the nation-state itself was largely contingent on a series of successive time-space compressions, including the canal system, the stage coach, railroads, the telegraph, and the calendar. Because these innovations allowed for an increasingly precise monitoring of social life (surveillance) by the state, they were important to its internal pacification, the monopolization of the means of violence by the state and its removal from the labor contract. In the same vein, literacy and printing were fundamental to the emergence of liberal democracies, nationalist politics, and the labor markets of the industrial revolution (Ong 1982); it was no accident that the Enlightenment coincided with age of print (Postman 1985). Both writing and printing, therefore, were strategic elements in the historical construction of new production systems, new power relations, new ideologies, and new forms of everyday life. Historically, it is apparent that increasingly elaborate forms of communication integrated ever larger numbers of people over progressively larger territories (i.e., they expanded the time-space distanciation of social relations and eroded the centrality of face-to-face contact). With the introduction of electronic communications, physical absence ceased to hinder system coordination (Giddens 1984, 35).

FROM SPACE TO HYPERSPACE: TIME-SPACE
CONVERGENCE AND COMPRESSION

Until the advent of electronic communications in the late nineteenth century, transportation and communications were synonymous. The resulting analytical emphasis on the human body was well merited, for all information was necessarily conveyed through the physical movement of bodies in time and space (at a maximum rate of roughly 40 miles per hour). Electronic communications, however, ruptured this unity, permitting out-of-body experiences and wreaking havoc with the coupling constraints of time-geographers. Previously, the indivisibility of the human body meant that information was largely confined to one locale at a time; with electronic communications, however, individuals no longer required presence availability to interact with one another. With electrification, the distances between linguistic transactions expanded infinitely, while the time necessary to transmit them shrank to zero. Electronic communications thus allowed for a dramatic reconfiguration of the spatial and temporal matrices of opportunities and constraints in which everyday life unfolded. Giddens's emphasis on speech (i.e., face-to-face contact), therefore, obscures the importance of communications mediated through channels such as electronic databases, television, the telephone, radio, and so forth and the ways in which human consciousness can be created and reproduced in nonlocal ways, often involving vast distances.

The introduction of electronic communications was an integral part of the historical construction of modernity and the commodification of time and space. The history of electronic communications is intimately interwined with the emergence and geography of industrial capitalism and is punctuated by the introduction of several innovations of far-reaching importance. Pred (1977) revealed how Morse's invention of the telegraph in the 1840s had immediate and widespread effects, particularly with regard to the uneven circulation of information among highly specialized commercial circuits, enhancing the status of some cities and eroding that of others. Electrical lighting and photography in the late nineteenth century inaugurated new rhythms of daily life and new ways of experiencing time and space (Marvin 1988). In the same vein, by the 1920s, radio became the public's most common source of news, entertainment, and commercial information.

Alexander Bell's invention of the telephone in 1876 created what is still by far the most commonly employed form of two-way telecommunications. The telephone had important repercussions for the structure of urban areas (Abler 1977), accelerating the explosion of suburbia. The telephone allowed the formation of "communities without propinquity," or groups of people sharing common interests but not common places and contributing to the dissolution of urban neighborhoods. From the beginning, however, the effects of this technology reverberated differentially across class and space, disproportionately enhancing the power of some social groups and disempowering others (Martin

1991). Marvin (1988) illustrates that the telephone did not simply allow communication over longer distances; it threatened class relations by extending the boundaries of who could speak with whom, altering modes of friendship, romance, business, and other formal and informal networks.

Today, it is difficult to exaggerate the role of electronic communications in the everyday life of people who inhabit the industrial world. Their perceptions of the world—and of themselves—are deeply shaped by the information that floods the electronic airways. News, entertainment, and advertising—all deeply ideological texts—are shaped by their electronic "wrapping." By providing much of the corpus of taken-for-granted knowledge that individuals draw on in their everyday lives, electronic media form a critical network of assets and constraints that structure the world of lived experience. In short, for many people in late-twentieth-century capitalism, electronic communications and practical consciousness have become inseparable (but not synonymous).

Television, for example, exerts a profound influence over most people's interpretations of the world and of themselves, shaping from infancy their perceptions, stereotypes, role models, wants and desires, morals, values and priorities, notions of sexuality, and the multiple ways in which they come to comprehend social issues and problems. In the United States, in which 99 percent of all households own televisions, the average television is on 7.5 hours per day; only work and sleep command more time. The average American child witnesses 18,000 murders and 17,000 sex acts on television by age eighteen, desensitizing many to the violence and eroticism of the real world (Kubey and Csikszentmihalyi 1990). There are, inevitably, powerful consequences of this exposure.

Television advertising, for example, which completes the circulation of commodities, was both part of the cultural formation of modernity and a major avenue for the penetration of commodity relations into everyday life (Marchand 1985); the average U.S. viewer sees 20,000 television commercials per year. Poster (1990, 48) notes that "so successful is the practice of the TV ad that it has expanded its domain from commodities to public service messages, political campaign tactics, military recruitment, and religious donations."

What television does best, however, is to entertain. By far the most common form of recreation in the industrialized West, and, increasingly, the Third World, television has become the model for all other forms of discourse, so that politics, education, religion, and other forms of communication must become entertaining in order to interest the public (Postman 1985). The alluring images transmitted through television range from cheap escapism (e.g., soap operas and sitcoms) to financial news and have varying impacts, including stress reduction, release from boredom, and serving as myth and ritual, all accomplished through the narcotic, entranced hypnotic stage that sustained television viewing induces. It is not accidental that a vast literature on television employs such terminology as "couch potato," "the electronic teat," and the "electronic wasteland." Sabbah (1985) notes that television reinforces social and spatial segregation, creating a "growing individual seclusion in a world of self-gratifying images"

(p. 223). These conclusions are hardly novel; Frankfurt School theorists argued long ago that the mass media render their audiences passive and one dimensional (Horkheimer and Adorno 1972; Marcuse 1964).

In short, television in large part structures the world of common everyday understandings and shared interpretations. Invoking Goffman's dramaturgical model of "front stages" and "back stages," an interpretation with which Giddens is much infatuated, Meyrowitz (1985) contends that by mixing audiences normally kept separate in the course of daily life (i.e., allowing a glimpse into the back stages of the relatively powerful), television nullifies temporal and spatial segregation, allowing for asynchronous gatherings of heterogeneous populations. Television thus does not simply alter the time-geography of everyday life because so many hours are spent in front of the tube; it is the medium through which enormously powerful social ideologies are produced, conveyed, and reproduced. As a shifting series of texts, television blurs the distinction between fantasy and reality, the possible and the impossible. For many people, television is more real than reality itself (Luke 1991). Curiously, given its enormous significance, the geographic literature on television is virtually nonexistent (but see Gould 1984); Adams (1992), however, argues that television functions as a gathering place in the sense of shared meanings.

At times, Giddens explicitly acknowledges the degree to which electronic communications radically expanded the time-space distanciation of social interaction: "The most radical disjuncture of relevance in modern history (whose implications are very far from being exhausted) is the separation of media of communication, by the development of electronic signalling from the media of transportation: the latter always having involved by some means or other, the mobility of the human body. Morse's invention of the electromagnetic telegraph marks as distinctive a transition in human cultural development as the wheel or any other technological innovation ever did" (1984, 123). However, Giddens's discussion of electronic communications generally focuses on the impacts on bureaucratic institutions (e.g., corporations) rather than the patterns of everyday life, other than to claim that coupling and capability constraints have become increasingly irrelevant. He offers little discussion, for example, about the specific effects of television, the telephone, radio, or any other such medium. This silence is particularly curious in light of the earlier emphasis on the body and presence availability found in structuration theory. Similarly, structuration theory suffers from an impoverished sense of technological change, often relying on simplistic diffusion approaches (Gregory 1985). In both cases, there is an inadequate conceptualization of how spaces are reconstituted by the ubiquitous but far from neutral impacts of electronic communications. Gregory (1989, 198) argues that "a sustained theorization of spatial structures of technical change would . . . convert Giddens's scattered accounts of the uneven development of capitalism from the prefunctory to the persuasive."

Although some electronic media such as television comprise a one-way form of communication, other forms (e.g., the telephone) allow discretionary, bilateral contact and, consequently, at least some degree of mutual policing of behavior over considerable distances. Thus, agents can glean at least some insight into the doings of others, and perceive that others are perceiving them as well, without sharing presence availability. Mutual knowledge is thus recalled at the level of practical consciousness while it is being transported across time and space, in the process unintentionally reproducing social practices. Geographically, opportunities for social association thus no longer depend on propinquity. Lost in the transformation, of course, are the numerous subtleties inherent in face-to-face communications. Cohen (1989, 103), for example, notes that the telephone "fails to transmit the physical gestures, facial expressions, and postural alignments that comprise routine means of conveying tacit information and emotional cues in full fledged social encounters." Such problems may indicate why presence availability is still so critical for information-intensive occupations in the managerial and administrative functions of large corporations. Despite these inconveniences, electronic communications allow agents engaged in bilateral, but uneven, power relations to remain in sufficiently close contact that the fundamental purposes of their interactions are fulfilled (e.g., supervision of subordinates, coordination of schedules, entertainment, etc.).

Within geography, the impacts of telecommunications have generally been approached from the perspective of time-space convergence (e.g., Brunn and Leinbach 1991; Janelle 1969). Harvey (1989, 1990) argues that the numerous telecommunications systems introduced during the late-twentieth-century transition to post-Fordism have accelerated the "annihilation of space by time" through an acceleration of the turnover time of capital (see also Swyngedouw 1989). The cultural and ideological appropriation of this transformation is manifested in the form of "time-space compression," the rapid integration of vast amounts of information from far-flung locales into the rhythms of everyday life. Time-space convergence or compression reflects capitalism's incessant tendency to produce new economic and social forms, new technologies, new ideologies, new political practices, and new geographies and has historical antecedents (Berman 1982). During the period in which modernist culture became hegemonic, for example, the introduction of railroads and the telegraph initiated new ways of experiencing time and space that found their ways into the fabric of everyday life as they were internalized, generally without critical reflection, by the masses of late eighteenth and early nineteenth century Europe and North America (Kern 1983).

The introduction of electronic communications necessarily obliterated much of the preelectronic social configuration; Poster (1990, 71) notes that "drastic changes in the means and relations of communication are making a shambles of the delicate balance of the social order that was negotiated and struggled over during the epochs of nineteenth-century industrial capitalism and twentieth-century welfare statism." In much the same way that Gutenberg's invention obliterated the traditions of handwriting, so too do electronic communications create new ways of interacting, destroying much of the culture that thrived with and depended on writing.

It should be abundantly apparent from this discussion that the electronic mediation of information does not simply expand the time-space parameters of social interaction, it qualitatively changes the nature of communication itself (Poster 1990). Just as written texts erect a certain distance between author and reader (the subject of much poststructuralist theorizing), allowing time for cool contemplation and repeated receptions of messages, so too do electronic communications alter the ways in which information is collected, represented, transmitted, and received. Unlike written texts or oral speech, electronic data, images, messages, advertisements, and texts can be splintered, shifted, and recombined in an infinite number of nonlinear ways. Poster (1990, 85) underscores the dramatic differences: "Words cannot any longer be located in space and time, whether it be the 'real time' of spoken utterance in a spatial context of presence or the abstract time of documents in a bureaucrat's file cabinet and library's archive. Speech is framed by space/time coordinates of dramatic action. Writing is framed by space/time coordinates of books and sheets of paper. . . . Electronic language, on the contrary, does not lend itself to being so framed. It is everywhere and nowhere, always and never. It is truly material/immaterial.'' The fact that information can and has become disembodied, therefore, has enormous implications for the time-space stretching of social relations.

ELECTRONIC COMMUNICATIONS AND THE TIME-SPACE MEDIATION OF PRODUCTION SYSTEMS

The social and spatial effects of electronic communications are not confined to entertainment and social reproduction. In the broad sphere of production, telecommunications systems have become a competitive necessity in many sectors (Gillespie and Williams 1988). A sizable literature has documented the emergence of globalized, post-Fordist "flexible production systems," which are typically characterized by computerization, just-in-time inventory systems, flexible labor practices, niche markets, and small, vertically disintegrated firms (see Storper and Walker 1989). Electronic communications constitute an integral part of this transformation (Harvey 1989).

Financial firms have been at the forefront of the construction of an extensive network of national and international communications systems. Because they are so information intensive in nature, banks and securities firms have turned to leased telephone networks (Langdale 1989) as well as satellites and fiber optics systems (Hepworth 1986; Warf 1989) in the formation of global capital markets. Electronic funds transfer systems form the nerve center of the international financial economy (Langdale 1985), allowing banks to move capital around at a moment's notice, arbitraging interest rate differentials, taking advantage of favorable exchange rates, and avoiding political unrest. In the securities markets, global telecommunications systems have also facilitated the emergence of the 24-hour trading day, linking stock markets through computerized trading programs. Subject to the process of digitization, therefore, information and capital become two sides of the same coin. The same process, of course, also heightens the susceptibility of these networks to disruptions (e.g., computer viruses and international transmissions of stock market disruptions).

Among the most profound geographic repercussions of the globalization of finance has been the growth of "world cities," particularly London, New York, and Tokyo (Moss 1987), each of which seems to be more closely attuned to the rhythms of the global economy than the nation-state in which it is located. London, for example, boomed under the impetus of the Euromarket in the 1980s and has become detached from the rest of Britain (Thrift 1987). Similarly, New York rebounded from the crisis of the mid-1970s with a massive influx of petrodollars and new investment funds (i.e., pension and mutual funds) that sustained a prolonged bull market on Wall Street. Tokyo, the epicenter of the gargantuan Japanese financial market, is likely the world's largest center of finance capital, with one third of the world's stocks by volume and twelve of its largest banks by assets. Given the extensive backward linkages of these firms, the effects are considerable. In each metropolitan area, a large agglomeration of banks and related firms generates well-paying jobs; in each, soaring incomes for a wealthy stratum of traders and professionals have sent real estate prices soaring, unleashing rounds of gentrification and a corresponding impoverishment for disadvantaged populations.

A related geographic manifestation of the new, hypermobile capital markets has been the growth of offshore banking, a reflection of the shift from traditional banking services (loans and deposits) to lucrative nontraditional functions, including debt repackaging, foreign exchange transactions, and cash management (Warf 1989). The growth of offshore banking, usually in response to favorable tax laws, has stimulated banking in such places as Panama, Bahrain, and the Netherlands Antilles.

Telecommunications have also allowed for the steady decentralization of "back offices," which perform tedious clerical and data entry functions (Moss and Dunau 1986). Traditionally clustered near headquarters in central business districts or in adjacent suburbs (Nelson 1986), back offices have become increasingly mobile and capable of seeking out pools of cheap, semiskilled labor around the world. For example, U.S. airlines and insurance firms have relocated large numbers of back office jobs to the Caribbean and to Ireland. In the formation of global office networks characterized by international linkages, back offices reveal many of the archetypal aspects of post-Fordist production.

Giddens (1981, 121) notes that this series of transformations has profound implications for locally based production complexes: "The vast extension of time-space mediations made structurally possible by the prevalence of money capital, by the commodification of labour and by the transformability of one into the other, undercuts the segregated and autonomous character of the local community of producers.'' The increasing mobility of firms and capital imparted by telecommunications systems casts considerable doubt on the recent emphasis on ''local dependence'' found in many circles (e.g., Cox and Mair 1988), in which locality cuts across class, tying workers and firms to places through intricate webs of input-output relations and the local reproduction of social relations. Rather, the electronic mediation of information indicates that the creation and dissolution of regional production structures is increasingly dictated by extralocal, increasingly global, processes.

In this light, Castells (1989) argues that the new information technologies, social relations, and geographies of late-twentieth-century capitalism are mutually transformative. The microelectronics revolutions so emblematic of post-Fordism opened new opportunities for many firms, allowing hypermobile industries to escape traditional place constraints and seek out low-cost locations on a global scale. Geographies thus become defined by the space of flows rather than the space of places. In the orthodox economic geography literature, this notion is recapitulated through the acknowledgment of profoundly greater levels of ''footlooseness'' among many firms.

What does this phenomenon signify for the people who inhabit the places progressively enveloped in a globalized matrix of telecommunications? While the consequences to this process have yet to be understood in their entirety, one observation is readily evident. Electronic communications not only accelerate the mobility of capital in time and space, they rework the networks of control on which the administration of capital depends, removing decision-making ability from the hands of local residents and concentrating it in distant centers of corporate control in what Logan and Molotch (1987) call a process of ''delocalization.'' Thus, decisions made in global command-and-control centers (New York, London, Tokyo) have far-reaching repercussions for people from Borneo to Birmingham. To this extent, telecommunications work to obscure the geography of power, dominance, and subordination and make the task of gaining control over the events in local areas qualitatively more difficult.

POWER, POLITICS, AND ELECTRONIC COMMUNICATIONS

The most obvious ways in which electronic media shape formal politics have been widely noted (Meyrowitz 1985). Television, for example, brought graphic images of the Vietnam War into America's living rooms; more recently, a prime illustration is the infamous ''sound bite,'' exemplar of the triumph of style over substance that defines the postmodernist age. The same medium deeply shapes popular stereotypes about gender, age, race, and place (Kubey and Csikszentmihalyi 1990; Meyrowitz 1985). Clearly the media are a central arena in which class and other conflicts are negotiated, loyalties are determined, conflicts are framed, and limits to socially acceptable discourse are established.

There is widespread disagreement, even among critical theorists, about the political consequences of the electronic transformation of the media. Luke (1991), for example, asserts that the power relations of electronic hyperreality require the simultaneous participation of diverse groups, while Sabbah (1985) argues that electronic media accelerate the withdrawal of citizens from public discourse and responsibilities, creating a world in which social obligations become increasingly confined to the self. The very pervasiveness of the politics of the electronic media, however, forces structuration theory to expand its conception of how power relations are territorially manifested.

An important dimension of Giddens's presentation of structuration theory concerns the role of administered power (Cohen 1989). Telecommunications systems have altered the time-space distanciation of such systems profoundly by allowing numerous localities to be monitored through centralized command functions. The growth of large corporations, for example, required the spatial disassociation of control and production (headquarters and branch plants). Similarly, large civil bureaucracies that were integral to the emergence of the nation-state rely heavily on the integration from multiple administrative offices in distant locations. These networks form a system of surveillance in which the masses of people willingly participate; to acquire a credit card or driver's license, for example, one must surrender vital information about one's self. Poster (1990) argues that electronic databases represent a disturbing extension of power relations as individuals communicate to centralized sources (e.g., banks, police departments, credit card companies, public utilities) detailed information about their views, lives, habits, and preferences. With computerized data, authorities enjoy considerably more control over subordinates than in preelectronic systems because "reproduction is exact, transmission is instantaneous, storage is permanent, and retrieval is effortless" (Poster 1990, 72). Telecommunications hence comprise a form of "remote control," extending Foucault's (1979) famous panopticon analogy to encompass global distances. The process of erecting these systems, Giddens (1984) argues, creates new forms of routinization geared to the schedules of administrative bureaucracies. Thus, commuting, shopping, meetings, and so forth are dictated by public, commercial, and educational organizations (Cohen 1989).

Contrary to the utopian and politically naive expectations of early postindustrial theorists, electronic communications do not play an inherently emancipatory role. While electronic communications eliminate the technical barriers to discourse, they do not necessarily liberate people from their prevailing social and political constraints (witness, for example, how television has been effectively deployed by dictatorships around the world). Indeed, as Luke (1991, 17) notes, "advanced communications can also reinforce existing social barriers tied to language, class inequalities, education, or basic code competencies." Electronic communications, therefore, are neither inherently confining nor emancipatory, but must be understood within specific political contexts; their effects are contingent and often unintentional.

CONCLUSION

Any view from an airplane serves as an effective reminder of how "horizontal" human societies are; that is, how thinly they are stretched over vast areas of the earth. This horizontality—geography—is central to the structure and reproduction of social relations. From this perspective, the role of electronic communications in annihilating space is powerful indeed.

The late twentieth century has been a period of immense technological, spatial, and socioeconomic restructuring in which electronic communications have played an instrumental role through what Nicol (1985) calls the on-line economy. By linking together actors in far-flung locales, these systems obliterate the need for presence availability and make vast quantities of information instantaneously available. The expansion of production and contact systems involves a significant time-space compression (Harvey 1990). From a structurationist perspective, in which only actors, not social structures, exert agency, time-space compression may be viewed as the unintended outcome of the efforts of capitalists as a class to deal with new conditions of profitability by introducing new technologies, accelerating the turnover of capital, and shifting production to new locations.

The geographies unleashed by these events at various spatial scales have been equally poorly understood. Because structuration theory suffers from a poorly developed sense of geography in general, space has been theorized simply as a constraint to action (i.e., something to be overcome), and distanciation has been subsequently conceived as a widening of territorial interaction. Clearly, Giddens's notion of the "packing" of locales and the central place it occupies in conceptions of social integration must be thoroughly revised and the baggage of time-geography decisively jettisoned. In their place, there should be inserted a sustained examination of the impacts of the electronic mediation of communication and production, which have had tremendous effects on the structures of everyday life and the social construction of individual life worlds.

In the terminology of critical theory, there has been a widespread decentering of the living subject as the self is continuously multiplied, decontextualized, and disperse (Poster 1990, 6), an important starting point for various debates about postmodernism (Harvey 1989). Given the astonishingly rapid rate of technological change in electronic communications, which will undoubtedly introduce a host of new innovations in the future including many in the earliest stages of use (e.g., fax machines, VCRs, electronic mail systems, artificial intelligence), there will most surely be further, largely unforeseeable effects. It is equally important to note that electronic communications are not simply an extension of writing, but qualitatively change the nature of information; to paraphase McLuhan's (1964) much-overused dictum, the medium and message are inseparable.

Electronically mediated communications systems are not chaotic or random in their consequences, nor do they generate predetermined effects. Actors using the telephone, watching television, or firms using fiber optics systems to connect distant offices are still engaged in the *patterned* reproduction of interactions over time and space. There is no guarantee that they will reproduce these interactions in the same way each time. The effects of electronic communications are contingent on who utilizes them for what purpose and under what conditions their messages are received (i.e., on praxis and social context).

What theoretical implications emerge from these comments? Poster's (1990) notion of a "mode of information," in contrast to the mode of production, explicitly confronts social theory with electronic communications, with mutually transformative consequences: not only are new theoretical structures necessary to comprehend the age of electronic communications, but these ontological shifts also reverberate to create powerful theoretical changes. In particular, the shifting constellations of signs that surround virtually everyone in everyday life—a "snowstorm of pixels" (Luke 1991, 17)—call for a critical semiotics capable of disclosing the sources of mystification and domination in the social production of meaning. The works of Baudrillard (1983) appear to offer significant promise in this regard: by linking the changing worlds of everyday experience to the political economy of advanced capitalism, arguing that individuals' behavior is largely produced through prepackaged cultural codes, Baudrillard reveals that it is increasingly problematic to ground an authentic conception of humanity outside of commodity exchange. Geographers working from a critical theory perspective have yet to make full use of the broader shift to semiotics and the deconstruction of meaning now widely prevalent in other disciplines. Clearly, however, the emergence of electronic hyperspaces makes this project a pressing analytical priority.

Part II

Empirical Applications

4

Small Towns as Historical Places: A Symbolic Interactionist Approach to Structuration Theory through the Study of Landscape

John A. Jakle

As a cultural geographer interested in the evolving built environments of North America, I have explored a wide range of cultural geographical topics. Initially, I came to my work from points of view espoused early by Carl Sauer (1925) and, more recently, by Wilbur Zelinsky (1992). To these individuals, culture was a shared bundle of values and technologies possessed by a people that shaped the immense diversity of human habitats. But culture, a kind of superorganic, could be given only vague definition and could not be measured precisely. Nevertheless, cultural landscapes were assumed to be decipherable through their observable material attributes. In this way, culture was seen to determine differences and similarities in landscapes observed across places. This traditional approach remains exciting as a motivation to discover meaning in the built environment, but seriously limits comprehension of place-oriented behavior sustained by the built environment. As James Duncan (1980) has argued, the superorganic mode of explanation in cultural geography reifies the notion of culture. It assigns this concept ontological status and causative power, with culture emerging as an entity above human beings mysteriously responding to its own laws.

Most cultural geographers interested in landscape have come to focus on the functional implications of material culture. Following substantially from the writings of J. B. Jackson (1980, 1984), the task has been to discover patterns in the built environment extrapolating back to underlying decision making steeped in cultural values. Significance is almost always assigned by assessing function: how and why a landscape is used. The visual (and especially the visually aesthetic) aspects of landscape are ignored on the assumption that the mere seeing of landscape contributes little to real comprehension. Questions about how users of landscape visualize the built environment are dismissed as irrelevant. Aesthetics is frequently pushed aside even when aesthetic appreciation is central to a landscape's use.

Early in my career I began to move away from traditional cultural geography by concerning myself less with the concept of landscape and more with the concept of place. I began to focus on place images: the conceptual structures of belief, attitude, and intentionality that defined place-oriented behavioral expectations and the physical objects of place that cued the same as icons or symbols (Jakle 1982, 1987). I have tried to focus on how individual human beings have conceptualized their geographic worlds. This emphasis required consideration of where cultural values were derived (including aesthetic appreciations), how they were shared, and how they were seen as playing out in actions that configured landscapes in distinctive ways. It required concern with decision making whereby places were created and sustained as dimensions of social context. These were considerations substantially different from those of traditional cultural geography, and of the larger human geography that dominated Anglo-America in the 1960s and 1970s.

This chapter explores the evolving cultural fabric of four small towns in the United States. I unearth the different social and cultural adjustments of these places as they work to resuscitate their eroding economic bases. In the context of a deteriorating small-town America induced by uneven capitalist development and associated patterns of migration, these places have sought to reconstruct their social identities. This process of redefining involved a human reconfiguring of place and function that was filtered through the lens of multiple individuals. In this exposition, therefore, my focus is the role of human beings in refashioning their geographic worlds amid changing structural circumstances. Unlike many other social analyses of U.S. small towns, I recognize the potency of individuals to define their evolving places. At the same time, I recognize the importance of the contextual conditions within which they operate. Put another way, both structure and agency are seen as important analytical variables in the process of place reconfiguration that I examine.

Two bodies of theory inform my analysis: structuration theory and symbolic interaction theory. Structuration theory posits that human behavior can be understood by looking both at individual actors and at the social structures through which individuals drive action. More than any other scholar, it has been Anthony Giddens (1976, 1977, 1984) who has fostered this point of view in current social criticism. His is a focus on social praxis: the production and reproduction of social life (Cohen 1987). Geographical decision making, for example, is seen to reflect both individual prerogatives in assessing options and making locational choices, and the institutional or social contexts through which these options are defined, evaluated, and acted on. Culture enters as the value sets that enable institutions to function. Cultural landscape, which reflects past decision making, is part of the context that influences present decision making. Thus landscape or built environment is both a social construction and a molder of future constructions. The place concept comes to the fore in that all human behavior is place oriented. It occurs in locales. Place construction nested in landscape becomes central to society's structuring, and vice versa.

Symbolic interactionism defines society as the sum total of all social interactions; processes of communication are emphasized whereby social realities are negotiated (see Denzin 1992). Fueled by the writings of George Mead (1934) and Herbert Blumer (1969), this approach presents part of human communication as direct and overt through face-to-face meetings of highly personalized interaction. From there the binding communications of society scale toward the anonymous and the latent as, for example, in the substantially impersonal messages contained in the landscape as built environment. These are messages embedded in the infrastructures of place that help define social contexts or situations for action. They are messages predicated on an interacting population's past experiences in similar places whereby anticipated place satisfactions and dissatisfactions are cued.

Giddens emphasizes the power of human actors to intervene in a course of events or state of affairs. In large measure, such leverage involves changing the meanings that attach to social situations, reorienting the context toward some new or different goal. Ira Cohen (1987, 284) writes that "social agency depends solely upon the capability of actors to 'make a difference' in the production of definite outcomes, regardless of whether or not they intend (are aware) that these outcomes occur." Mead's notions achieve relevance with realization that social acts are generated through symbolically mediated behavior between actors. Members of a society maintain standard expectations about the character and consequences of social action. Standardized actions are discovered, created, and sustained by social actors during the course of their actions (Cohen 1987, 291). Social institutions are routinized practices that are sustained by the majority of the members of a collectivity. Actors develop an unconscious sense of trust in the fabric of social activities and the physical world that comprises the circumstances of their daily lives (Cohen 1987, 302).

SMALL TOWNS AS HISTORICAL PLACES

Places are locales that may be seen to contain and, indeed, invite ongoing behavior. Place image or stereotype of locale is central to this process. As I have explored elsewhere, place images may be analyzed according to at least four dimensions of meaning: belief, attitude, icon, and intentionality (Jakle 1990). Beliefs establish in the minds of place users (both actual and potential) what a place is and what a place is not. Attitudes reflect positively or negatively vis-à-vis the place so conceptualized. Beliefs and attitudes are symbolized by objects of material place—what I have called icons. Beliefs, attitudes, and icons have relevancy only when examined in the context of behavioral intentions. That a place is believed to be old, rooted in its past, or otherwise seen to convey historical value stands as belief. That such oldness, pastness, or historicity is either good or bad (inviting or uninviting, etc.) is an attitudinal stance. Beliefs and attitudes come to be symbolized by icons (buildings, streets, etc.), the stuff of landscape as built environment. Historic preservationists have established an extensive iconography of historical values in this regard. The essence of a locale as a historical place, however, is very much dependent on the intentions that users bring to the place as promoter-capitalists, citizen-residents, or visitor-tourists by way of example. It is the iconography of historical place that I emphasize in this chapter.

The small town has stood as a distinctive place type in the American experience beloved by some for its idealized friendliness as a sort of extended family or highly personalized community setting, and damned by others for its parochial ways as a kind of cultural backwater (Hilfer 1969; Jakle 1982). Most Americans would agree that small towns and small-town people no longer exert the influence that they once enjoyed in molding American cultural values. Metropolises exert the greatest leverage on lifestyles today, and small towns have been substantially reshaped in recent decades to conform to big-city values. New subdivisions filled with ranch houses and new businesses spread out in peripheral highway strips serve to symbolize a universal modernity. Nonetheless, in some towns time has apparently stood still. Although towns are variously part of the modern urban-oriented system, strong icons of the past may remain in these places suggestive of old beliefs and attitudes. Townscapes speak of previous ways of doing and being. Such towns are seen to possess historical value for the residual images of past life that they convey. Indeed, many such towns promote themselves as historical places by managing their landscapes as historical resources attractive not only to residents but, more especially, to tourists (Ziegler 1980).

Small-town America has fallen on hard times as fundamental changes have affected the agricultural and industrial sectors of the American economy. Farm consolidation and abandonment has reduced the farm population, eroding the market base for most farm towns as central places (Davidson 1990). Decline of heavy industry in a shift to postindustrial economic emphases has wrought decline in mill or factory towns, and in mining towns that once supplied industrial raw materials (Bluestone and Harrison 1982). True, some small towns near large cities continue to grow as suburbs. And some farm towns remain vigorous for the persistence of ethnically based communities that sustain a rootedness in place in apparent defiance of economic logic: for example, the rootedness of German-Americans in rural "covenanted" communities across the Middle West (Salamon 1985). Beyond these exceptions small-town America is substantially in decline. A profound inequality has developed between metropolitan areas and nonmetropolitan areas, with the small towns of nonmetropolitan America especially disadvantaged.

Small towns are being marginalized in fundamental ways as economic bases erode, with populations continuing the now three quarters of a century shift cityward. Many small-town landscapes stand relatively unchanged, communities lacking the economic energy to change materially. But some towns have discovered resource value in their antiquated, now relic landscapes and have begun to promote themselves as historic places attractive to tourists. Other towns have used historical amenities to boost suburban potentialities. Some towns have sought to showcase historical landscapes as attractive to prospective new employers and their employees. Cultural landscape has been made the focus of overcoming the deficits, actual and perceived, of small-town misfortune.

In the past, Americans have tended to view history as something apart from life's mainstream (Lowenthal 1966). History and things historical have tended to be viewed as past—as no longer of real significance. The future has been valued more. America's penchant for newness and change (or "progress") remains a basic dimension of a highly materialistic, technologically oriented society. Pastness, where it survives in contemporary landscape, is still generally ignored although things truly significant from the past—places associated with celebrated personages or important events—may be enshrined as historic sites.

Relic objects in landscape may be valued for their historical symbolism. The historic preservation movement has matured rapidly over the past half century as a process for manipulating these symbols (Hosmer 1981). And a concern for things past recently has begun to assume some importance in the American experience. The saving of old buildings, especially houses, was initially largely an elitist's endeavor. House museums and private residences were promoted as status symbols (Lowenthal 1985). In finite supply, relic gentry architecture (as with art and antiques) has come to serve as an excellent social marker for status and class distinction. Indeed, the penchant for historically rooted social symbolism has begun to filter down the social scale, affecting more broadly what might be considered American popular culture. Corporate America has taken heed of history, commodifying the same in theme parks, for example. As I will demonstrate, small-town boosters variously have turned to history in landscape in order to promote economic development.

I examine historic landscape awareness of residents in four small towns as they seek to keep their places economically viable (Map 4.1). Specifically, I look at the strength of local dedication to principles of architectural integrity and historical authenticity (traditional values among most historic preservationists) and concern for visual aesthetics (what, I argue, really makes historical landscapes truly valuable for preservation). Georgetown, Kentucky in the 1980s was substantially endowed with relic landscape features. Residents valued highly certain individual structures, especially houses, but valued little the total landscape as context. Marshall, Michigan residents, in contrast, had developed an appreciation for both individual buildings and the way that those buildings in-

Map 4.1
Case Study Towns: Georgetown, Kentucky; Marshall, Michigan; Jacksonville, Oregon; and Keystone, South Dakota

tegrated as landscape. They had sought integrity and authenticity through architectural design controls in specially zoned historic districts. Jacksonville, Oregon presented an added dimension in relic landscape management: substantial re-creation of a past landscape to simulate not the past of actuality so much as an idealized past as purveyed by contemporary media. The people of Keystone, South Dakota coupled benign neglect with aggressive contrivance. Keystone stood not only as a caricature of the past, but, more specifically, as caricature of itself as a historical landscape. Historical places are not of a single genre, but display real distinctiveness case to case.

My attention in this chapter is drawn not to the small town of the past, but to the small town of today seemingly rooted in the past—historical places defined in the cognizance of current residents and visitors. Along which dimensions of meaning are these places defined as historical? Who does the defining? How? Why? And to what purpose? My first concern is to define the symbolic dimensions of pastness as it plays out in places as historical value. My next concern is to suggest how and why individual agency drives such values through' systems of governance, development, and promotion. My intention is exploratory—to use historical place as a topic to outline the even larger concerns of place distinctiveness. My intention is to suggest how structuration theory might provide a suitable context for analyzing the symbolic aspects of place. For the student of structuration theory, I suggest a focus for empirical application: the study of symbolic representation whereby icons in landscape are manipulated toward social ends. For the cultural geographer, on the other hand, I direct attention to structurationist and symbolic interactionist stances as means of energizing the study of cultural landscape.

Georgetown, Kentucky

In the 1980s the visitor to Georgetown driving north the twelve miles from Lexington entered a place seemingly stuck in the past. At least in basic outline the town's traditional physical aspects appeared remarkably preserved. At the center, Main Street retained its principal buildings from the late nineteenth century. Along Main Street to the east, Georgetown College stood on its hill keeping a kind of vigil with town houses of the 1830s and 1840 fronting the college gate. Where Main Street topped the heights to the west, occupants of gentry houses built in the 1870s and 1880s could still gaze directly down on the business district. Residents still valued these structures as architecture, and, since these buildings were in relatively short supply and carried implications of high social status from the past, they continued to serve well as symbols of social prestige. But the fabric of the landscape that contained these architectural threads was in danger of unraveling. Civic leadership had little valued the larger landscape as a distinctive environment worth protecting. No historic zoning or other protective devices had been set in place. Relic landscape survived through inertia, inaction, and conservatism born of decades of economic stability. Georgetown's

Georgetown, Kentucky. The town's main street was anchored visually by the court house. The renovated bank building on the left disrupted what otherwise stood as a street of integrated red brick commercial facades.

unique historical qualities appeared more as afterthoughts in the minds of the few and not as forethoughts in the minds of the many.

A close look at Georgetown would have disclosed the neglect. Main Street, although relatively untarnished from the Gilded Age of the past century, had been negatively affected by a bank renovation of the 1960s. The building's azure blue skin with its arches of prepressed concrete disrupted the continuity of the street as integrated red brick architecture. The bank building seemed intended to draw maximum attention to the bank, the bankers intending to dominate visually the town's center as they might have hoped to dominate the town's economy. Elsewhere on Main Street business facades had been refurbished with glass, plastic, and aluminum. Layers of modernization clung to first stories, making Georgetown's Main Street a carnival of modern signage. The town's main cross street had been widened to accommodate increased traffic, and gasoline stations and other automobile convenient businesses had begun to dominate the street, depreciating adjacent residential areas.

Today, Georgetown enjoys an economic boom. A Japanese automaker has located a large assembly plant east of town. For decades Georgetown business and civic leadership sought economic development through preoccupation with road, airport, and other improvements potentially attractive to industry. Avail-

Georgetown, Kentucky. The automobile's accommodation had vastly altered the traditional image of this street through elimination of shade trees and the reduction of front yards.

able land for development, a regional situation near parts suppliers, a location central to the American automobile market, state subsidy, and the ambiance of a reasonably well-preserved town situated in the attractive Kentucky Blue Grass region worked an economic miracle for Georgetown. In this regard, the sense of time-depth that gave Georgetown a distinctive American stamp should not be undervalued. History has played a role, although a subsidiary one, in Japanese manufacturers selecting places like Georgetown for new plants. Georgetown is a place that looks American and is an attractive place for plant managers to live.

Marshall, Michigan

The visitor to Marshall in the 1980s would have been struck not only by the relic quality of the townscape, but by evidence of effective landscape management that successfully related old and new construction to harmonize the built environment. Marshall also had been successful in attracting businesses such as the regional office of a large insurance company. Unlike Georgetown, however, it had done so by forcefully emphasizing its image as a quality residential place firmly rooted in the past. Here the preservation ethic prevailed

Marshall, Michigan. The Harold C. Brooks House, a visually prominent landmark, had become an icon of Marshall as a historical place just as Brooks, himself, had become a symbol of enlightened, local leadership.

thanks largely to the efforts of a single person, Harold Brooks, a local businessman and one-time mayor of the town (Collins 1978). Brooks had focused the town's attention on its landscape, especially the historical qualities of the built environment. What Brooks could not accomplish through political means or through his influence in the local business community, he had accomplished through outright gift. When in the 1940s Calhoun County demolished the court house and the state highway department converted the court house square to a traffic circle, Brooks gave the community a large fountain to serve as a new centerpiece and directed the landscaping of this area as a park. Brooks thwarted plans to level two buildings facing the circle for gasoline stations, and he renovated a former livery stable and gave it to the town for a municipal building. He subsidized the historical society, thus salvaging another important town centerpiece. Construction of a new post office in the 1950s prompted Brooks to provide materials and subsidize an architect. In the 1970s he initiated a tree planting program on Main Street and a program to preserve the original facades of Main Street buildings. Marshall is now carefully zoned, with much of its area in a designated historic district.

Marshall had sought the tourist dollar, although only on a limited basis. Tourism rooted in historical landscape appeal was used to promote the town's

Marshall, Michigan. The traditional juxtapositioning of buildings in Marshall created positive visual tension. Here the Honolulu House (occupied by the historical society) combined with the National House (a restored coaching inn) to anchor visually the public square on the west.

image as a desirable place to live. Nonetheless, Marshall's leaders had been unwilling to compromise the town's residential character to touristic excesses. The visitor sought was the educated viewer of historical architecture who enjoyed fine meals and novel accommodations in a relaxed, gentrified atmosphere (Grimes 1991). Nor did Marshall present itself as a museum. The town did not pretend to represent a single historical period. Instead, the best of several succeeding periods had been preserved. New construction reflected prevailing tastes, but with some exceptions was carefully integrated with the old. Contrivance had been held to a minimum; quality visual display had become a watchword.

Jacksonville, Oregon

Visitors to Jacksonville in the 1980s found a relic town that had vigorously promoted tourism for several decades (Ross 1972). A former mining town and former seat of Jackson County, the town had little if any pretense to industrial development since it was located off major transportation routes well up in the hills of the coastal range. There was little space for commercial development.

Marshall, Michigan. Tree planting along Michigan Avenue, the town's main street created an attractive visual environment for the pedestrian.

Unlike Marshall and Georgetown, retail trade was oriented primarily to tourists—not just those seeking gentry satisfactions but those in search of the popular culture of the American West. Through building renovation, the main street appeared to be quintessentially western as rooted in the late nineteenth-century frontier mystique. The narrow street, lined by brick and frame buildings, and the sidewalks, shaded by porches, invited tourists to stroll into the past, albeit a highly fictional past. Modern signs had been stripped away, exposing old advertisements, or had been replaced with modern simulations of the old. Only the highway markers and the modern pavements detracted overtly from the sense of pastness. Historic zoning had encouraged renovation and new development compatible with the wild west theme. Jacksonville, unlike Marshall, was in the process of being fossilized to an ideal. The town was rapidly becoming a museum through contrivance.

Jacksonville stood for something much larger than itself. It was not only the Jacksonville of the frontier period that was being celebrated, but the frontier period itself through an archetype townscape. The inspiration for this celebration came not so much through understanding the town's actual history as through regional stereotypes conveyed in the contemporary popular media. It was the West of the dime novel, the motion picture, and of television that was being created here. Only the occasional sign alerted visitors to the pretense. In 1970 Jacksonville's main street had been renovated for the filming of Universal Stu-

Jacksonville, Oregon. Sufficient architecture survived the business district to give Jacksonville the look of the stereotyped western mining town of the late nineteenth century.

dio's *The Great Northfield Raid*. Much of this renovation, which had made the town into a facsimile of nineteenth-century Northfield in Minnesota, remains today. Of course, signs establishing this fact added significance to the town, for image making by the contemporary popular media was, and is, very much celebrated among tourists for its own value.

Keystone, South Dakota

Keystone, in South Dakota's Black Hills, presented the visitor with two realities. Another derelict mining town like Jacksonville, Keystone had also sought to use the western frontier theme to attract tourists. Not satisfied with the town's old dirt streets lined with storefronts and miner's cabins, entrepreneurs had developed a new Main Street along a peripheral highway. Here developers had little regard for authenticity. Most tourists, they realized, were easily satisfied with imitations of reality, especially imitations that heightened a distinctive sense of place. In the new Keystone, mansard roofs mixed with bay windows, gas lamps, and other paraphernalia thought symbolic of the past. The past represented a gimmick that the town used to define a distinctive image for itself irrespective of truth in packaging. Keystone had created a suburbanlike shopping street for the sale of souvenirs and services as blatantly pseudo as the street itself. Unlike Jacksonville, the new Keystone made no effort to root its historical image in an

Keystone, South Dakota. The main street of Keystone offered the image of a make-believe western frontier town. The Ruby House was only a decade old.

authentic past. Valid and invalid messages about the past thus were not confused as at Jacksonville. Everything was blatantly unreal.

As outlined earlier, the image of a place is a function of the beliefs, attitudes, and intentionalities that people share in place conceptualization, dimensions of meaning that attach to physical aspects of place—objects that stand symbolic of a place as icons (Jakle 1987, 1990). Place meaning is cued by icons. Changing the meaning of a place requires either new icons or changing the meaning of old icons. The latter is what the historic preservation movement is all about. Preservationists strive to develop for old buildings new associations, renewing the lives of old structures by giving them new symbolic implications. There are at least three interrelated evaluative dimensions that preservationists—the promoters of historical value in landscape—use in promoting preservation. They are integrity, authenticity, and aesthetics. Icons selected for development variously carry these characteristics, informing directly developmental outcomes.

INTEGRITY, AUTHENTICITY, AND AESTHETICS IN HISTORICAL PLACES

Historical place making involves the overt use of material culture. In this process, the physical objects of place are actively manipulated. Icons do not merely symbolize prevailing social belief and attitude. They are, themselves, the focus of intentionality as social agendas are set deliberately according to the contrivance and/or preservation of these objects as icons. They can be made the focus of economic development and other initiatives gauged to overcome the perceived deficiencies of a place. Historical landscapes are social displays that reflect varying social agendas as, for example, those of business opportunity.

Integrity, authenticity, and aesthetics are three interrelated evaluative dimensions applicable to understanding the use of the past in small towns and other settings. Integrity relates to honesty. A townscape of high historical integrity is seen by preservationists to be complete in its principal parts. It exists in a state of innocence that clearly reflects changing place functions over time—an unpretentious accumulation of functionally related structure and spaces. Authenticity reflects origins. The town appears to be a genuine article well rooted in its regional culture as opposed to being false, fictitious, or counterfeit. It is real as opposed to being a caricature for some special purpose. Aesthetics is a matter of pleasing the eye. Much historical value in a place derives not so much from integrity and authenticity of time-rootedness as from the harmonious relating of structures and spaces, especially as they convey an ambiance reflective of past as opposed to modern places. The aesthetic place is tasteful visually according to codes of taste usually arbitrated by predominant social classes. In an automobile world, the values of genteel pedestrianism communicate a sense of pastness through the structuring of places intended for humans rather than automobiles or other machines.

Of the four towns, Georgetown would seem to have ranked highest on the scale of integrity. The town had made no pretense to being other than itself. Its landscape had evolved to display elements of each succeeding period of growth, stability, or decline. Its origins were visibly present in its current fabric. Marshall displayed authenticity, but the town's integrity as a place rooted in prevailing place functions of the past was masked by historical pretense driven by its better educated and more affluent residents. The town had sought to develop its land-scape in the image of a preautomobile age, thus significantly improving the town as aesthetic display. Jacksonville lacked integrity and authenticity while preserving a measure of the aesthetic. Keystone, in its fabricated Main Street, was totally contrived as a display of the past. It lacked integrity, authenticity, and even aesthetic value. Keystone did not pretend to be a real town, but rather an exaggerated entertainment where tourists willingly played at being in the Old West.

Integrity results when civic action promotes values traditional to a locality. Economic boosterism is the value system prevalent in most American localities and, where an expansive attitude does not prevail, pessimism, the reverse of boosterism (or boosterism failed), often prevails. The line between success and failure is thin, with most small towns in an era of metropolitan dominance clearly showing both boom and bust in residual landscapes. The traditional fabric of a town cannot survive either impulse long. Successful boosterism leads to new construction often at the expense of old buildings and the integrity of traditional landscape. Pessimism leads to delayed maintenance and physical decay and the removal of buildings without benefit of replacement—the unraveling of landscape. These latter landscapes may lack visual appeal and, as unattractive places, may prove incapable of economic regeneration. Pessimism frequently dissolves into inertia and unplanned chaos that, although blatantly honest is a cancer of decay and decline.

Integrity suffers where historic preservation is practiced vigorously. Historic preservation is a form of boosterism given to visual and historical as well as economic considerations. Preservationists are concerned to enhance the functional life of a place in an economic sense; however, they are concerned to do so by respecting authentic historical values reflected in relic landscape. They are also concerned to enhance the visual quality of environment as pictorial display. Preservation, like pure economic boosterism, proceeds by fad and fashion. Thus places like Marshall and Jacksonville reflected as much the 1980s as the 1880s (or earlier decades) from which landscape relics survive. Historical authenticity becomes a factor when old buildings, indeed whole neighborhoods, are being recycled. To what extent are buildings to retain their antique look? To what extent should contemporary styles in restoration refashion visual appearance?

Places preserved as historical attract attention visually as they deviate from contemporary scenes dominated more fully by present-day building technologies. Preserved places carry a sense of continuity with the past. Where the past has been truncated through the eradication of a traditional landscape, modernity fully prevails. Preserved places, whether preserved for tourism or not, attract tourists for being different. Indeed, tourists become part of the pretense to historical if not social class significance. Tourist towns, if successful, usually become fossilized around the relic landscapes managed and those images of historical significance prevailing at the time of preservation.

The majority of tourists in the United States neither demand nor appreciate integrity and authenticity in historical displays. Indeed, the pseudoplace, like Keystone, serves the typical tourist better for thè exaggerated view of the past and for qualities that put the self-indulging tourist's comfort first (Boorstin 1961; Jakle 1985). Tourists travel to validate expectations that are necessarily stereotyped and, accordingly, stereotyped places serve more readily to please. Keystone's leadership has realized this and has remade the town. To promote tourism less than vigorously generates its own outcomes. Tourism can translate directly into commercial success through the gross of dollars expended, but tourism also can be indirectly translated into economic development. Tourism can be used to create a desirable image for a place and this image used to attract new jobs and new residents. Marshall plays this game. Development is thus variously rationalized around concern for historic place.

Contrivance is antithetical to authenticity. The tendency to distort historical reality knows no bounds when the overwhelming purpose is image mongering for pecuniary reward. Jacksonville's leadership has discovered this truth. Irrespective of the original intentions to effectuate authentic architectural restoration, the town's very success as a tourist center has created a momentum that has carried it forcibly toward contrivance. Once tourism is used to justify preservation, success in attracting tourists creates demand for more attractive goods and services thus to entice even more tourists. Each cycle of development makes the community more and more into a contrived place until an unauthentic landscape ultimately prevails. Success in tourism hastens decline of place authenticity as development obscures amenities.

FOCUS ON AESTHETICS

Formulating developmental plans necessitates agreement as to how questions of integrity, authenticity, and aesthetics are to be resolved. Integrity is a concept that comes to the fore when preservationists discover architectural value in landscape. Integrity and authenticity, however, are values that do not always survive the historic preservationist's intentions since preservation, itself, is not without fads and fashions destructive of the residual past. Integrity and authenticity also prove weak as values when confronted with the economic realities of development. It may be time that concern with integrity and authenticity in historic preservation give way to a primary consideration of aesthetics, specifically the visual appreciation of landscape. It may be visual preservation and not historic preservation that holds the key to truly effective landscape management through the preservation ethic.

Until the late 1970s, American preservationists were preoccupied with the restoration and rehabilitation of individual buildings. In recent years concern with entire landscapes, often defined as historic districts, has focused attention on how buildings relate to one another through spatial proximity. Historic districts, however, continue to be defined legally in terms of building clusters, and little consideration has been given to the visual values of proxemics: the manner by which buildings relate visually to streets and other public spaces as well as to each other. To preserve individual buildings and even clusters of buildings is not enough. What gives a landscape real character is its peculiar visual assemblage whereby sense of scale and texture, among other distinguishing characteristics, are defined. In other words, the visual relationships between buildings need to be preserved as well as the buildings themselves. This lesson has been learned in Marshall, where the preservation of old buildings was first generated out of fear of visual landscape disruption. Preservation in Marshall has meant infilling key spaces in the visual fabric of the town as much as it has meant structural restoration and rehabilitation.

Among scholars, a philosophy of visual landscape management has not yet been fully formulated. Relatively little has been written about how people see landscape as visual display. Speculation regarding the discovery of beauty in the visual environment remains tentative. Geographer Jay Appleton (1975) sees the quest for prospect (the ability to view long distances) and the quest for refuge (the sense of being protected in one's viewing) as basic. The preservationist needs to identify the principal prospects and areas of refuge by which a place is known. He or she needs to identify the important vistas by which a town, for example, is seen and remembered. These vistas, usually defined by streets as paths along which movement occurs, are anchored by key buildings as focal points. In Georgetown the view down the main street, as anchored by the court-house, forms an important public scene. In Jacksonville, the view up the main street likewise dominates the overall image of the town. Preservationists also need to identify the important places of refuge (e.g., the public squares where a sense of pause outside the stream of pedestrian and vehicular flow is suggested). Marshall's former court house square is such a place.

Important also is the sense of detail by which the eye fills the broad outlines of landscape (Jakle 1987). Details of building facade, street furniture, vegetation, and, indeed, anything and everything that gives a place character (what some authors call "sense of place," "genius loci," or "spirit of place") deserves consideration (Durrell 1969; Norberg-Schultz 1980; Tuan 1977). The distinct visual relationships between trees, sidewalks, signs, windows, and doorways give Marshall's Michigan Avenue, as seen by the pedestrian, a distinctive char-acter. The juxtaposed detail of the roughly textured brick facades and the signs, both old and new, define a uniqueness for Jacksonville. Preservationists might determine which details of place are central to its visual character and undertake to preserve those details accordingly.

In visualizing landscape, people compose pictures by analogy to the visual arts (Jakle 1987). In modern society photography is especially influential in determining what people consider pictorial or scenic (Dondis 1973). People take the broad outlines of landscape and fill in significant visual detail toward the composition of pictures in the mind's eye. Most of what is seen is forgotten. It evolves and occludes visually as part of a passing kaleidoscope of imagery. But certain scenes in every place, for the frequency of their encounter, stand as important remembered views. As a town's populace shares these views, the pictures derived come to define the icons of place, giving them strong social connotation. For example, the Brooks house, elevated on its wooded hill over-looking Marshall, has become an important icon of that town. A historical marker located in front reinforces the location's significance in celebrating Brooks's role as local preservationist.

The pictures of place prevalent in the mind's eye enable people to recognize landscape as geography: to establish a mental map of a town as a place. Some features serve to tie a town together geographically because they are visually prominent. That is, they are pictured frequently from different vantage points. The town hall and historical society in Marshall are such features as viewed at various angles from around the public square. The aesthetic landscape confronts the eye and suggests beauty through harmony. Buildings and spaces fit together as a gestalt, the whole being a pleasing sum greater than its parts. An aesthetic landscape appears to be in balance. Nothing can be taken away or added without disrupting the sense of appropriateness whereby the parts combine to form the whole. Such pictures become significant in driving developmental schemes forward.

STRUCTURATION, SYMBOLIC INTERACTION, AND HISTORIC PLACE

The emergence of structuration theory should excite cultural geographers on several fronts. First, the approach rejects the narrow stance of many positivists who have tended to expunge from social analysis direct concern with human decision making, preferring instead to think in terms of abstracted processes (established primarily on grounds of statistical regularity observed using population aggregates). Human beings have been treated as parts of a social machine. Anthony Giddens, on the other hand, posits the individual as a reasoning agent who, in interacting with others, creates and sustains social situations amid being shaped by them (Giddens 1984). Society is thus simultaneously object and subject, being forged by the interconnections of society, institutions, and interpretive individuals. Focus is placed on individuals as actors or interactors. Second, his approach requires concern not only with the temporal dimensions of social behavior, but, as importantly, with its geographical dimensions. All interaction takes place in locales: social situations lodged in temporal and spatial specificity. Following from previous discussion, how might actors drive the valuing of things historical to the forefront of small-town life?

The symbolic interactionism of George Mead (1934) and Herbert Blumer (1969) enters when consideration focuses on the manipulation of icons. Individuals negotiate the meaning of places in daily social life. Giddens emphasizes the power of significant actors to intervene in a course of events or a state of affairs as engendered by regularities of praxis (Cohen 1987). Places as social situations have value as centers of mutual interest where interacting populations seek known satisfactions (or, conversely, avoid known dissatisfactions). Rules of behavior, traditionally validated, impose constraints. Nonetheless, actors do enjoy degrees of freedom in changing the meanings of places. Agendas for locales can and do get reconfigured. Rules, or tacitly understood social procedures, are changed and places redefined thereby. Again, in light of the preceeding discussion, how is it that a place suddenly becomes historical and, in its redefinition, new categories of social behavior emerge?

In structuration theory, social institutions unfold as routinized practices carried forward by a majority of an interacting collectivity. Social structure, as such, only exists as it is instantiated in social practices (Cohen 1987). Otherwise, it persists between instances of social interaction only as memory traces sustained by the actors themselves. From these memories comes a sense of trust in a fabric of social activity seemingly more stable than dynamic. Especially important to a sense of social stability are the anchored relationships whereby individuals are tightly bound within family, workplace, club, and other situations. How do distinctly historical orientations to a place get institutionalized? How do historically charged beliefs and attitudes get attached to specific icons of place and come to the fore in changing intentionality?

In approaching an understanding of places—historical places included—structuration urges first that emphasis be placed on individuals as actors. Of special interest to geographers would be the individuals who negotiate the social construction of places as locales for socialization. Again, people have the power to intervene in the structuring of place through the values that they assert—places in their physical manifestations coming to symbolize those values, and vice versa. It bears repeating that built environments are not merely containers for society, but help from what society becomes through their construction. Of greatest interest to geographers, perhaps, are those regularized behaviors that drive institutionalization overtly organized around the icons of place.

Historical places are created by individuals as they act in concert toward certain agreed-on social goals. I have emphasized in this chapter the goals of economic development. In Keystone and in Jacksonville the creation of and the preservation of historically charged icons of place was intended to drive tourism. In Marshall, place making embracing historical icons was intended first to create residential quality, which, in turn, was intended to drive development, tourism remaining subsidiary. In Georgetown, development was foremost, with environmental ambiance rooted historically serving only as a facilitating factor leading to development.

Although I have named only one specific individual—Harold Brooks of Marshall—each of these towns has had its equivalent actors and it is to them that scholarly attention should be drawn. Brooks's role in Marshall cannot be understated. As a member of the town's gentry, he worked to cultivate and refine that group's aesthetic sympathies and to make those sympathies predominant in the town. He worked to drive an awareness of local historical architecture and landscape resources within varied institutions: chamber of commerce, city government, service clubs, and so on. Brooks's values were clearly rooted in an appreciation of art and architectural history fostered in a privileged Ivy League education. He subsidized travel excursions for friends and business associates as far afield as Europe thus to push to the forefront appreciation of selected architectural and landscape values in Marshall's political, economic, and social evolution. The way that Harold Brooks looked at and saw Marshall came to be shared.

Brooks drove specific agendas through various institutional settings until a cult or culture of historical landscape appreciation evolved to subsume the town's very personality as a place. Marshall's society can be seen to have coalesced around the historic preservation ethic toward making and keeping Marshall a distinctive residential place. The town has become an attraction to households interested in developing distinctive lifestyles around the symbols of historical place. Perhaps more so than in most towns, social integration in Marshall hinges around icons of historical significance. These objects have come not only to symbolize the locale's past, but, more importantly, to symbolize the ways of life now possible in this place. From Marshall's peculiar ambiance derive satisfactions of class and status implication. Marshall residents build social identities around historical allusions materialistically based. Individual and family identities are built around living in a place viewed as distinctive if not exclusive—the idealized gentry place in which to live, to raise children, to grow old. These sentiments attached to the place reflect clearly in local definitions of what constitutes integrity, authenticity, and aesthetics in landscape.

The Harold Brookses of the other towns drove differing agendas through the institutions of their respective towns, forming and reforming economic, political, and other social institutions in the process. Where were their values learned? Upon what power base did they operate? Concern with architecture and landscape historically defined differed substantially from place to place, and the belief and attitudinal systems that evolved were clearly distinctive. Iconographies differed with regard to issues of integrity, authenticity, and aesthetics. Respective places were made to appear historical in different ways for different reasons. Thus history was negotiated to suit the temper of time and place.

Those in pursuit of a scientific geography in the 1960s and 1970s tended to ignore the significance of human agency in producing place distinctiveness. Their search was to generate regularities that ran through places. Aggregated data were analyzed relating to testable propositions. The amount and density of rehabilitated housing might be seen as a function of changing income, property values, or the occupation levels of resident populations by way of example. Theirs was not a grappling with personal biographies playing out in public and private arenas for social action. Their product was not explanation hinged on specific actors driving agendas through evolving community institutions. Theirs was not a search for emplotments of cause and effect operating within shifting social circumstances. Their product said little about what made places distinctive as human habitats.

Structuration and symbolic interactionism would seem to invite the instincts of the historian to geographical research. However, the careful assembling and validating of evidence, and as well the creation of explanatory sketches focused on causative chains of events, would consider contemporary social scenes as opposed to those of the distant past as in current historical geography. For respective social situations, who are the key players and how have they defined the game? How have they pushed specific agendas through emergent institutional fabrics? How have goals been defined and according to whose values? For what purpose? And with what results, both intended and unintended? More specifically, how have symbols been manipulated toward social goals? Which beliefs and attitudes have been fostered and under which divergent circumstances of intentionality? How has the physical environment been manipulated toward goal achievement? What in the environment stands symbolic of the whole as icon? How were the basic inequalities between places faced?

Consideration should be given to appearances—what places appear to be as visual displays. Places are settings configured to encourage ongoing, regularized activities. They are structured physically to reinforce expectations as to the kinds of satisfaction obtainable (or dissatisfactions avoidable). As social expectations attach to the icons of place, places come, as a function of their physical reality, to carry much of the memory load whereby appropriate social interaction is sustained. Out of the rules of such interaction comes a sense of social structuring. Physical objects abide to form the loci for repeated social situations that in their trajectories over time come to be viewed as structural. Icons facilitate the recall and renewal of social relationships. Changing the icons helps to foster social change through changed appearances. Overcoming the deficiencies of place in a world of profound place inequalities can be accomplished through focus on built environment as aesthetic awareness.

When the meanings attached to a place change, the essential question becomes, "Who benefits?" In many but not all instances gainers may be offset by losers. Are some people denied? Are lives marginalized? Historic preservation has been made suspect in many large cities, where gentrification is seen to displace in many neighborhoods incumbent residents (Smith 1979b). To what extent are there winners and losers in small towns when history becomes a force for development? Those who can afford to enhance lifestyle and, indirectly, social status through the preservation of buildings and landscapes would benefit. Those who find employment and business opportunities enhanced would benefit. But successful development often inflates property values, inflating taxes and rents. Higher costs of living can discourage low-income people from continued residence in a town. In none of the towns treated here are such circumstances evident except, perhaps, in Georgetown, where a new automobile plant, and not historic preservation, now provides the leading icon of change.

The regularized behaviors within social institutions hinge on the creation and sustaining of place meanings through the manipulation of icons. Such is the case with places of all kinds defined at various scales of social organization. Small towns as historical places have been discussed here. The embracing of environmental tastes substantially rooted in former times, intrinsically interesting as a subject in its own right, has served, nonetheless, to illustrate the essence of place as locale for social interaction. In Georgetown, Marshall, Jacksonville, and Keystone appearances have been manipulated toward defining and maintaining locales conducive to achieving specific developmental goals advanced and brought to predominance by key actors.

The traditional cultural geographer might engage landscapes in diverse places, recognizing similarities in function and form place to place. Historical landscapes might be discovered and described as they are characterized by relic material culture. But relic landscapes in different places invariably reflect different social agendas irrespective of parallels in form and function. It is the symbolic aspect of material culture seen as icon that counts in explaining such cultural landscapes. The built environment does not simply reflect culture, being explained thereby. Rather, objects of the built environment are negotiated as carriers of social meaning. Therein lies deeper explanation. How landscapes appear as visual display should be emphasized, for it is in the seeing or reading of landscapes that iconography comes to the fore in cuing place as a part of human socialization.

The basic questions remain: who drives the defining of place? How? Why? Along which dimensions of meaning are places defined as social settings? What are the important dimensions of belief, attitude, and intentionality? How are icons created to carry the symbolism of place? The stance of the structurationist looms important as emphasis is given to agents of change as they act and react within structures socially negotiated. The stance of the symbolic interactionist is implicit as emphasis is given to the negotiation of social value. A traditional concern of cultural geography enters when the focus is on the material culture of landscape—when the built environment is taken as the thing to be explained. As the built environment is given social meaning (as it physical appearances are managed as iconography), it drives and is driven by social context. The notion that key actors actively manipulate symbolically the icons of place toward specific social ends is an important one. I believe that it may provide a significant handle by which to steer structuration theory into the realm of empirical analysis.

5

Context Is Everywhere: Structuration, Community, and Social Order

John Eyles

AN ENGAGEMENT WITH STRUCTURATION THEORY

Structuration theory and I go back a long way. I began reading and thinking about applying the theory in my research in the late 1970s and early 1980s. At the time, I was interested in neobehavioral, neomaterialist, and neohumanist approaches to the study of place. Everything I looked at seemed wanting in some ways. Despite Golledge's (1981) spirited defenses of behavioral approaches, they seemed still to underemphasize the social and concentrate on deductive reasoning. Materialist approaches, as current in the late 1970s, seemed to emphasize structure to the exclusion of the human subject (cf. Althusser 1965); Harvey 1973) while humanist perspectives seemed to lead to the attitude that values and meanings are important (Entrikin 1976; Smith 1979a). I was interested in carrying out an investigation into how and why place was important in people's lives. In other words, I wanted to study place as implicated in place-in-the-world, meaning as embodied in structure, locale as part of the negotiated totality of everyday life. And so I discovered structuration.

Structuration theory seemed to offer a way of considering place as one phenomenon, among many, as part of a structured totality (Eyles 1981a). It seemed to provide therefore the possibility of recognizing structures, forces, and processes outside of everyday experience that were not necessarily observable in a strictly empiricist way. As I conceptualized sense of place (Eyles 1985), I thought of the mechanisms that shape existence and experience as being irreducible to the individual level but being manifested at it. Sense of place may only be one small dimension of this manifestation, but it may demonstrate the nature of the relationships between the conduct of life and the forms and structures it produces and those that product it. Reality is, therefore, a social construction that acts back on its subjects, sometimes in unseen and taken-for-granted ways. Giddens's (1979) ideas concerning the duality of structure seemed most appropriate, with social life exhibiting a basic recursiveness.

This notion of the mutual dependence of structure (rules and resources organized as properties of social systems) and agency (continuous flow of conduct) also seemed to provide a way of bridging the increasingly sterile, parallel arguments of the materialists and the humanists. Giddens had elucidated in this protoversion of structuration theory what appeared to me to be a fundamental truth of social life; that individuals make societies and societies make individuals—a conception that owes as much to Berger (1963) and Berger and Luckmann (1967) as it does to Giddens. For me all the arguments were well summarized by Bhaskar (1979, 45): "people do not create society for it always pre-exists them and is a necessary condition for their activity. Rather, society must be regarded as an ensemble of structures, practices and conventions which individuals reproduce or transform, but which would not exist unless they did so. Society does not exist independently of human activity (the error of reification). But it is not the product of it (the error of voluntarism)." I did not realize it at the time, but the ideas in this quotation would draw me to other theories to help me in my work on the microsocial processes that shape the social world—Bourdieu on social practice and Blumer on interactionism, to cite the two reported in this chapter. But that is to leap ahead, although I should add that the purpose or the outcome of thinking about and writing this chapter has been to position more explicitly the insight on the one hand and practical utility on the other offered by structuration for my work. But armed with protostructuration theory and some ideas about place and place-in-the-world, I entered the field (circa 1981) to investigate sense of place.

This chapter is an exploration of my investigation into the complexities of sense of place. At the heart of this exploration is an attempt to convey to the reader my struggle to understand situated human affiliations in geographic place and how structuration theory as now codified has helped in this endeavor. In the first part, I briefly explore the range of senses of place that I encountered in an introductory research project. I then discuss two case studies that I have conducted on this topic and probe the utility of structuration theory and competing theoretical perspectives to understand these situated unfoldings. The first study concerns the household survival strategies of poor Italian-Canadians in a large industrial city; the second involves the disruption of everyday routines among stigmatized rural Canadians and how they seek to recapture "normality." Finally, I reflect on my recent engagement with structuration and discuss this perspective's importance to my research.

SENSES OF PLACE

In part, the purposes of an early study on sense of place—a logical precursor to the two case studies I later discuss—were to show how findings derived by different methods but concerning the same phenomena provide different pictures of the social world. But of immediate concern were the senses of places that were identified, their significance, and the comments they allow us to make about structuration theory. In fact, on the basis of in-depth interview responses with 162 individuals, it was possible to identify ten ideal-typical senses (Eyles 1985). All ten were firmly located in the sources of identity and forces and structures of the material worlds that shape how people live. They had greater or lesser impact depending on individual circumstances and attributes, which greatly influenced how people shape their social worlds and reshape their environments. It is in this shaping and reshaping that the significance of a lay sense of place may be observed. The most important sense of place was social—that place had little meaning without reference to social ties and interactions. Place was shaped by it being the location of family, neighbors, and friends. In some instances, family dominated this shaping of environment in terms of either interactions or where the family's roots could be identified. Others gave the social a different meaning, seeing people and place as dimensions of a stage on which a particular lifestyle could be played. These individuals significantly reshaped and redefined what was present to suit their own ideas on how life should be lived. They did, however, tend to do this in a positive way, contributing to the social life of the place. Others used people and place more instrumentally, wanting a village-type existence without the interactions and obligations that such existence brings. They viewed people and places as commodities, as things to be acquired, used, and ultimately discarded. While their reshaping was social in orientation, they shared a perspective with those who saw place as a means to an end, in terms simply of what it provided (or did not provide).

While those who possessed an ecological sense of place (with environment important in its own right) were few in number, two other reshapings were more significant. One group, consisting almost entirely of elderly people, saw their living space in terms of the past. They lived nostalgically, with the past being the most significant element in life. The other appeared to have no sense of place at all, seeming to be apathetic about where they lived. They simply acquiesced to life and place as they were, not because they believed life was particularly good, but often because they felt they could not change anything themselves. But their silence and acceptance of what they have been given should not be taken as approval. The burdens of life leave little time, will, or resources to effect a reshaping of the place. Life is there to be lived through and put up with. Further, this group may not have played out its significant events in physical locations or places but may have ordered the world through messages received through the mass media. As Meyrowitz (1985) puts it, the texture of everyday experience is shaped by the electronic media. In such a world, people have no sense of place.

This study, however, concentrated on seeing how people defined community through negotiating or imposing their own definitions of place. While the sample was a mixed one in terms of income and occupational characteristics, it was primarily a nonmarginalized rural community that was defining and managing the environment for itself (Eyles 1990). This setting was very different from impoverished social environments, where the evidence of external manipulation is everywhere. For instance, places of the poor are substantially modified or destroyed by design professionals in exercises of rezoning or redevelopment. Their places are also substantially altered by the operation of market forces. The growth of central commercial areas, the desire of many elements of the service class to live close to work, and the destruction of many traditional industries in the process of economic restructuring have meant that many working class groups are more manipulated than manipulating. Such changes can lead to the destruction of places, early examples of which can be found in Boston (Fried 1966); their changing social composition as with the gentrification of some of the inner areas of such cities as London, Toronto, Sydney, and Auckland; and their decline to house an acquiescent population hit hard by high levels of unemployment and reductions in social support services. In the main, such places are backwaters bypassed by "progress" and are seen as marginal in the dominant view of the social, economic, and environmental system. This does not mean that in such localities people have no sense of identity or place, but it may mean that the raw materials at their disposal to remake places are mainly themselves. The constraints of context underline the social nature of experience. The ability to shape and manipulate place is thus constrained by occupational structure and work position. Individuals and groups may physically and psychologically re-make space as well as use their social worlds to do so, but for most (not only the poor), economic, political, and ideological dimensions provide insistent answers to existential questions, concerning our place-in-the-world (Eyles 1990).

But what has the discovery of these senses of community to do with structuration theory? I can only answer that in terms of what structuration theory meant to me. As I have suggested, I saw its importance in terms of relating agency and structure. Thus in one respect, sense of place embodies what place means to people. But in another respect, there is more to it than that because experience need not be explicable only in its own terms and by reference to its everyday world but also in terms of structural constraints. Place is not then simply the experience of conceptualization of place. Life, existence, place-in-the-world seem to intrude and become manifest in sense of place.

The implication of place-in-the-world in so many of the descriptions of the forms of senses of place means that place itself is therefore seen in a dialectical relation with what an individual is and what he or she sees himself or herself to be. In short, sense of place and place-in-the-world both suggest the centrality of material existence and identity in explicating these forms. The relationships are still not necessarily straightforward because material existence and identity may not be related in an unproblematic way. Identity is no mere reflection of existence. It may be used to transcend aspects of materiality. In other words, identity may be a way of escaping a reality that is seen as enclosing and constraining. The quest for identity in place, community, or wherever may simply be a technique of mental management, of negotiation, to make the routines, regularities, and objectifications of everyday life livable (see Cohen and Taylor 1976). Further, this implicating of identity and material existence may be seen as an alternative way of saying that agency, the flow of conduct, is implicated in and by structure, the rules, resources, and properties of social systems (i.e., as part of the process of structuration). Structure (or material existence) does not exist independently of agency (or identity). But neither is it a product of it. Society and the material basis from which it emanates are constituted as a collection of structures that individuals reproduce or transform through their activities and searches for sources of identity. These structures do not determine identity and indeed may be expressed through it. A similar relation was noted by Cohen (1980), who found, in the context of the Notting Hill Carnival (London), that economic and political structures were identified through ethnicity. Sense of place may thus be regarded as an integral dimension of those processes of reproduction and transformation that also ensure the continued existence of the structures. The place-identity-material existence relation is a necessary relation for the production and reproduction of society.

So how had I utilized structuration theory? Or more specifically, what use had it been to me, remembering that I was working before the codifying of the theory in Giddens (1984)? Uncharitably, structuration theory was useful in providing a theoretical prop for exploring relationships that lie at the center of human geography. More charitably, there were obvious parallels between my interests and structuration theory as an approach to investigating social activities. Its relevance is clear if we adopt Thrift's (1986) notion that structuration theory is not an attempt to put together a theory of the chief causal mechanisms and contingencies relevant to a particular time and place but rather a statement of a set of basic principles of social analysis. Key in this set is the duality of structure (see Gregson 1986; Sayer 1983). But what else can be said after it has been affirmed that agency and structure are linked? As Gregory (1984, 129) comments, "it is one thing to grasp what the theory of structuration entails . . . but quite another to incorporate its theorems into substantive accounts in such a way that one captures the engagements between agency and structure."

Structuration theory tells us of the connection. And of course it tells us a lot more about the nature of agency, acts, and actions on the one hand and system and structure on the other (Giddens 1984). Further, it may be, as Gregson (1989) argues, that the expectation that structuration concepts can be transferred directly into empirical analysis is misconceived. But I am left convinced by two of Thrift's (1986) criticisms of "The Constitution of Society," namely the treatment of the human agent and the relationship between structuration and empirical research. I fully appreciate the detail with which Giddens (1985, 1989) has worked through the operation of society at the macro level through the incorporation of time-space concepts and the empirical work that rests on those workings (e.g., Gregory 1982; Pred 1986). But as Thrift (1986) comments, Giddens's human agents are curiously anonymous creatures. Creativity and conflict seem lacking. The point has been reinforced by Gregory (1989, 213): "Giddens has so far not shown how the transformative capacities of human beings vary according to the specific circumstances in which they find themselves and through which they are constituted as knowledgeable and capable human subjects. His preoccupation with an abstract account of human subjectivity . . . prevents him from following through the consequences of his own insight into the way in which social structures enable as well as constrain." Given this variability, the forms that the outcome of the relationship between structure and agency will take depend on circumstances, on contingency. For me, structuration theory is important because it is contextualizing. But as such, it is hardly startling or unique. As Thrift (1983a) says, a contextual approach attempts to recapture the flow of human conduct as a series of situated events in time and space. It is in the level of detail that structuration theory differs from Hagerstrand's (1984) time-geography, Ley's (1981) humanistically influenced contextualized meanings, and Soja's (1980) contextual space. But Giddens has provided real insight especially for the operation of the world system and of individual motivation and behavior. For my own interests in the empirical investigation of negotiated and contested social worlds, other theories have proved to be more useful. I want to illustrate these before concluding with another engagement with structuration theory.

FEELING SECURE AS A MIGRANT: SOCIAL PRACTICES IN A NEW WORLD

My case study work on Italian-Canadians in a large industrial city (see Eyles and Perri 1993; Perri 1990) was inspired by the "making do" literature (i.e., by that which tried to assess the importance of household survival strategies among marginalized populations, particularly in times of financial hardship; see Edwards and Ribbens 1991; Mingione 1985; Pahl 1984). It seemed worthwhile to investigate these issues among a particular population group in a city undergoing significant industrial restructuring. But as often happens, our respondents redefined our research problem for us, seeing the social practices of the Italian family as crucial in defining themselves and their place not only in the changing city but also in life itself. The family was used to create order, but the responses of individuals were quite diverse, as the following quotations demonstrate:

I love my family. In Italy we were so close. I had 15 aunts and uncles and I loved them all. . . . There has to be respect in family. If my kids are late they call me. . . . I love my kids and family. They have education, better jobs, more money, who can complain? I'd do anything for them. I cook, clean, wash, I work too. All I want for my kids is good health and for them to get married. The responsibilities of a mother are never over.

Family helped all the time. As a father you think for your kids. The family must always stay united. If the children leave home it's very sad. . . . Collaboration is the key. . . . If you are good with me I'm good with you. I need respect. This is what family is.

I have always been part of a tight family. I lived with my brother for years. My brother found me work, gave me a job and fed me. He meant everything. . . . I want to do the same for my family. When my kids get married I want them to live with me to save money. I don't think this will happen. In our days children were more educated, we were poor but had respect. Now kids don't give a shit. . . . I don't understand.

All the children today want one house, two cars, two women and to work a little and earn a lot. Money talks here in Canada. My daughter is divorced. This is tough on us. My son-in-law fell in love with another woman. Sacrifices even now for my kids. . . . We must sacrifice to stay united. If it hurts my kids, it hurts me. I live for my kids to be happy.

My parents struggled a great deal. They were frugal and knew how to stretch a dollar. There was not credit; it was on honour. They had no money, there were no presents at Christmas, but we had respect; we never answered back. I always learned to help them out. . . . Today, the children take everything for granted. . . . In the past women were treated like women, respect for them. Today, kids don't open doors for elderly women or give up their seats in buses. . . . I baby sit my great niece whose mother is divorced. I try to instill in her values, but the niece is brought up by three or four families. . . . The family is very important but its importance has diminished over time. The family doesn't come around as much, only maybe at mass and at Christmas. The parents drew the family together. They always lived for their children.

What can help explain this attachment to the private world of the family and its home, particularly among different generations? It appears that over the last forty years, more Italian-Canadians have re-created home anew in the New World (see Bagnell 1989; Breton et al. 1990), as have many migrant groups before them. Important in understanding the role of family and home are the processes of obtaining and retaining ethnic identity. Breton et al. (1990, 87) identify different forms of ethnic identity and societal incorporation in their study of several different ethnic groups in Toronto:

1. an identity revolving around concrete objects, as symbols, including food and artistic articles;
2. an identity revolving around having friends of the same ethnicity and marrying within the group;
3. an identity revolving around the practice of customs and community participation;
4. an identity revolving around the language itself; and
5. an identity related to giving support to the group's causes or needs and/or helping group members with a job.

We argued in this project that all social forms observed may manifest themselves through the Italian-Canadian family (Eyles and Perri 1993). Family is a way of making a home—as place. But despite the obvious love of and commitment to home and family, there are tensions between first and second, on the one hand, and third generation Italian-Canadians, on the other. As such, this group is not unusual. Indeed, in a recent essay on the Canadese, Bagnell's (1989) concluding chapter is entitled, "Home Is where the Heart Is: But where's the Heart?" One of his final quotations points out, "It is because the Italian community is too often a community built around the buck. Making it big in material well being has come to mean too much. . . . Young people see their father having made a lot of money without education. But their fathers were too busy struggling to pay off the mortgage to get an education. . . . We have failed somewhere. . . . Too many young people of potential have simply settled for the easy dollar" (p. 264). In this, young Italian-Canadians again do not greatly differ from many other migrant descendants. The issue may therefore be understood as a problem of ethnic identity retention with a waxing and waning of interest in mother tongue, ethnic institutions, and so on. But it is also possible to see the issue in terms of the meaning and importance of home and being at home in an *apparently* individualized world and the relations between the public and the private realms.

How then may we explain home and at-homeness? One influential scheme from the psychological literature, taken up by among others Porteous (1976), is that of Cooper (1974), who argued that the self is the most basic of archetypes and that the house is its frequent symbol (i.e., its manifestation of the here and now in time and space). For Cooper, the strict identity between house and self is natural (and not socially influenced) and static (arbitrarily abstracted from social context). Pratt's (1981) criticisms of the self-house relation are quite telling. She comments that Cooper naturalizes a potentially objectified, alienating, and reified world in which objects (i.e., the house) come to represent the self without any reference to the social production of those objects.

Dovey (1985) provides a more useful starting point with her essay on home and homelessness. She argues that the home as distinct from the house has three properties: as order—a patterning of experience so individuals are oriented within a spatial, temporal, and sociocultural order they understand; as identity—an identification with the place in which individuals dwell with a binding of person and place (including those at that place)—order and identity are joined as connectedness (the making of relationships as meaningful with home connecting people, place, past, and future); and as becoming, with home being situated with respect to such categories as insider-outsider, home-journey, order-chaos, self-other, private-public, and us-them (i.e., as defining place-in-the-world). Home is where the heart is, and these properties of home describe the (stereo) typical home life of Italian families in Canada (see Bagnell 1989; Jansen 1981; Sturino 1978). Dovey's scheme is conceptually important. Her last property—home as becoming—shows particularly how the home (and with it home life, which is—ideally at least—equated with family life for Italian-Canadians) is not an isolated phenomenon but embedded in the daily social fabric. In Giddens's terms structure is embedded in agency and agency in structure. But why does home (family) *appear* to be isolated and not part of the wider society?

The answer may be in the idea that these linkages are all pervasive and taken for granted, as Gregory (1989, 200–201) perceptively puts it "accepted-as-legitimate." He goes on: "Just because actors are bound into time-space routines, it does not automatically follow that they internalize the values of the social institutions which are reproduced through them. . . . to accentuate the recursiveness of time-space routines without opening a conceptual space for deroutinization 'from the inside' is, I think, to short change the transformation model embedded within structuration theory." I will reserve comment on this point until later, but the pervasiveness of family-home among Italian-Canadians may be either taken for granted or accepted as legitimate depending on generation and personal circumstances and predilections. The ideas of diversity in the yet taken-for-granted nature of everyday life are captured in Bourdieu's (1977) idea of habitus, which is an array of common-sense, taken-for-granted ways for acting in the world. Further, "As an acquired system of generative schemes, the habitus engenders all the thoughts, all the perceptions and all the actions consistent with those conditions and no others" (Bourdieu 1977, 95). It simultaneously generates and is generated by social classifications reproduced in practice. It is similar to Giddens's duality of structure but emphasizes home and the relation between space and actions (or practice) more clearly in that it conceptualizes this recursive embedding of agency and structure. Habitus conceptualizes practice as ways of coping, of dealing with everyday things. But "the schemes of habitus, the primary forms of classification, owe their specific efficacy to the fact that they function below the level of consciousness and language, beyond the introspective scrutiny or control by will" (Bourdieu 1984, 466).

If this taken for grantedness also seems right and familiar (as is the case with an ethnic cluster or family acting as a haven of peace, security, and comfort in an alien world [Boal 1976] until challenged intergenerationally), the schemes of habitus become reinforced. This reinforcement may be intensified by the sharing of homes by many migrant families in linguistically alien cultures. Bourdieu's (1977) commentary on the significance of the house resonates for many Italian-Canadians: "In a social formation in which the absence of the symbolic product-conserving techniques associated with literacy retards the objectification of symbolic particularly cultural capital, inhabited space—and above all the house—is the principal locus for the objectification of generative schemes; and, through the intermediary of the divisions and hierarchies it sets up between things, persons and practices, this tangible classifying system continuously inculcates and reinforces the taxonomic principles underlying all the arbitrary provisions of this culture" (p. 83). It works. And home (family) becomes the taken-for-granted basis of understanding and operating in the social world.

But Bourdieu's scheme implies an overarching hegemony for habitus. But as Robben (1989) points out, its reproduction in practice is always a contextual interpretation and open to structural and interactional diversity. Structural diversity may result from which of the various meanings of home are more or less dominant (see Rybczynski 1987). In other words, home is not necessarily a unitary construct. Its inhabitants may have different reasons for their attachment to it and be differentially affected by forces apparently external to it but embedded within it in terms of their effects on well-being, providing opportunities for advancement, and so on.

Not only is practice open to different interpretations, it is itself diverse. Robben (1989) argues that three processes shape diversity of practice within the habitus, namely obligation (referring to the mutual expectations of two parties with respect to the reciprocal content of their social relationship); consideration (the anticipation of another person's needs without seeing their fulfillment as a duty or obligation); and media (an emotional barometer that evaluates the mood and temperament of people in everyday interactions). Obligation predominates in the economic domain, consideration in domestic relations, and media in the public sphere. But a family (particularly a migrant family) is all these spheres. And if "contextual ambiguities and classificatory disagreements about social relations are major sources of conflict" (Robben 1989, 577), the family and home become sources of tensions, particularly where relations of consideration become infected with demands of obligation with reference, for example, to finding work or using influence for sons and daughters. Thus structural and interactional diversity point to the external means and internal responses by which habitus may be disrupted.

How might the relation between home-family and external means be conceptualized? Dovey's (1985) idea of homelessness—the processes and conditions that can erode the experience of home and paralyze its emergence in the modern world (cf. Relph 1976, 1981)—is important. In the main, her properties of homelessness are macrosocial. But particularly important is the erosion of communal space, which emphasizes the relations between the micro and the macro, individual and societal, and the public and the private. Dovey argues that a sense of home has been eroded by the decline of communally shared open space. Further, Aries (1978, 233) argues that the city "has become a mass of small islands . . . all separated from one another by a great void. The interstitial space has been vanished." But the erosion is more widespread than Dovey suggests, involving the erosion of lived space or common experience in societies that are becoming increasingly segmented and pluralistic in terms of core-periphery, men-women, black-white, young-old, and so on. In the case of the home-family of Italian-Canadians, this erosion manifests itself in intergenerational differences that are all the more intense or deep seated because of this process's layering with issues of ethnic identity. But the layering is a reason why the erosion does not become a schism. Another is the need for home itself.

This is the main reason why in the ideal (and often the real) home and family remain central to Italian-Canadians. It may mean that the tensions become conflicts or that its activities become ritualized in dinners, annual get togethers, and so on (see Devos and Romanucci-Ross 1975). It may also mean that the home-family (habitus) is not doomed to perish but must be renegotiated so that its meaning has a shifting but not unstable property. There is, in fact, stability in the very use of the terms *home* and *family*. Despite its shifting differentiated meaning, home gives a place in the world: a personal place where we feel at home in a potentially frightening public world. But defining away the public does not mean that it ceases to exist. As Sennett (1977, 310–311) puts it,

The refusal to deal with, absorb, and exploit reality outside the parochial scale is in the sense a universal human desire, being a simple fear of the unknown. Community feeling formed by the sharing of impulses has the special role of reinforcing the fear of the unknown, converting claustrophobia into an ethical principle. . . . This is the peculiar sectarianism of a secular society. It is the result of converting the immediate experience of sharing with others into a social principle. Unfortunately, large scale forces in society may psychologically be kept at a distance, but do not therefore go away.

The emphasis on the personal—home-family—is understandable, bringing meaning to a confusing world and being reinforced by the taken for grantedness or acquiescence (and security) of habitus. Italian-Canadians are no more or less different in this process, although questions of ethnicity and ethnic identity retention of different generations (and possibly genders) complicate the issue. Home serves an intensely personal purpose, but through habitus and language (with home being constantly appropriated in and by social practices) it also serves to naturalize the personal and decouple it from the public. Home may be where the heart is, and we may be unsure where the heart is. But we do not, on this argument, want to know what lies outside the home. More correctly, we may not want to know some of the things that are embedded within it because its practices represent structures in this apparent world of agency. And it is because of this embedded nature of agency and structure as played out in the everyday that the conceptualizations of Dovey and Bourdieu seemed more useful than the duality of structure. For me and this project, while Giddens's distinction is as insightful as Berger and Luckmann's (1967) ideas of individual-in-society and society-in-the-individual, it was found limited in terms of practical utility for explaining the diversity in the everyday lives of a migrant group. I shall return to these themes in the concluding section.

BACK TO NORMAL: NEGOTIATING RISK AWAY

If the first case study examined the complex textures of everyday life among a marginalized group, the second one looked at the disruption of the routines of everyday life and how potentially stigmatized people return to normality. This then was an event-driven piece of research (see Baxter et al. 1992; Eyles et al. 1992, 1993), in that it was being conducted on the psychosocial impacts of living close to solid waste disposal facilities (Taylor et al. 1993) when a tire fire broke out in the early hours of February 12, 1990, close to the small Ontario town of Hagersville, some 100 kilometers southwest of Toronto. Between 13 and 14 million tires had been assembled on the site since the late 1970s. The fire burned for seventeen days before it was successfully extinguished on February 28, 1990. We were awarded another contract from the Ontario Ministry of Environment (MoE) to examine the impacts of responses to the fire. This event also provided me with a chance to look at how people cope with a disruption to routine in this rural setting.

In fact, the study population totaled 2100 and was located in scattered dwellings and small settlements. The rural setting and the population's sociodemographic profile had implications for possible responses to stressful events. Several factors implied an enhanced capacity to cope with stressful situations. These included the stability of the population (Lazarus and Folkman 1984); the rural context, social structure, and lifestyle (Tremblay and Anderson 1970); the conventional family structure (Cobb 1976; Hodge and Qadeer 1983); and, following from the previous characteristics, the potential for well-developed social and community support networks (Bromet et al. 1982). Other dimensions of the sociodemo-graphic structure in the population implied greater susceptibility to environmental stress. These included the high percentage of households with children, the relatively low socioeconomic status of area residents, and the high proportion of home owners. Families in early stages of the life cycle were likely to be sensitive to environmental stress (Levine and Stone 1986). Studies by Dohren-wend et al. (1981), Kessler and Cleary (1980), and Kessler (1982) indicate that those in lower status groups are more likely to develop symptoms of distress. Home owners are also more likely to be affected by psychosocial impacts than renters. Thus the population is such that a diversity of reactions to the fire could be expected with different subgroups experiencing different levels of anxiety, stress, access to support and resources, and therefore capacities to cope.

Initially, the fire was thought to be a barn ablaze, a rare but not out of the ordinary occurrence in a rural community. Interest and concern intensified as the blaze continued and as media reports on radio and television and in the local press informed people that the Tire King tire dump was on fire. There followed, for many, a period of confusion as they were unsure of the likely effects of the plume and whether they should leave their homes. There was also uncertainty as to which authority or department should be contacted to help decide about evacuation. There appeared to be no systematic, coordinated strategy to put into place if a disaster occurred, although plans were drawn up and implemented by local and regional officials and politicians. According to a local resident, Mrs. Farmer, "They didn't give us any idea whatsoever how long we would still be away from home. . . . Nobody had any idea how long it was gonna be so . . . the next night or the day after we just said to heck with it, we're going home. . . . At that time we didn't know we were going to be reimbursed for leaving home, eh? So we just thought rather than trying to run [our kids] back and forth every day such a distance we, uh, just came home."

Uncertainty and its concomitant anxiety were further intensified by the evac-

uation call. People were upset that despite the fire burning all day, they were
not visited by the police until very late at night or the early hours of the morning,
which meant that children would have to be awakened and that it would be
difficult to contact friends or relatives who might help. Further, the evacuation
call was phrased in such a way that the decision was left to individual households.
Most evacuees chose to go and stay with family, usually in homes some distance
from the area. For some this compounded the distress because of overcrowding
and the disruption of other people's lives.

After the fire and its plume had disappeared, confusion tended to be replaced
by inconvenience—a further disruption to everyday life. For many, particularly
those who had been upwind of the fire and those at some distance away, the
disaster or bases for concern ceased to be visible. With this invisibility, their
perception of risk was lessened, meaning that their main concerns were the
problems of access along particular concession lines and local travel convenience
in general. Inconvenience resulted from the police blockading various routes
around the fire. This particularly affected those living or working on these routes.
School bus schedules had to be revised, and a system of identification was
established. This system was praised in general. It was seen as necessary to
bring some security to evacuated properties. The police were regarded more
sympathetically than the local firefighters. Although there was praise for their
work, particularly in the conditions that existed on the site, some thought that
the locals wanted to maintain control over the firefighting effort despite not
having an overall strategy or all the necessary equipment. This variable attitude
toward the firefighters points to just one of the divisions that emerged in the area
after the fire.

Carried out three months after the fire, the research interviews with forty-
three households obtained a complex picture about disruption, coping, and concerns relating not only to the fire and evacuation but to the cleanup as well.[1]
The family, both immediate and extended, was used, not surprisingly, as a major
resource when people required accommodation and other forms of assistance.
Further, many of the anxieties and uncertainties were played out within the
family unit, as this was the social unit most affected by the disruption. Husbands,
wives, partners, and children were reciprocally used as sources of support to
militate against stress, to talk through problems, and so on. Such intense, stress-
related interaction was not always positive. Members of the same family disagreed about how to deal with anxieties, what certain things meant, and how the
unit should respond. Some existing tensions were exacerbated by having to
respond to the fire and the cleanup. The difficulties and intensities were found
especially among those closest to the fire site. Mrs. Vonderheufel admitted, "I
can tell that I'm a little more on edge, especially with the kids, not quite as
patient as you'd like to be—not that you ever are—but it's hard; you lose it a
lot quicker."

Others thought that there was little need to continue to cope. Their lives had
been disrupted for a few days, but all had returned to normal. Coping thus really

meant the continuous and incremental adjustment to changing life circumstances. The fire was only one element in these circumstances. And such adjustments were natural. So once the fire and the worst of the cleanup had been lived through, life had to go on as it had before: work had to be carried out, children looked after, the home tended. Mrs. Vonderheufel said, "You cope with what you have to cope with and you have friends and family and you have your church and that helps a whole lot. . . . Just moral support you know if you need something . . . but you know for us our faith helps a lot because we know we're going to come through it all right in the end. It's just getting that far: that's the hard part, but it has been tough."

But there was a further diverse set of impacts from the fire that variably acted as disruptions to everyday life. Some had to ensure that their livelihoods, especially produce if they farmed, would still be accepted at market. Some other businesses relied on positive public perceptions (e.g., dog kennels). All were affected by concern about water quality. In the main, the Ministry of Agriculture through product testing and advisories helped minimize these disruptions. More lives, however, were disrupted by compensation claims that prevented life from getting back to normal.

Compensation became a divisive issue in the community. Understandably, the MoE was able to process small claims for out-of-pocket expenses caused by the evacuation and minor damage claims more quickly than major claims. All residents were satisfied with compensation for the evacuation, although it often resulted in uneasy feelings inside the extended family as the evacuees had to demand that their relatives bill them for food and accommodation. Very few people thought that the MoE should compensate them for any disruption caused by the stress or anxiety that they suffered during the fire or evacuation and their aftermath. Major claims for damage to homes and goods and for buying out those who felt that they could not return to their homes were processed slowly. This resentment was exacerbated by the perceived insensitivity with which the MoE rehoused them. They were housed in trailers near Townsend. Some families spent over a year in these cramped conditions. Negotiations over goods were particularly slow and only resolved in the summer of 1991. These negotiations involved only those closest to the fire site. Those in the outlying areas thought that those who moved out of their homes settled for handsome sums. There is some envy and indeed a more general feeling that some of their neighbors were golddiggers, claiming damages that were not fire related. Most offered stories of this golddigging, which had the potential for being a continuing, divisive issue. Mr. Zimmerman said, "They're using this to their advantage. . . . They just bought that for 62 thousand, six or seven months ago—less than a year. . . . Now they want a hundred and sixty-eight for it; almost triple the money they bought it for six months ago, no way. . . . They're asking that much and the government will probably give them a hundred thousand and they're still gonna walk away laughing, and they're living for free over in, uh, well, Townsend, yeah, that little quarry—they got all set up over there. They're living for free now.'' In some respects life was and will be very slow in returning to normality. Indeed, it may have changed irreversibly.

There were few concerns about the health effects of the tire fire, except indirectly through water quality issues. Virtually everyone expressed concerns about water quality, fear about the effects of the toxic runoff from the site. According to the Barkers,

M: It burned for almost three weeks, . . . thousands of thousands of gallons of oil went someplace. And they kept saying, "we sucked it all up." And you say, no you didn't. We know you didn't; you couldn't have sucked it all up, you didn't get into the middle of that pile for almost a week and a half, two weeks, so where'd it go?

F: There's going to be long term effects—tons of long term effects that they are going to have to deal with and hopefully they will deal with it so it won't harm the people.

There was uncertainty in which direction and at what rate the heavy oils and metals from the melted tires would run through the bedrock. If the process is slow, it may be years before the full consequences are known. The December 1991 deadline for long-term compensation was, therefore, regarded as inappropriate. There was also general dissatisfaction about water quality testing that has been and continues to be carried out by the MoE. The site has been ringed with test wells to monitor for toxins and pollutants. But most were dissatisfied, wanting their own well water to be tested. There seems to be a schism between the scientific reasoning, which argues that if nearby wells are clean, far ones should be, and the popular view that no one knows what is happening underground and pollutants can show up anyplace. But even if residents' wells were tested, there was dissatisfaction with the testing itself. The testing has found low quality but potable water and poor quality well construction and maintenance. The residents felt that they were being blamed for present water quality concerns and inferentially for potential future problems. But the latency of the water quality issue suggests that, at this level, life for some will never return to normal.

While water quality is the dominant long-term impact from the residents' point of view, water testing may also be used to illustrate their attitudes toward government, related to reflections on causes of the fire and accountability. There was a widespread mistrust of government in the region and the province. With respect to the fire, government was seen as insensitive, uncoordinated, slow, and uncaring. According to Mr. Krieger, "I don't know how good people's words are, who do you believe? . . . One time, they say one thing and the next time they say something else. So . . . the government is supposed to be good people aren't they? I guess they're just as shifty as everybody else." Parts of its apparatus were viewed positively, but many held government in contempt not only for the cleanup difficulties but also for allowing the fire to happen in the first place. In fact, few blamed the site owner for the fire. He was primarily seen as a businessman trying to earn a living but constrained by government and court inaction. Some saw him as fulfilling a community need for taking the tires.

There is a degree of fatalism in some residents' views on causation. The site was seen as an accident waiting to happen. It was inevitable that something would occur, although it must be added the site did not loom large in people's prefire minds. The pile was simply part of the landscape. But it was a pile for which the government was held largely accountable in that its various agencies should have listened to the owner's petitions more attentively, policed him more effectively, and ensured speedier court action. The government was held accountable for the circumstances that allowed the fire to happen, not for the fire itself (although the government was not completely absolved for the fire). There were comments that the Young Offenders Act and the probation service were not tough or efficient enough. The youths who started the fire were seen merely as the literal and metaphorical spark. With respect to causation, we again see the fire as a potentially divisive force in the community. But in terms of overall accountability, the government is less highly regarded by those in the Hagersville area than it was before.

From this analysis of accounts of the fire and its cleanup, the forms of disruption may be discerned—evacuation, return, product quality, water issues, divisive community relations, and so on. But a dominant subtext in the stories, except for those households ($n = 6$) closest to the fire site, is getting back to normal. In this respect, people used themselves, their immediate and extended families and friendship networks, and some governmental assistance. In the main, they used themselves by, for example, reestablishing prefire patterns of behavior and interaction, by downplaying the significance of the event (indeed, no lives were lost and property damage was minimal), and by wondering what all the fuss was about. Most of their lives were affected and in some respects continue to be affected—the unknown effects on well water and its impacts on health (particularly that of their children) and the consequences of their mistrust of public officials. But the risks are downplayed, minimized, defined away. What conceptual frameworks may assist in understanding these empirically derived generalizations?

I am uncertain as to whether the duality of structure gets over the idea of the transformation of the social world through disrupted routines and the renormalization of the world in diverse ways through different strategies to reduce risk. Initially we turned to the empirically derived risk perception literature, much of which refers to toxic events and contaminated communities. Thus Edelstein (1988) argues that the social and psychological impacts of toxic exposure involve complex interactions among various levels of society and vary across time and environmental context; that these impacts have short- and long-term effects on how the exposed population behaves and perceives and understands their lives; that toxic exposure incidents are stressful, forcing those involved to adopt some coping response; and that contamination is inherently stigmatizing, arousing anticipatory fears. This stigma may be amplified by circumstances surrounding the event, mainly the ways in which information is transferred and the type of response mechanisms present (Kasperson et al. 1988). Generalizing from many studies, Hance et al. (1989) infer that imposed risks are seen as more severe than voluntary ones; risks under individual control are accepted more readily than those under government control, thus raising issues of trust-mistrust in authority (e.g., Short 1984; Slovic et al. 1991); risks that are perceived as fair are more acceptable than those that seem unfair; and perception of risk is affected by the perceived trustworthiness of information sources. Personal experience and degree of personal control are also important (e.g., Stallen and Tomas 1988), as are acceptance or denial of vulnerability (Baird 1986) and global feelings about well-being and the social legitimacy of the activities involving risk (Bastide et al. 1989). In sum, risk has many attributes that are perceived to be greater if it is thought to be uncontrollable, involuntary, involves dread, is unknown to those exposed, is new, has delayed (or latent) effects, is potentially catastrophic, and is especially problematic for future generations (see Slovic 1987).

Risk is now widely recognized to be socially constructed; appraisal and management are determined by people's place-in-the-world and how they see and act in the world (Kahneman et al. 1982). All ideas about the world are in fact rooted in experience, and different forms of social organization and their underlying value systems will influence risk perceptions (Douglas and Wildavsky 1982). In fact, community perceptions act as filters through which individuals perceive risk and on the basis of which they respond to that which is seen as risky (see Fitchen et al. 1987). This complex interplay of social, economic, and psychological dimensions shapes attitudes and responses concerning risk.

Seeing risk and risk perceptions in these ways is to adopt implicitly an interactionist perspective on social life. As Denzin (1992) remarks, it has been followed more than it has been formulated. But Blumer (1969) has specified the basic premises of the approach, namely that human beings act toward things on the basis of the meanings that the things have for them and that these meanings are the product of social interaction in human society and are modified and handled through an interpretive process. Thus meanings are worked out in encounters, and while these are tentatively agreed on they are never fixed. From this viewpoint, the social order and individual lives are open and negotiable. Thus individuals living their lives are not moving through a set of predefined steps. Interaction is improvised by being built around themes and ideas that are modified to meet particular circumstances. Thus disruption to everyday life is met by improvising responses to achieve the desired goal of returning to normality. Risks are, therefore, downplayed or seen as not particularly extraordinary but as part and parcel of the negotiation of everyday life. Disruption that brings ambiguity and uncertainty intensifies negotiation to bring life back to normal. Thus while the whole of social life may be seen as negotiated order (Hall and Spencer-Hall 1982; Strauss, 1978; Strauss et al. 1964), order is itself negotiated in the course of everyday life through individuals defining their situations as, say, risky or not risky, problematic or unproblematic, and so on. Over the course of the Hagersville tire fire and its aftermath, the negotiation and defining of situations excluded most risks (except the unknown consequences of future water quality and children's health).

Interactionism thus emphasizes the individual and his or her world of meaning and experience as embedded in structures and rules, or in, as Day and Day (1977) put it, the situational context of social actions. By stressing definition of the situation and negotiation, interactionism places on center stage people's reactions to circumstances as they see them. Different people see circumstances differently (golddigging versus fair compensation). But the significance of circumstances (structure) is recognized. Interactionism allows for social order—and through that people's places-in-the-world and sense of community—to emerge as an ongoing process. This order is subject to endless modification through the continuing and fluid negotiations that take place among community members in a variety of circumstances and that, therefore, lead to diverse outcomes.

CONCLUSION: A LATE ENGAGEMENT WITH STRUCTURATION

In the two case studies, I have tried to outline the theoretical schemes that have been useful in helping me understand these empirical settings. My work has been largely concerned with the everyday and how people live the everyday (see Eyles 1989). In these examples, I have examined two different groups— one marginalized by its migrant status in its attempts to find a home and a community, the other potentially stigmatized by a toxic contamination and with a need to respond to this disruption to daily life to restore its senses of order and community.

Why have I not used structuration theory? Certainly the frameworks I have used have detractors as well as supporters. Certainly there have been major developments to, applications of, and critiques concerning structuration. Giddens's (1976) work was central to me in beginning an exploration of interpretive sociologies. Further, in appeals to utilize contextual theories, structuration is seen as valuable as notions such as habitus (see Kuper 1992; Robben 1989). Why then no explicit use of structuration theory?

My answer will appear to place me in a time warp of early Giddens, or structuration I. I continue to be much taken by the notion of duality of structure. This concept, however, has been found wanting both empirically and theoretically. Theoretically, Sewell (1992) joins together the duality of structure and habitus to develop a theory of structure, while empirically Layder et al. (1991) in their work on the transition from school to work argue that agency and structure have to be seen as loci of powers rooted in partly independent domains that interpenetrate at particular times and places. The conclusion from my case studies is that agency and structure are embedded within each other, but this interpenetration takes diverse forms and may only be visible to the actors at particular times and places. In other words, as Mann (1986) puts it, societies (and individuals' places in society) tend to be messier than seems to be allowed for in structuration theory.

Further, my lack of engagement with structuration II (see Cloke et al. 1991) is that the project seems less relevant than structuration I to the research questions that interest me. In attempting to explicate society in general (Giddens 1985, 1989) and the nature of modernity (Giddens 1990), structuration theory and its extensions are grand theorizing. And as an interpretive geographer, I concur with Denzin's (1992, 22–23) remarks:

Interpretive (and symbolic) interactionists don't think that general theories are useful. They do not write . . . grand or global theories of societies. They take this position because they believe that "society" is an abstract term which refers to something that sociologists have invented in order to have a subject matter. They understand society to be something that is lived in the here and now, in the face to face and mediated interactions that connect persons to one another. Society, as it is lived, known, felt, and written about, goes on behind people's backs. . . . Interactionists believe they should write about how people are constrained by the constructions they build and inherit from the past.

A touch of hyperbole but a challenging comment. But this is not to say that grand theorizing is always unhelpful. For example, the empirical investigations of parts of Parsons's (1951) theory of the social system long after it was written (e.g., Gallagher 1976; Gerhardt 1989; Wolinsky 1981) continue to demonstrate the relevance of the sick role. Perhaps, however, I should be more circumspect about the structuration project. I do this in the full knowledge that whatever I say will have little impact on the Giddens phenomenon. As Clegg (1992) says, there is little point in embracing or spurning Giddens; his works are now institutionalized as phenomena. But I am struck by what Giddens (1991) has to say about the uses of structuration theory. He says that he likes least works in which authors attempts to import the whole theory. The sparing use of concepts is applauded while the overall framework is relevant to anyone writing broadly about social organization and transformation. Indeed, I have found the duality of structure notion thought- and research-provoking, although I have gone elsewhere for conceptual schemes. For the understanding of everyday life, the intersecting of agency and structure are paramount. As Pred (1985, 344), in his propositional statement of place as a historically contingent process argued, "any place or region expresses a process whereby the reproduction of social and cultural forms, the formation of biographies, and the transformation of nature and space ceaselessly become one another at the same time that power relations and time-space specific path-project intersections continuously become one another in ways that are not subject to universal laws but vary with historical circumstances." Duality of structure provided for me the clarion call for investigating the daily circumstances of marginalized and stigmatized groups; notions of habitus and negotiation, diversity and definition were necessary to comprehend the messy textures of everyday life.

NOTE

1. Interviewees who participated in this study include: Mrs. Farmer, local resident; Mrs. Vonderheufel, local resident; Mr. Zimmerman, local resident; Mr. and Mrs. Barker, local residents; and Mr. Krieger, local resident. Fictitious names have been used to ensure confidentiality.

6

Taking Control in the American West: An Application of Pred's Theory of Place

Jefferson S. Rogers

The history of the West, in many respects, is a history of exploitation. From its very beginning, the life of the West never has been its own. Westerners settled the land, lived on it, died on it. But they seldom owned it. Small prospectors found its gold and silver, but it was eastern corporations with capital and technology that seized the field—and fortune—from them. Sodbusters nested on the prairies and built a civilization out of dust. But it was cattle kings and eastern syndicates that dominated their land, and eastern banks that bled them of their profits. Throughout its history, the West was filled with little men with big dreams. They blazed the trails, dammed the rivers, built the cities. But it was eastern power—mining combines, cattle cartels, railroads, banks, smelters, and political coalitions—that ruled. (Lamm and McCarthy 1982, 6)

The settlement and development of the American West has been a continuous struggle for control over land, water, and minerals. Corporate organizations have been on the winning side for the past century. Vast tracts of agricultural land, thousands of acres of forests, and many of the energy and precious metal deposits located in the West are now owned or controlled by large firms. The federal government, often influenced by corporate interests, has facilitated this consolidation of power. Through public land leases, agricultural subsidies, water redistribution projects, military spending, environmental policies, and other means, the federal government has structured development in the West such that large, capital-rich firms are most favored (Mayer and Riley 1985). As a number of writers have pointed out over the past decades, the American West is a colony (e.g., Caughey 1959; Lamm and McCarthy 1982; Webb 1937). With extralocally based corporations and the federal government controlling a major portion of its assets, the West has long been and remains dependent on investment and political decisions made outside its boundaries.

Yet, at the same time, corporate and federal power over the West has never been absolute. Western activists and political leaders have found ways to modify various projects initiated by extralocal organizations. American Indians, environmentalists, farm workers, and state governors, for example, have pressured companies and federal agencies to change the ways in which projects were enacted. Through local legal requirements, strikes, media campaigns, and even guerrilla warfare, local actors and organizations have influenced the making of the American West. Nevertheless, the making of the American West has been and remains an unbalanced dialectic. Since it is doubtful that extralocally based private and federal organizations will relinquish control over their portion of the region's assets in the near future, Westerners will have to utilize further the financial, legal, and natural resources they possess to acquire a more powerful role for themselves in the development process.

In this chapter, I present a case study of Rifle, Colorado where a grass-roots organization is attempting to gain more control over the processes shaping the community. Between the 1890s and 1970s, Rifle was a relatively stable commercial and social center for west-central Colorado. During the 1980s, however, the town was disrupted by the boom and bust of a major oil shale project operated by Exxon Corporation. Irresponsible and insensitive use of resource-based power by Exxon set a number of destructive processes into motion. In response to the problems that have plagued Rifle since the boom and bust of oil shale, members of a local grass-roots organization have initiated a process of their own. Since 1991, they have been planning the construction of a special events center. The people behind this project hope that this facility will encourage the development of other locally controlled projects. The most promising future for Rifle, in their opinion, is one in which local residents—and not extralocally based corporations—can design the town's form and functions.

The theoretical framework I use to interpret Rifle's history and the grass-roots initiative is Allan Pred's theory of place. In part a variant of structuration, the theory of place integrates the ontological notions of social action and structure with conceptualizations of time-space geography and landscape. Pred has established a framework that specifies the essential components and interrelationships of place-making processes. Projects, divisions of labor, social and cultural forms, biography, the physical environment, power relations, and other components continuously interact with and across space; places are the ever-becoming "products" of their synthesis. I use the theory of place in this study to understand how places in the American West such as Rifle, Colorado have been and can be fundamentally changed by both local and extralocal agents. I suggest that residents can become more powerful agents if they learn about and take control of the processes shaping their communities.

This chapter comprises four sections. In the next section, I provide a review of the theory of place. I then present a conventional history of Rifle with emphasis on the events of the 1980s. In the third section, I draw on the theory of place to interpret the special events center initiative. I conclude the chapter with a brief discussion that reaffirms the view that local residents have important roles in the becoming of their communities. My presentation of the events taking place in Rifle is derived from local histories, newspaper accounts, survey data, and interviews with members of the town's business community.[1]

THE THEORY OF PLACE

Place is a construct that has been defined and applied by geographers in various ways and contexts over the past several decades. Economic geographers, for example, designated places as service centers geometrically situated within contrived hinterlands (e.g., Berry and Garrison 1958). In sharp contrast, some social, urban, and cultural geographers using humanistic approaches have defined places as landscapes of meaning constructed by the experiences and imaginations of individuals (cf. Gibson 1978; Tuan 1975). More recently, however, geographers and other scholars have tried to integrate humanistic and structuralist perspectives to explain the development and form of various locales; in their view, places are both products of and contributing factors to conscious human activities and continuously evolving structures (e.g., Anderson 1988; Smith 1988; Warf 1988).

The most comprehensive articulation of this dynamic and inclusive conceptualization of place has been authored by Allan Pred (1984, 1985, 1986, 1990b). According to Pred (1985, 344) any place or region expresses a *process* in which "the reproduction of social and cultural forms, the formation of biographies, and the transformation of nature ceaselessly become one another at the same time that power relations and time-space specific path project intersections continuously become one another in ways that are not subject to universal laws, but vary with historical circumstances." Places thus are more than functional analytical units; they are also active systems comprised of conscious individuals, events, social formations, relationships, and physical features that continuously interact over time and across space.

The theory of place is conceptually and ontologically based on several theoretical frameworks: Vidal's *la geographie humaine*, Hagerstrand's time-geography, and Giddens's structuration theory. More specifically, the theory of place is structuration *informed* by the other two frameworks. As such, the theory of place is both an expansion and critique of structuration in several ways. First, Giddens has failed to explain how the physical arrangements and symbolic significance of spaces and places develop. "To go beyond Giddens," as Pred (1990b, 26) puts it, is to acknowledge that the situated formation of durable, symbolic artifacts, and the creation and evolution of meaning-filled settings (i.e., the social production of space itself) are part of the structuration process. The contexts that encompass human agency are not merely frozen backdrops; they, too, are both the mediums and outcomes of structuration.

Second, Pred argues that Giddens has not fully explicated the role of the material continuity of the body through time and space. Pred contends that every individual—every body—must take an uninterrupted path through historical-geographical contexts from birth to death. To go beyond Giddens is to emphasize explicitly that "the joint time-space constitution of society and the subject is perpetually spelled out, is objectively embodied, without cessation, by the intersection of particular paths with particular institutional projects occurring at specific temporal and spatial locations" (Pred 1990, 27). In this sense, social systems are always associated with biographically, spatially, and temporally specific points of convergence.

Finally, Giddens does not fully reveal the basis of the transformation of practices. Pred argues that greater emphasis should be placed on the individual's or collectivity's ability to change the properties of structures. Since individuals are exposed to different structuring processes and inherently possess imaginative capacities, they have the ability to "not merely follow rules, but occasionally undermine . . . , negotiate, and create them" (Pred 1990b, 29).

The place-process (my own term) can be understood as a system of five interacting components: projects, social and cultural forms, biography, the physical environment, and power relations. Some general sense of the theory of place can be provided through sample descriptions of the following project-oriented relationships:

Project—Biography: Dominant institutional projects (i.e., operations of locally significant modes of production) are the foci of the place-process. Their impact on biography is considerable in that they require substantial allocations of time by individuals. Once an individual makes a commitment to participate in a project, he or she is precluded from exposure to many other projects or place-situated experiences.

Projects—Division of Labor: Dominant institutional projects almost inevitably result in spatial and social divisions of labor. Spatial divisions of labor occur because the tasks of production and distribution cannot take place in the same specific setting; social divisions of labor occur because participation in specific tasks is determined by perceived differences in the skills of knowledge of the individual. Pred (1985, 342) argues that "neither the spatial nor the social division of labor can exist or emerge independently of one another." These divisions can come to affect project formation and transformation as well. As successive rounds of projects are played out over time, spatial and social patterns of interaction tend to solidify and influence how and where new projects will be operated.

Projects—Social and Cultural Forms: What projects are undertaken are also affected by social and cultural forms such as language and religion. Language, for example, enables and constrains projects in that it (1) sets the parameters for describing, grouping, and differentiating objects, events, and experiences; (2) is an essential element in the legitimation and sustenance of social domination; and (3) acts as the medium through which the elements of project tasks are defined, made understandable to all involved, and eventually recounted (cf. Pred 1984, 285).

Projects—Physical Environment: Like language, the physical environment enables and constrains how and where projects operate. A locale's climate, topography, mineral deposits, hydrography, ecological diversity, and other natural characteristics influence what type of production can take place. What Pred emphasizes, however, is how the physical environment (as well as the built environment) reflects projects. Landscapes that are somehow tied to projects are "not lifeless, not without biographies of their own. . . . Instead, their existence and state of newness or decrepitude, their active use or abandonment (as well as their symbolic meanings), are always seen as the outcome of previous projects, or previous path convergences and path divergences involving people, human-made objects and natural phenomena" (Pred 1986, 24). Moreover, as these landscapes are further transformed by human activities, subsequent project operations or developments are inevitably affected.

Projects—Power Relations: In the theory of place, power relations are "the invisible structural cement holding individual, society, and nature together in the time-specific practices by which places continuously become" (Pred 1984, 289). They become more discernable in the operation of projects where their content, administration, and participants are determined by the individuals who control the rules and resources needed to carry out project tasks. In this context, power relations are developed and reproduced by the establishment and repeated application of project definitions and rules, the accumulation of resources by power wielders, and the predisposition of power subjects to accept the project definitions and rules put before them. The implication of this relationship is that, given the validity of the aforementioned relationships, power relations strongly influence the other components of the place-process such as biography, social and cultural forms, and the physical environment. It follows, then, that transformations of the place-process are often attributable to shifts in power relations. According to Pred, power relations are usually modified by either (1) conflicts between power wielders, power subjects, and/or institutional units over the definitions, rules, and resources involved in a project; or (2) contradictions between project goals and outcomes that, in turn, create disruptive crisis situations.

What Pred offers through the theory of place is not a new way to think of agency, the physical environment, power relations, or other specific elements that construct human geographies. Cloke et al. (1991), for example, note that Pred's conceptualizations and applications can be seen as reformulations of existing theory and research already presented under different headings by various scholars.[2] Instead, Pred makes a distinct contribution by collecting these known concepts into a logical ontological framework. Through the theory of place, events and settings can be viewed as being situated within a dynamic process involving the interactive relationships between projects, biographies, divisions of labor, physical environment, and power relations. Accordingly, Pred has given scholars a total framework with which to interpret observations of individuals, organizations, events, landscapes, and relationships in the real world.

BOOM AND BUST IN RIFLE, COLORADO

As described at the beginning of this chapter, control over the place-process in the American West has been most powerfully exercised by extralocally based organizations. In the negotiation over how Western towns evolve, residents have tended to be the reactive participants in projects that exploit the bases of natural resources. While residents do possess proactive roles in these projects in that they can manipulate various elements of localized structures (e.g., wages, profits, severance tax funds, zoning ordinances) and thus affect local place-processes, their powers are limited since they usually do not own or control the base means of production. Whether a project takes place is often largely determined by people and organizations situated well outside small communities. Indeed, the American West is littered with towns that have grown and declined as extralocally based organizations have developed, downsized, and abandoned major projects. During the 1970s and 1980s, many towns that hosted energy-related projects experienced this all too familiar sequence. Places such as Gillette, and Rock Springs, Wyoming; Grants, New Mexico; and Beulah, North Dakota boomed and busted as energy companies operationalized and curtailed huge energy development projects. The small town of Rifle, Colorado also experienced a similar fate (Map 6.1).

The Oil Shale Experience

Rifle's changing situation is, as the theory of place suggests, based on the relationships between the components of the place-process. As with an energy-impacted community, the natural environment has played a fundamental role. For most of its existence, Rifle served as the commercial center for the region's farming, ranching, and mining communities. Fertile valley soils, extensive lands suitable for grazing, abundant amounts of Colorado River water, and a relatively mild climate encouraged the development of a successful agricultural economy. Mineral deposits also supported a number of other important economic projects in the Rifle area. Coal was mined from deposits in the nearby Grand Hog Back Range between the 1930s and 1960s; rich and extensive vanadium and uranium deposits were mined and processed during most of the Cold War years (Reading Club of Rifle 1973). The most significant natural resource to affect Rifle's place-process, however, was oil shale.

Rifle is situated along the southeastern edge of a vast oil shale region. The Green River formation, a 16,500 square mile area covering the connecting bor-

Map 6.1
Selected Towns and Oil Shale Development Sites

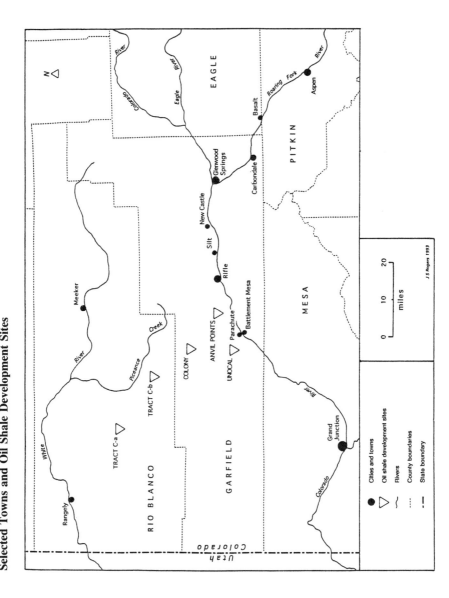

Cities and towns

Oil shale development sites

Rivers

County boundaries

State boundary

miles

0   10   20

J.S Rogers 1993

ders of Colorado, Utah, and Wyoming, contains the United States' largest oil shale deposit. The formation holds approximately 600 billion barrels of recoverable shale oil. About 80 percent of this reserve is located in Colorado's Piceance Creek Basin (Sullivan 1983).[3]

Oil shale's great promise as a long-term energy source has lured many individuals and multinational corporations to the isolated ranch lands of west-central Colorado. It was the federal government, however, that took the first steps to secure access to the resource. During World War I, concerns over access to petroleum supplies prompted President Woodrow Wilson to designate regions with significant energy deposits as federal reserves. Over 45,000 acres of federally held land in west-central Colorado and some 85,000 acres in northeastern Utah were withdrawn by the federal government in 1916 to form the Naval Oil Shale Reserve. News of Colorado's oil shale deposits and their potential value spread across the nation and attracted a rush of speculators. According to Gulliford (1989), 30,000 oil shale claims were patented and over 250 companies had incorporated to sell oil shale stock by 1920; 150 of these firms were chartered to develop oil shale on an exclusive basis. The legacy of the post-World War I oil shale boom was not the production of synthetic fuels but, rather, a transfer of land ownership. With the federal government prohibiting further private acquisition of oil-shale-bearing lands through the Mineral Leasing Act of 1920, the claims staked prior to that year significantly increased in value. Several of west-central Colorado's more affluent families purchased parcels from various claimholders and then sold or leased them to major oil companies at a considerable profit. By the late 1970s, fifteen firms controlled nearly all shale-bearing tracts not already reserved by the federal government (Gulliford 1989; Mayer and Riley 1985; Taylor and Mumby 1982).

Various oil companies, oil shale development consortiums, and the federal government operated small-scale experimental facilities between the 1940s and the 1970s. High production costs and ample supplies of cheap crude oil stifled commercial-scale expansion of the industry during the period. In 1980, however, a second major oil shale boom hit the region. Several key events prompted it. First, the 1979 Iranian revolution prompted a new oil crisis that pushed energy prices up sharply.[4] Oil shale development was once again seen as a potentially feasible commercial enterprise. Second, the federal government began to heavily subsidize alternative energy development projects. In 1980, President Carter signed the Energy Security Act, which authorized an initial $18 billion allocation for the formation of the Synthetic Fuels Corporation. The SFC provided land, loan guarantees, purchase agreements, joint ventures, acquisition and lease-back of synthetic fuel projects, and price guarantees to oil companies engaged in synthetic fuel production. Third, Exxon Corporation purchased controlling interest in the Colony Oil Shale Project north of Parachute, Colorado for $400 million from Atlantic Richfield. Colony, established in 1964 by Standard Oil of Ohio and several other companies, consisted of a shale mine and processing plant. After several changes in ownership and some production of shale oil in the late 1960s and early 1970s, Colony was closed in 1974 due to prohibitively high capital costs. Since the Colony site was already relatively well developed and had environmental impact statements approved by federal and state agencies, Exxon was able to move ahead relatively quickly (Gulliford 1989; Mehls 1988; Schantz and Perry 1978).

Exxon had great expectations for oil shale. In a report on the future of oil shale development, the company predicted that it and other oil companies would eventually invest approximately $500 billion in synthetic fuel development production over a twenty- to thirty-year period. Exxon also anticipated that these projects would create major changes to the production region.[5]

Exxon did not waste any time initiating its plan. In August 1980, the company commenced operations at Colony and at Battlement Mesa, a new town across the Colorado River from the village of Parachute. Battlement Mesa, designed for 7000 residential units, several schools, a complete shopping center, recreational facilities, churches, and other amenities, was intended to house many of the workers of the Colony project as it progressed over the years. For both projects, Exxon spent an average of $1 million per day. Other energy companies such as Chevron, Mobil, and Occidental were active in the region as well. Union Oil of California (UNOCAL), continuously involved in oil shale research and production in the region since the 1920s, also began construction of a major oil shale mining, processing, and refining facility north of Parachute in the early 1980s.

While the most intensive development of oil shale occurred near Parachute, the greatest economic and social impacts were felt in other communities. Grand Junction's economy surged as it became a command, control, and resource distribution nexus for the oil shale companies. Rifle became the home for many of the blue collar workers and the hundreds of entrepreneurs who came in to take advantage of the rapid growth. Within about a year's time, Rifle's population increased significantly (Table 6.1). As Gulliford (1989, 119) observed, the rapid influx of money and people changed the character of Rifle and the rest of the region:

In western Colorado, the boom took on epic proportions. Cafes flooded with out-of-town job seekers, white collar professionals, bikers wearing black leather and chains, and young, single men looking for a good job and a good time in the Rockies. Restaurants that had always closed at 8 P.M. now stayed open until one in the morning. School districts hired extra bus drivers to accommodate the hundreds of new school children whose parents worked time-and-a-half and double time. Vacant spaces for house trailers evaporated. Rents for houses doubled. Liquor stores had empty shelves. Traffic and crime increased, yet so did the boomtown euphoria and the feeling of excitement—of being in the right place at the right time.

Local leaders may have felt the opposite. The shale boom forced them to handle problems they had never anticipated or been trained to solve. Severe housing shortages, mass housing development schemes, overtaxed sewer and water sys-

Table 6.1
Rifle, Colorado: Selected Statistics

Year.	Population	Retail Sales (millions $)	Sales & Use Tax Revenues (millions $)
1978	2288	28.723	0.340
1979	2320	37.150	0.435
1980	3215	48.229	n/a
1981	3994	71.435	n/a
1982	5143	76.675	0.941
1983	4871	53.269	0.693
1984	4084	41.704	0.554
1985	4354	38.616	0.543
1986	4560	40.347	0.548
1987	4580	40.871	0.543
1988	4759	53.431	0.592
1989	4952	58.219	0.656
1990	4636	67.453	0.640

Source: Colorado Department of Local Affairs. Annual 1978–1990.

tems, overcrowded schools, inadequate fire protection, higher crime rates, protests by environmentalists, and zoning controversies confronted town and county government officials. Yet, as Gulliford also noted, the leaders learned how to deal with the problems in remarkably short order by following policies developed in the 1970s for oil and coal boomtowns, coordinating efforts across the county, and quickly channeling newly acquired resources to the most urgent cases.

Just as the citizens and leaders of Rifle and other shale communities began to adjust to the demands brought on by rapid growth, the boom came to a sudden and largely unexpected end. At 5:00 P.M. on May 2, 1982, a day now known in the region as "Black Sunday," Exxon announced that it was immediately closing the Colony project. Unsolved technological problems with processing and refining, cost overruns, and an apparent long-term glut of cheap oil in the world energy markets prompted Exxon's decision.[6] With the Colony shutdown, approximately 1000 Exxon employees were laid off on May 3; another 1100 lost their jobs within the following two weeks. About 7500 support workers employed by subcontractors were eventually given their pink slips over the following year. Eighty-five million dollars in annual wages evaporated from west-central Colorado's economy. Contracts with other firms for millions of dollars worth of support projects also were canceled (Crowell 1982; Gulliford 1989).

The oil shale bust not only cost workers in the oil shale industry their jobs, but it also hurt those who had less direct ties to the Colony project. The Colony shutdown shattered many individual expectations that the oil shale industry would continue to grow and increasingly dominate the region's economy well into the twenty-first century. Exxon's public relations campaign, which stressed its progress with and long-term commitment to oil shale development, had many believing in an extended growth scenario. Residents acted on their beliefs by entering into home mortgage agreements. Entrepreneurs bought property and expanded businesses. Officials spent funds on infrastructure designed to handle demands considerably larger than needed at the time. As the influx of Exxon capital ceased and as the population dropped by 20 percent, many of these projects collapsed: "Social services were greatly reduced. Church memberships declined dramatically as people moved away, leaving congregations that had expanded into new facilities with large debts spread out over a much smaller segment of membership. . . . Eighteen months after [Exxon's announcement] many local businesses had failed including over 200 in Rifle alone. Bars that had been receiving five busloads of miners after every shift closed their doors for lack of customers" (Gulliford 1989, 181). Casualties in Rifle also included hundreds of households that could not maintain mortgage payments, one of the two local newspapers, a drugstore that had been in business since the 1950s, and the First National Bank of Rifle, which had, fifty years earlier, survived the Great Depression. The bank's losses were so severe and complex that the federal banking agency overseeing its dissolution took six years to settle debts and other accounts. Local officials were affected as well; every member of the Garfield County Commission was voted out of office in 1983 and many of the administrators working for local governments in west-central Colorado were forced to take substantial pay cuts or resign.[7]

Transformation to a Bedroom Community

For several months after Black Sunday, many residents hoped that another oil company would acquire Colony and resurrect the shale boom. Others believed that Rifle could revert to its former status as a central place for the agricultural community. Colony, however, remained idle and, as Gulliford (1989, 187) observed, there was no going back. In the mid-1980s,

government officials and city council members told citizens to be patient and wait for the return of the pre-boom economy, but other factors . . . entered into the picture. . . . Businesses that had successfully operated for generations folded. The value of ranchers' agricultural products declined, coal became less valuable, and the oil and gas industry continued to spiral downward. People in the Colorado River Valley ruefully realized that, after stretching and expanding to accommodate boomtown growth, [their] communities and business [could] not rebound and take their former shape.

One result of the oil shale bust was probably what few residents expected or wanted: Rifle became a bedroom community. Two interrelated processes appear to be most responsible for this outcome. First, the collapse of the Colony project and many of the businesses and projects that were dependent on the energy economy forced a significant portion of the local workforce to seek employment outside of the community. One woman who has lived in Rifle since the early 1960s explained her household's not so uncommon situation: "In order to help support my family after my husband lost his job because of city budget cuts, I had to work 100 miles away from here. My husband then had to work 8 months in California to pay medical and other bills. I was not able to find work in my profession and had to make career changes. We didn't have the money to permanently relocate and find new jobs." By 1992, an estimated 40 percent of all working adults who resided in Rifle commuted to other towns and cities on a daily basis. One resident quipped that one of the busiest intersections in Rifle is the Interstate 70 on-ramp at 6 A.M.

Second, Rifle's transformation into a bedroom community has been caused by an unevenness in the housing costs across the region. During the oil shale boom, real estate developers significantly expanded Rifle's housing stock to take advantage of rapidly growing demand. The bust at Colony and the ensuing outmigration of well-paid workers created high vacancy rates and falling real estate values. At the same time, Aspen, Colorado's growing role as a playground for the world's elite spurred the construction of expensive homes and tourism-oriented commercial buildings within its limited buildable areas. With the combination of strong upscale demand and decreasing land availability, Aspen's property values rose rapidly in the 1980s to the point that only the most wealthy or short rental visitors could afford to reside there. A recent growth moratorium pushed land and rent costs up even further. These processes, in turn, sent an inflationary wave of housing and rent costs northward down the Roaring Fork Valley toward Glenwood Springs. Rifle, with its devalued housing stock and commutable proximity to the Glenwood-Aspen growth corridor, became the affordable housing alternative for the region's less affluent households. According to a long-time Rifle resident, after the 1982 collapse of the oil shale industry "people moved out and property values declined to such a low price range that the majority of people living upvalley—Carbondale, Glenwood Springs on up, which is a very high area for rent and property—moved to Rifle and bought houses and property that were at one time selling for $125,000, $130,000, $150,000 during the boom for only $60,000. So, now that they've bought these houses down here and still work upvalley, they do nothing but drive back and forth to work." By 1990, shortages of affordable housing once again became a problem in Rifle.

The rebound in population and housing occupancy has not been matched in the retail and service sectors. Retail sales and city revenues are still well below boom-era levels and Rifle's downtown remains pockmarked with vacancies; businesses that survived the oil shale bust continue to have difficulty making profits. Indoor malls and mass merchandise stores that were built in Grand Junction and Glenwood Springs during the 1980s have lured Rifle's consumers away from the town's small, independent shops. Moreover, commuters who are employed in or near Glenwood Springs are shopping there for convenience or by necessity. Not only are prices marginally lower and selection greater in Glenwood Springs, but many of Rifle's shops are closed by the time commuters can get home from work.

An additional symptom of Rifle's transformation into a bedroom community is a sense of declining community spirit. One merchant told me it was one of the town's most fundamental postboom problems: "What's wrong with Rifle? There's no community spirit in Rifle. . . . When I came to this community 13–14 years ago, there was a feeling in this town of community spirit. We used to have sales down on 3rd Street, we had pick-fiddlin' contests, we had Apple Pie Queen Days that had been going on for years and years. People have grown apart. The attitude's become: 'This is my world—don't bother me!' " Changing work and shopping-related paths appear to be part of this phenomenon. One resident who commutes to the Glenwood Springs area on a daily basis told me that the one remaining place and time people tend to meet is the chain grocery store in the early evenings, after they return from their upvalley workplaces. A business owner also quipped that when he wants to socialize with townspeople, he goes to the mall in Grand Junction: "I go buy a book there at Dalton's and sit there in the main area and read it. People from Rifle come walking by and they say 'Hi—! What are you doing here?' And I say, 'Oh, I don't get to see too many people from Rifle at my store, so I thought I'd come down here and see everyone.' "

Summary

In a Depression era guidebook for the state of Colorado, Rifle was tersely described as a "Saturday-night town" (WPA Guide 1987, 240). For the first ninety years of its existence, Rifle was a rather typical Western central place. The town served as the principal rail shipping point for cattle raised across northwestern Colorado, the sourcepoint for agricultural and household supplies, the home for workers of intermittent mining enterprises situated in the region, and the meeting place where friends and relatives could share stories and good times. It was on Saturdays in Rifle when the region's economic and social transactions were most frequent, the point in the week when people had or made time to break away from the everyday routines of work.

The Exxon-led oil shale boom changed this scenario by 1980. With the company's massive investments in Colony and Battlement Mesa, oil shale production became the dominant project in Rifle and other parts of west-central Colorado. Tasks once related to serving the needs of agricultural and other smaller projects became less important as the needs of shale production overwhelmed them in number. The influx of workers realigned the social and spatial divisions of labor

Interaction among newcomers and oldtimers created new syntheses of knowledge. The natural environment, providing the oil shale that geographically situated the entire process, was forever changed by mining, building construction, water consumption, and additional pollution. Most importantly, perhaps, power relations shifted into the hands of extralocally situated organizations. Exxon, with its access to vast financial resources, used its power to define what would occur. Not only did Exxon redefine Rifle's place-process, it attempted to create one from scratch through the construction of Battlement Mesa.

With Exxon's abandonment of its project, interaction between these components was severely disrupted. The capital and the project tasks that had drawn people into the region, financed the addition and expansion of other public and private projects, transformed the environment, and realigned power relations virtually disappeared. The place-process that quickly evolved in the early 1980s that was based on the assumption that the capital would continue to enter it for years to come fell into crisis. The result was, in part, changes in the life and daily paths of residents. Many workers left the region or tapped into the resources distributed from projects in other locales within commuting distance. Private and public projects were either totally abandoned or significantly downsized. As entrepreneurial projects—stores, shops, and services—became fewer and fewer, consumers chose to participate in the new opportunities located elsewhere; socializing activities followed. With a greater segment of the population now commuting, shopping, and spending leisure and recreation time elsewhere, Rifle is all but the Saturday-night town it once was. As one owner of a small business told me, "no one shops in town on Saturday. I don't even keep my own business open on Saturdays anymore. Everyone's in Glenwood Springs or Grand Junction."

TAKING CONTROL IN RIFLE, COLORADO

In his description of the theory of place, Pred explains that institutional projects tend to dominate limited time resources of resident individuals and thus affect their abilities to act, know, and interact across time and space. In modern capitalist societies where production and distribution projects dominate the lives of most individuals, the biographies of individuals are connected to the dialectics of macrolevel structuration processes since their work activities are ultimately a part of a global system. According to Pred (1986, 14), the "most central practices in these processes are the locational decisions knowingly and unknowingly made by job-providing institutions in conjunction with investment, purchasing, and subcontracting activity." These decisions, conditioned by patterns built up over time through past decisions, gradually shift spatial patterns of labor. In many cases, an unevenness in the spatial division of labor tasks, skills, wages, and other attributes evolves. When imbalances in labor capacity and/or related factors emerge from these decisions, migration to or from a place occurs that, in turn, affects successive decisions of production.

Rifle's deteriorating relationship to Grand Junction and Glenwood Springs as a central place is a result of the processes Pred describes. Locational and operational decisions regarding oil shale that were predicated on a complex series of production, distribution, and political decisions in the energy industry radically changed the configuration of labor-project opportunities for working adults in Rifle. Locational decisions regarding the placement of mass merchandise outlets in the region changed the configuration of labor-project and supply-acquisition opportunities for workers and consumers. Locational decisions regarding investment of housing and entertainment facilities for the world's elite in the Aspen area also changed the configuration of labor-project and housing opportunities for workers and their households. Hence, locational decisions made extralocally have created new sets of opportunities and constraints in Rifle and west-central Colorado.

Many of the business owners have not prospered as Rifle's residents have responded to and reinforced these locational decisions. Yet, as the established business community has come to accept and understand why Rifle has declined as a central place in west-central Colorado, some of its members have also begun attempts to reestablish the town's capacity to employ its working population and rebuild demand for locally provided goods and services. The method by which they hope to reconfigure Rifle's economic base and, thus, redirect the spatial patterns of work-, consumer-, and leisure-related behavior is tourism development.

The Expo Center Project

By the early 1990s, several tourism-related projects were underway. A visitor information center and riverine wetlands park adjacent to the Interstate 70 interchange and the Colorado River were opened in 1992. A recreational parkway along Rifle Creek that would extend from the Colorado River, through town, and to Rifle Gap State Recreational Area has been planned. A rodeo museum that would celebrate the history of the professional rodeo industry and its participants has been proposed as well.

The project that stands to change most significantly Rifle's potential as a tourist destination is the proposed Expo Center. Estimated to cost approximately $5 million, the Expo Center is expected to become western Colorado's premier convention, special events, and exhibition facility. Flexibility is a key design feature. In a promotional brochure published by the organization that initiated the project, this aspect is emphasized: "The Expo Center is envisioned to be a true multi-purpose facility with an indoor arena, convention space, and exhibition area. Maximum adaptability of the building is the goal so that a wide variety of groups will be able to use the facility. A dustless, compactable floor material makes horse shows, as well as dancing, possible in the arena. Convention rooms will be adjustable to any size group. It will be located on the Garfield County Fairgrounds and increase use of existing stalls, track, exhibition, and rodeo capabilities'' (Garfield County Capital Investments, Inc. 1992). The 70,000 square foot building is planned to have a 7000 seat capacity, banquet rooms with two kitchens, dressing rooms, and theatrical lighting fixtures. Parking areas will accommodate over 3700 vehicles within 2000 feet of the facility.

The Expo Center project began in the spring of 1991 and was still active at the time of this volume's publication. Like many similar initiatives undertaken in other communities, the Expo Center project is primarily an attempt to create new jobs and wealth. Yet, in the process of promoting and planning the facility, the organization responsible for the Expo Center initiative has set forces into motion that may produce more profound changes.

This organization's efforts and the actual or anticipated transformations to Rifle's place-process can be portrayed as a *series* of effects (Figure 6.1). Although the place-process is, as Pred describes, a continuous and simultaneous scenario of interactions between all the elements that are involved in the becoming of place, I suggest that its planned transformation may be better understood as having a sequential logic. As I describe later, the Expo Center project is an enterprise where activities are directed toward modification of certain components of the place-process at different points in time. Before the general, interrelated goals of new project formations and more spatially confined daily paths (i.e., greater numbers of local employment opportunities and reduced extralocal commuting and shopping trips) can be realized, several changes in the place-process must occur. First, biographical aspects come into play as individuals negotiate an experiential and ideological consensus to form the organized decision to commence a new project. Second, a project with which to operationalize their ideas and contain their allocations of time must be created. Third, power wielders of the project must build their base of support by gaining control over available resources. How the process has unfolded in Rifle and how the Expo Center might further change the town's place-process are as follows:

Project genesis: The role of agents: In a discussion of the origins of projects, Pred (1986, 15) makes this observation: ''The decisions leading to locally placed investments . . . must . . . in some way derive from the practical knowledge, situation-specific information, and motivating ideologies possessed by the decision-makers themselves.'' That is, actors base place-transforming actions such as investments on their understandings of how best to act and interpret everyday life, the facts associated with particular contexts, and their own values and beliefs. Actors perceive the place-process in progress around them and respond. Similarly, the Expo Center is the idea of a Rifle business owner who felt he had to respond to the town's deteriorating status as a central place and to the needs of an organization of which he was a member.

In the mid-1980s, the Colorado Quarter Horse Show Association (CQHSA), which had regularly held competitions at the Garfield County Fairgrounds in Rifle, needed an all-weather venue to hold more events and enhance show environments. In 1986, CQHSA attempted to have the arena built with county funds. Its initiative failed along with another proposal for a multimillion-dollar

Figure 6.1
Transformation of the Place-Process

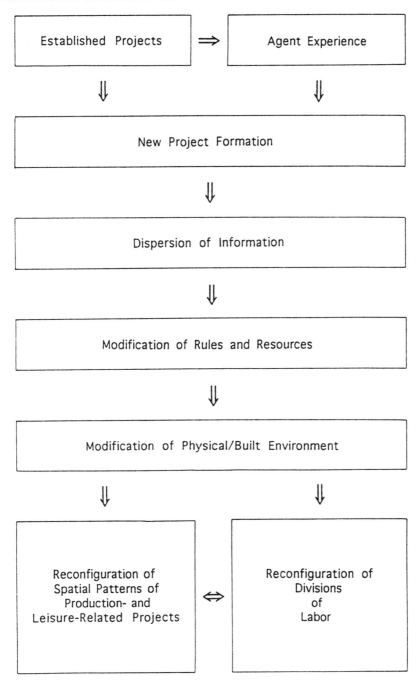

county indoor recreation center. The idea for the indoor arena was revived in 1988 but financial problems again stifled the initiative. In the spring of 1991, CQHSA's board of directors raised the issue once again at an executive meeting in Rifle. The Rifle business owner argued to the other board members that the organization needed to reconceptualize the proposed facility to win public support:

That night I told them that a horse arena would never fly. We would never get the financing for it unless it was a multipurpose facility where we could have other things than just horse shows or rodeos. My view was that a horse arena would only be used for several days out of the year; the rest of the time it would be sitting idle. The facility would never pay for itself. So I said we needed to have a building where we could have concerts, dances, horse shows, trade shows, or just about anything. . . . People wouldn't pay for a covered horse barn just like they didn't pay for the [proposed] recreation center [in 1986].

Having learned through his experiences during the boom and bust years that product diversity was the best way to survive in a small, unstable market, the business owner insisted that a multipurpose facility would be the only politically viable solution to the dilemma. He also believed that the benefits of such a facility went beyond the needs of CQHSA. Like other business owners in Rifle, he disliked the town's transformation into a bedroom community and its deteriorating commercial and social environment. A multipurpose center, in his opinion, represented a potential solution: "It is a project which makes sense. It would stabilize the economy, it would get it away from dependence on energy development, it would create jobs, it would change the overall well-being of the town." Moreover, he believed that the center could be more than a physical improvement to the town; it could also be the means by which Rifle's business community could being to rebuild and increase local control over the town's economy.

At the meeting, CQHSA's board gave the business owner the responsibility of operationalizing his proposal. For the remainder of the spring of 1991, he and several other CQHSA members toured existing special event centers in Utah to ascertain potential designs, construction costs, and economic benefits. He also contacted state and local government agencies to determine the availability of grants and other funding mechanisms. As the business owner expanded his efforts and as local interest in his idea for the facility increased, he realized that the project had outgrown CQHSA. In June 1991, he established Garfield County Capital Improvements, Incorporated (GCCI) as the organization through which the growing number of tasks associated with the Expo project could be delegated. Attracted by the idea of a facility that had the potential to reverse the town's deteriorating commercial fortunes, other members of the Rifle business community became active participants in the project.

Project promotion: Using information to gain power. Power to carry out a project is predicated on capacity to organize and manipulate the necessary resources. As noted previously in this chapter, such capacity is established by the creation and repeated use of project rules, accumulation of resources, and acceptance by power subjects of project rules and definitions. The question thus becomes, What actions need to be taken by would-be power wielders to accumulate the resources needed to build a power base?

The members of GCCI spent over a year establishing their collective power base by trying to convince other local and regional power wielders to share resources. Between the summer of 1991 and fall of 1992, GCCI's main efforts were directed toward the interrelated tasks of promotion and fund-raising. GCCI's officers conducted a field trip to a successful special events center located in Vernal, Utah with a group of twenty-four business owners and government officials from Garfield County, produced a video program on the Expo Center proposal for broadcast on a local cable television station, gave presentations to local clubs and organizations, sent letters to area newspapers, and canvassed voters through telephone solicitations (Glanz 1991a, 1991c; Parker and Bernhardt 1991). Rifle's history and eroding commercial base were used as key selling points in GCCI's promotional campaign. An illustration on a brochure produced in 1992, for example, depicts a team of horses (symbolizing Expo Center events) pulling a wagon loaded with cargo labeled "stability," "growth," and "diversity." Within the brochure, the illustration's message is articulated:

Why do we need Expo?

Expo will:

• Provide economic stability, impacting the entire county by creating a year round flow of users to the facility.

• Increase economic diversity by allowing established businesses to expand and new businesses to locate.

• Decrease dependence on energy related employment.

(Garfield County Capital Improvements, Inc., 1992)

Fund-raising efforts included GCCI membership drives, sales tax referendums, and planning development grant proposals. The group was successful in all three activities. In August 1991, GCCI raised $1500 within a week from new membership fees. A little over a year later, Rifle's voters approved a three-quarter cent sales tax increase that now generates approximately $85,000 per year for Expo Center planning and construction expenses (Anderson 1992; Glanz 1991b). In January 1993, GCCI was awarded a grant by a major telecommunications firm that provided funds to acquire the services of professional planning consultants (Anderson 1993). At the time of this writing, GCCI continues to seek additional funding sources and to develop site and architectural plans. Although the organization has a considerable amount of work ahead, the Expo Center project has already gained the funding and momentum needed to keep it a viable enterprise through the mid-1990s.

Project maturation: Reconfiguring spatial patterns. The production of space and place, according to Pred (1990b, 10) involves "the construction of an unevenly developed built environment, the shaping of the landscape and land-use patterns, the appropriation and transformation of nature, the organization and use of specialized locations for the conduct of economic, cultural and social practices, the generation of patterns of movement and interdependence between such localized activities, and the formation of symbolically laden, meaning-filled, ideology-projecting sites and areas." How we design the tangible features of our world strongly influences the courses we can and cannot take later.

Similarly, if the Expo Center is eventually built, several significant changes to Rifle's place-process may occur. First the facility would alter the geography of path-project intersections in the region. With trade shows, auctions, conferences, concerts, competitions, dances, and other events taking place in Rifle in addition to or instead of another location, both residents and nonresidents will spend more time in Rifle than they might have without the Expo Center. At the same time, both groups that would have normally spent their disposable income on activities located elsewhere may, instead, attend Expo Center events and direct their resources into the Rifle economy. A preliminary study conducted by the Colorado Department of Local Affairs estimated that if the Expo Center holds five two-day events per year (with 1000 visitors and 200 event participants per event), approximately $6.8 million in direct, indirect, and induced spending would be generated annually (Garfield County Capital Improvements Committee 1992).

An additional outcome resulting from the Expo Center's existence, an influx of visitors, and repatriation of resident expenditures would be a regional reconfiguration of the spatial division of labor. As event participants arrive in Rifle, they will bring with them demands for lodging, food, fuel, souvenirs, and other goods and services. Existing and newly established businesses will, as they grow, hire additional workers. GCCI members expect that commuters who hold service jobs in the Glenwood Springs and Aspen areas will gladly take the new positions in that they will save considerable amounts of time and money spent on the road. The Expo Center stands to become a significant intersection in the regional place-process. As such, it is expected to alter the paths of individuals and the sociospatial distribution of resources.

GCCI's members also hope that their efforts will enhance the community's capacity to continue locally based development. This capacity, in their view, will come from benefits generated by the Expo Center's operation. Tax revenues, for example, would give the city of Rifle the capacity to invest in general improvements that would help accommodate a greater daily tourist population and in new tourism-related projects designed to keep Expo Center event participants in town longer. GCCI's hopes are based on the experiences in Vernal, Utah. During the first year of operation of their special events facility, Vernal's city sales tax revenues increased by 19 percent and Uintah County sales taxes increased by 23 percent (Glanz 1992). In a similar vein, GCCI's members (many of whom own businesses) hope that increased profits will allow them the opportunities to expand their own operations. The Expo Center would be a growth pole, generating the resources needed to spread and maintain the economic revitalization process.

Beyond the Expo Center

The hopes for Rifle's future do go beyond the aforementioned economic improvements. Proponents also hope that the effects of the Expo Center—new money, visitors and events, fewer commuters, new projects—will revitalize Rifle's community spirit. One GCCI member envisions a rather vibrant scenario in which economic growth induces a joyous atmosphere: "It'll be like a carnival down on the main street. I think we'll have our Expo Center built, we'll have some trails coming from the information center through here and out on the Bookcliffs. And, we'll be having races and all kinds of events and there'll be people standing in line to get in the restaurants."

Other visions of the consequences of tourism development are more cautious. If there is any dissent to the Expo Center and the other tourism-related proposals, it is expressed toward the leaders' and residents' abilities to manage the projects and to handle possible impacts. The director of the city of Rifle's Tourism and Trade Board is a strong backer of the Expo Center projects but remains concerned about its long-term viability: "The only thing that scares me about the Expo is the longevity. Is it going to be a novelty? Is it something that's going to be able to be promoted year after year after year? Is it going to pack the people in? We only have a small draw here as compared to Denver. They have enough people that no matter what event's being held there, they're going to have a crowd. We're going to have to work harder. We'll probably have to draw from Vail to Moab, from southern Wyoming to Montrose." The vice-president of Rifle's Downtown Development Authority is, in contrast, more worried about its potential success. She cautions that a shift toward a tourism-oriented economy will only provide working adults low-paying, somewhat degrading service sector jobs. More importantly, in her opinion, inviting visitors to the Rifle area through the Expo Center and other attractions could ruin the town's positive amenities: "Rifle's biggest asset is that nobody's here. The whole tourism thing is kind of a joke. We want to push tourism, but on the other hand, we like the fact that this isn't a tourist town and that we do have all of these places to ourselves." The spokesperson for GCCI (an owner of a successful business) acknowledges this argument; tourism development or any other revitalization project is bound "to change the status quo." She adds, however, that it remains the best alternative; "Tourism's a far better industry, far cleaner industry, and far less detrimental industry to the value of the lifestyle here ... than other types of industry—especially oil shale. Tourism would not force [the type of growth that accompanied the oil shale boom] and would allow preservation of the quality of life to a fair degree.''

The driving force behind the Expo Center project and the other tourism initiatives is, in fact, the desire to overthrow the process, further strengthening the status quo. While the preservation of Rifle's quality of life is a concern, the greater emphasis is on how to break the town's dependency on extralocally directed projects. According to the GCCI spokesperson, this more radical view is the fundamental goal of the organization: "Obviously, as business people . . . we know that any increase in revenues is going to fall to all of us to some extent. You can say there's that much selfish interest. But I think that the major interest is that—hey—we live here and we want this to be a strong community, not a faltering one and we think we can make it that way. We want to control our destiny rather than react to it.'' Most succinctly, the Expo Center is more than an economic development projects, it also is a struggle for power over the place-process.

CONCLUSION

A fundamental problem faces places like Rifle, Colorado: extralocally situated organizations have control over many of the assets required for economic production. In Pred's terms, they are power wielders in that they can strongly influence what the dominant projects will be at given places and times. Because the organizations are extralocal, not all of the outcomes of their decisions are perceived as being relevant; as long as corporate or policy objects occur within tolerable limits, little else matters. When Exxon Corporation closed its Colony Oil Shale Project in 1982, it was not concerned about the workers it fired overnight, the residents who suffered through the rapid growth they did not choose to experience, or the local government administrators who rose to the challenges of quickly changing needs and demands. Exxon was concerned about it own immediate financial interests. People in towns and cities across the United States realized the perils of this type of power relationship in the early 1990s as both corporations and government agencies restructured their globally situated enterprises. Witness the factory and military installation closure "hit lists" printed periodically in newspapers.

As community development advocates have asserted, residents of towns and cities who are confronting the prospects or consequences of major economic downturns due to the loss of major employers need to take more proactive roles (e.g., Fendley and Christenson 1989; Fitzgerald and Meyer 1986; Ryan 1988; Swinth and Alexander 1990). Among the various alternatives, they suggest initiation of projects that are designed, owned, and operated by the residents themselves. By starting such projects, a number of interrelated effects may be induced. First, residents can become more powerful participants in the processes shaping their communities. What projects occur, how they are run, and the distribution of resources can be more directly determined. Second, people are more likely to be exposed to new concepts, conditions, and issues since they are responsible for more aspects of the projects that affect their economic and personal lives. Power is conducive to experiential growth. Third, there is greater potential for a reduction in the divisions of labor that have continuously marginalized segments of society. If more projects can be controlled by local participants and designed such that all participants are given the power to provide managerial input, divisions defined by class, ethnicity, or relative location can be more effectively minimized. Fourth, the physical environment may come to be more carefully understood and appreciated. As participants see the physical environment as a factor that can contribute to project success, they will become more aware of the need to protect and conserve it. Community-based economic development is a potentially powerful method of changing the place-process. Projects, power relations, biography, division of labor, and environment can be affected in positive ways.

Local efforts to create and control new projects may not always succeed. More importantly, they cannot immediately change historically embedded and functionally entrenched national or international power relations. Corporations and the federal government will continue to control the assets of the American West and other regions. At best, local initiatives can only partially modify place-making processes. The Expo Center project and the other tourism-related projects underway in Rifle, Colorado have the potential to change the spatial patterns of economic and social interaction; they will not change the ownership patterns of oil shale lands, Aspen's housing market, or other external circumstances. Nevertheless, if the relationships between participants of dominant projects are to be made less destructive and more democratic, local actors must exercise the powers they possess.

NOTES

1. The survey data are derived from a return-mail questionnaire sent to a randomly selected sample of Rifle residents in February 1992. Long interviews with fifteen business owners were conducted in September 1991 and July 1992. Names of respondents are withheld due to confidentiality agreements.

2. Pred's theory of place and his empirical applications have also been criticized by a number of scholars. See, for example, Earle (1987), McLennan (1990), and Warde (1987).

3. Oil shale is a sedimentary rock that holds oil in the form of a thick, organic substance called kerogen. When the rock is heated above 700 degrees Fahrenheit, the kerogen decomposes and a vapor of oil is released. When the vapor cools, it condenses into a liquid that can be refined into synthetic fuels. About one third of the oil shale locked in the Green River formation is considered "recoverable" (Sullivan 1983, 6; see also Taylor 1987 for a comprehensive technical review of oil shale).

4. At the time of the 1979 oil crisis, crude oil cost refiners an average of $13.41 per barrel; in 1980 it cost $25.93. Oil prices peaked during the first quarter of 1981 at $36.54 per barrel (Hunt 1987, 60).

5. Exxon predicted construction of 150 oil shale processing plants, six massive strip mines, employment for hundreds of thousands of workers, and an output of 8 million barrels of oil per day by 2010. The company also expected that synfuel development would create significant changes to the social geography of the region. For its twenty- to thirty-year planning horizon, Exxon anticipated that population would increase by 50,000 per year, 18,000 new housing units and twenty new schools would have to be built each year, and 200 police officers would have to be added to community law enforcement agencies annually (Gulliford 1989, 121–125).

6. Between the first quarter of 1981 and the second quarter of 1983, the average price paid by refiners for crude oil decreased from $36.54 to $28.61 per barrel. It eventually fell to approximately $13.00 per barrel by the second quarter of 1986 (Hunt 1987, 60).

7. Exxon may have been a casualty to some degree as well. Exxon invested somewhere between $700 and $920 million on Colony and Battlement Mesa. The company was also forced to pay substantial amounts of money to various Colorado municipal and county governments due to court settlements (Gulliford 1989; Isenberg 1984).

7

Gender Relations in Urban Growth Politics

Lynn A. Staeheli

Boulder badly needs anti-monopoly laws. Ultra-liberal profs took full control of [the University of Colorado] long ago. Now their "liberal spouses" are doing the same thing on city council.

—Woman, owner of a real estate loan company (cited in P. Smith 1981, 195)

We asked her to run for office because she looked like a motherly, housewife type, not because of her environmental policies.

—Man, PLAN-Boulder member[1]

My wife and I joined PLAN-Boulder when we moved here because we were asked and as a way of getting involved in the community. We made friends with a number of other couples in the group.

—Man, PLAN-Boulder member

When the temporary growth commission was appointed, all of the people had titles—Professor this and Professor that—except me; I didn't have a title. So when they announced the names in the paper, after my name they wrote "speaks at meetings."

—Woman, PLAN-Boulder member and growth study commission member

It was the women who did the work on the growth study commission. The men either went to their jobs and did this in their spare time or they only

worked in their area of expertise. The basic work was done by the three of
us.

—Woman, PLAN-Boulder member and
growth study commission member

Urban political theorists have paid little attention to the role of gender and gender
relations in structuring cities and politics (Staeheli and Clarke 1994). Some
analysts identify women as community activists, but often do so in a dismissive
way. Their analyses have been instrumental in reinforcing stereotypes of women
activists as dilettantes fulfilling some obligation to civic work, or as merely
following their husband's class interests, or as becoming involved for social
reasons. Such analyses take at face value comments such as the first four of
those made by community activists in Boulder, Colorado (cited at the beginning
of this chapter). The final comment, however, reveals another, less explored
side of gender relations in urban politics—namely the commitment and expertise
brought by some women to political activism. This chapter is part of a larger
effort emerging in feminist studies, geography, and other social sciences to
refocus urban political analyses to include gender and gender relations. More
specifically, it is an attempt to unravel the impacts of women's political activism
on the empowerment of women and the transformation of gender relations. This
unraveling involves understanding the values, systems of meaning, and goals
that are brought to political activism by women (in all their diversity), the abilities
of women to effect changes in the political system, and the ways in which women
and political systems are mutually transformed by the actions of women.

The analysis presented in this chapter is based on the feminist and structurationist premise that politics are situated. That is, the political, economic, social,
and spatial contexts of activity condition both the values and intentions brought
by actors and the outcomes (empirical and structural) of activism (cf. McDowell
1988; Moos and Dear 1986; Pred 1984). Thus, the empirical research is focused
on one example of gender-based distinctions in framing issues and in the ability
to act on issues, rather than on the dynamics of gender and political structures
writ large. The example is that of the growth control movement in Boulder,
Colorado during the 1960s and 1970s. However, the gender relations expressed
in the comments of Boulderites that began this chapter are not unique to Boulder.
The goal of this chapter is to demonstrate the ways in which the activities of
women in this particular case have modified both the political opportunity structure for women in Boulder and gender relations more generally. These modifications have occurred even as women have been constrained by patriarchal
relations.

The chapter is organized into five sections. In the first, I examine the com-
plementarities between feminist and structurationist approaches in analyzing gender relations and their relevance to this study. In the second section, some of
the critical methodological issues these approaches raise in examining women's
political participation are considered. The third section establishes the context

of activism in the debates over growth in Boulder in the 1960s and 1970s. This was a period of rapid transformation in the United States and in Boulder in terms of the economy, social relations, and civil rights. Regulska et al. (1991) have suggested that periods of destabilization, as this was, may weaken structural barriers to women's political participation. In the fourth section, the reasons that women and men became involved in Boulder's growth control movement are examined. The gender relations reflected in these reasons are highlighted. Finally, I examine the agency of activists in Boulder's growth control debates. While women's participation shaped the outcomes of the growth debates and the political opportunity structure for women, the success of their efforts in terms of achieving the outcomes they desired is unclear. Thus, the meaning of these women's activism for the empowerment of women remains ambiguous.

A FEMINIST, STRUCTURATIONIST APPROACH TO GROWTH POLITICS

Feminism encourages us to understand the ways in which social groups and identities interact with political, economic, and social processes. The purpose of feminist research is to transform structures of domination. Thus, feminists seek to construct praxis, in which theory, research, and practice are fused. The emphases within structuration theory on agency and the duality of structures provide a complementary framework for analyzing the web of power relations (Giddens 1984) that marginalize women and the ways in which the actions of women and men may change those relations. As such, a feminist, structurationist approach can help avoid the pitfalls of voluntarism on the one hand and structural determination on the other; it reorients us to understand the relationship between practice and process and thereby narrows the gap between academic research and political practice (Messer-Davidow 1991).

A feminist, structurationist approach can enrich analyses of growth politics through the application of four basic principles. The first three of these principles have been developed in geography by Moos and Dear (1986, 232), who argue for "the hermeneutic nature of social investigation, stressing the importance of 'mutual knowledge'; the need to treat the individual as knowledgeable in the reproduction of social practices; and understanding the major role of the unintended outcomes that result from intentional human activity." The final principle has been developed by feminist standpoint theorists, who argue for the importance of thinking from the standpoints, or social locations, of women to understand the motives, goals, and constraints that inform the agency of those in subordinate positions (e.g., Harding 1991).

Applying these principles to the analysis of urban growth politics will make it possible to uncover the interconnections between gender relations and political structures that shape the activism and outcomes of activism for women and men. These interconnections remain unexamined in much of the research in urban political theory and, somewhat ironically, in much of the research about women in politics. For example, research related to urban growth politics is often focused on the efforts of businesses, elites, and government officials (most of whom are men) to persuade the general public that growth is in their interests. In essence, these growth coalitions attempt to equate or link the interests of all interest groups in the city. Public conflicts over growth, therefore, represent a failure on the part of the growth coalition to maintain this linkage. More specifically, growth management debates are cast as a breakdown in the ability of growth coalitions to present their own attempts to maximize *exchange* values as being in the best interests of the public's effort to maintain their *use* values (Warner and Molotch 1990). The analytical focus of this research is often on the commonality or complementarity of interests held by participants in the growth coalition. When interests are deconstructed, it is typically done along class lines, not on the basis of race or gender (e.g., Cox and Mair 1988; Elkin 1987; Gottdiener 1987; Logan and Molotch 1987; Stone 1987). In fact, in one of the few analyses of growth politics in which gender was mentioned, the authors were at a loss when it came to explaining why the sex of voters entered their discriminant function describing electoral support for a growth control initiative. Even though this variable was the third most powerful in terms of ability to discriminate between supporters and opponents (women generally supported the initiative), the authors address only a short paragraph to gender and conclude that its importance is "puzzling" (Gottdiener and Neiman 1981, 66). Perhaps this is only puzzling, however, because the authors did not attempt to think from the social locations of women to consider the ways in which women might use and value environments. Application of the principles identified previously should be useful in such an attempt.

Application of feminist and structurationist principles should also make it possible to expand our understanding of women's political activism. Much of the research in this area has developed around one of three foci: (1) the numbers of women involved in local politics (e.g., Bullock and MacManus 1987; Karnig and Welch 1979); (2) issues that are stereotypically women's issues (Ackelsberg and Breitbart 1987/1988; Halford 1989; Mark-Lawson et al. 1985); or (3) settings in which women were clearly and often self-consciously operating from a subordinate position within the movement or society (e.g., Daniels 1988; Mackenzie 1988; Nelson 1984; Pardo 1990). These foci often encourage the researcher and the reader to concentrate either on the distinctiveness of women's political participation or on the subordination of women in politics. However, we misrepresent the true status of women as political agents if we imply that these are the only terms under which women operate. Rather, we need to recognize that the influence of gender relations in urban politics is broadly based, multifaceted, and complex. It is broadly based in that it is present in so many settings, including those that may not obviously be gendered. It is multifaceted in that women are located on many axes of oppression and may be marginalized on one axis and privileged on another. It is complex because the meanings and expressions of women's locations in the web of power relations make it necessary continually to reconceptualize issues and actions as the visions of each subgroup of women are integrated into the knowledge of all (Gorelick 1991, 473). Such integration, however, requires analysis at several conceptual and empirical levels. In the next section, these levels are discussed and a strategy for their analysis is developed.

ANALYZING GENDERED POLITICS

Feminism and structuration theory challenge researchers to develop methods to identify and analyze the positionality of individuals with respect to the structures that shape and define societies. In this study, for instance, participants in the debates over growth may have been simultaneously parents, spouses, workers, and political activists; they also have identities based in gender, class, race, and sexuality. None of these roles and identities should be analyzed in isolation because people do not live them in isolation; the locations of activists on a variety of axes may shape their goals, their actions, and the outcomes of their activism. In turn, each of these roles and identities may be conditioned by power relations at several scales and settings (i.e., the home, workplace, political organization, city, and society).

In this analysis, the household and political roles of participants in the growth debates are shaped by relations at four scales—the household, the neighborhood, the Boulder region, and American society. The reasons women and men became involved in the debates may stem from relations at any combination of these scales, or from conditions emanating from the way these scales are linked. This makes for messy analyses, since combinations and linkages may not be direct or follow simple transformation rules. The story of one woman with whom I spoke is illustrative of these complicated connections. She told me that she became involved in PLAN-Boulder and other local planning activities as a way of creating her own identity—an identity that was separate from those of her children and her husband (a scientist who was influential in his own way in shaping Boulder's future). This woman had a forty-year career in public service that included positions on the planning board and city council in the 1950s and then again in the 1970s. She said that for a long time she ''truly enjoyed being 'one of the men,' doing work that was not traditionally women's work, and not being associated with women. Over the years, however, she said she had come to realize that while she wanted to distance herself from her family and domestic work (a reaction to household relations and socially defined roles), she found that her personal situation influenced her career and her attitudes. She evaluated the impacts of growth in terms of fairness and quality of life, and she believes her reactions to Boulder's experience were shaped in part by a set of attitudes fostered by socialization as a woman in American society. The women's movement of the 1970s was important in helping her see that and in helping her reevaluate her actions and motivations. It is notable that on a personal level this woman had achieved a new consciousness that gave her insights into a variety of gender and political relations, but that this consciousness did not allow her to *escape* from these relations. One man told me that the reason a delegation of PLAN-Boulder members asked her to run for City Council was not her environmentalism, but rather her image as a "motherly, housewife type." Thus, this woman's career was shaped by her roles within her household, by the reactions of her male colleagues, by the opportunities afforded to her in Boulder, and by her socialization as a woman.

Clearly, the relations and conditions that give rise to particular interests and behaviors are complicated, and not everyone is able to articulate them in the way the aforementioned woman has. Nevertheless, the activists themselves are the only ones who can explain the ways in which those relations and conditions are experienced. Interviews with women and men who participated in Boulder's growth control movement are used to illustrate how structural relations that may be identified theoretically were experienced and were changed by the activists in Boulder.

All of the people with whom I spoke were members of PLAN-Boulder, the most prominent of the citizens' organizations that were formed to reassert the primacy of use values in the face of development pressures. PLAN-Boulder has been involved in virtually every major and minor land use decision since its founding in 1959 to prevent development on the scenic backdrop for the town that is provided by the Flatiron Mountains. Its members attend city council, county commission, parks and open space, and planning board meetings and regularly speak at them. Members also work with the professional staffs of these boards or actually serve on the boards to ensure that their positions are heard. Beginning with the 1971 election, an endorsement by PLAN-Boulder came to be seen as a political necessity, as PLAN-Boulder-backed candidates regularly defeated Chamber candidates (a term used in disdain by PLAN-Boulder members for progrowth candidates backed by the Chamber of Commerce). Thus, even while maintaining its citizen base, PLAN-Boulder was, and continues to be, a major force in land use and growth planning in Boulder (Robertson 1986).

As one might expect with a citizens' organization, membership information is sketchy, particularly for the 1960s and 1970s. Membership is generally at about 300, but at any given time there are far fewer who are active in the organization. For example, the weekly luncheon meetings are typically attended by about twenty-five members. Generally, members are white and middle to upper middle class. Its initial leaders were faculty of the University of Colorado or were from the town's scientific community, but there are many members, indeed many well-known members, who have no affiliation with the university or the scientific community. Significantly, PLAN-Boulder seems always to have had many women involved in its leadership, on boards and in positions in which they could influence organizational and government policies. For example, over 45 percent of the members of PLAN-Boulder's Boards of Directors from 1959 to 1990 have been women (Brownlee and Jones 1990; Robertson 1986). Further, women served as chairs of the organization for five of the seven years (1970 to 1976) that the growth control debate was at its peak.

Names of potential participants in the study were collected from news accounts at the time, the list of PLAN-Boulder board members and officers, and key informant techniques. It was, however, difficult to trace people fifteen years after the growth control debates lost intensity. Some people had moved away, died, or become very ill. Women, in particular, were difficult to trace in the absence of old membership mailing lists, since many use their husbands' names and cannot be traced through phone directories. In addition, seven people declined to be interviewed. Three cited time constraints due to their jobs (both volunteer and waged). Four women declined because they were unshakable in their belief that they ''didn't know anything useful.''

In all, twelve individuals were interviewed, eight of whom are women. The individuals were guaranteed confidentiality. While some individuals did not care if their names were made public, four of the individuals expressed concern that their criticisms of PLAN-Boulder might be misconstrued and did not want their names revealed. The interviews generally lasted between two and three hours. Everyone discussed their involvement in the growth control movement, their reasons for becoming involved, and their beliefs about the effectiveness of growth control and growth management in Boulder. Some people recounted their experiences in a personal way (such as linking their environmentalism to their spiritual beliefs), while others saw their actions in the context of national and world problems.

All of the people with whom I spoke were white, upper middle class, and over sixty. Most were raising families in Boulder at the time of their involvement in the growth control movement. Three of the four men were tenured faculty at the University of Colorado; the other man was a former business executive who moved to Boulder after retirement. None of the women had waged employment during their involvement in the movement. However, one woman was a freelance writer, and several had careers as volunteers that often demanded more than forty hours of work per week. Those women with children all commented that they were fortunate to be in a position to have other people assume their child care and household responsibilities. This comment serves as a reminder that identities other than gender shaped the growth control debates in Boulder. The social locations of the activists with respect to class and race may have made it easier for them to gain acceptance, both personally and for their ideas. I will suggest, however, that their social locations also may have limited the ability of some of the women activists to reach across locations and to identify and act on the issues most relevant to other groups; the difficulty of doing so was reflected in the ambivalence they felt about the outcomes of their activism.

The interviews were intensive but loosely structured. I chose this form because the personal and political nature of people's motivations and situations are often inaccessible to researchers using highly structured techniques (Personal Narratives Group 1989). Pred (1990a) argues that people respond to the power relations in interpersonal communications. As a result, researchers unwittingly may condition the information they receive through their control of the questions. Thus, it was more revealing when people more or less spontaneously began to think about why they became involved in PLAN-Boulder and what they hoped growth control would accomplish than it would have been if I had suggested possible answers and let respondents choose from among them. Accordingly, I have remained as true to these individuals' words and meanings as possible. Perhaps equally important, this was a research strategy that was consistent with the beliefs of at least some of the participants in the study. For example, two of the women interviewed were responsible for gathering citizen ideas about what Boulder should become. In their study, the women fought Housing and Urban Development pressure to administer a mail survey and insisted on community meetings in which "people could tell us what they wanted directly . . . they could tell us their aspirations for their own lives, for their lives in the community, and what they expected in the community. We wanted to ask different questions than the people at HUD and in the city planning office wanted, and we didn't think a survey would give us the answers."

CONTEXT OF GROWTH DEBATES IN BOULDER

The catalyst for Boulder's growth debates and the questions the woman quoted above wanted to ask regarded the explosive population growth the town experienced in the 1950s and 1960s. Boulder's population in 1940 was 12,958, but by 1970 it was 66,870—an increase of over 500 percent in thirty years. In the 1950s and 1960s, the annual growth rates were approximately 9 percent and 8 percent, respectively. In the context of rapid growth in the Denver metropolitan region as a whole, it was understandable that many people were concerned both that Boulder was losing its small-town nature and that it would become just another suburb of Denver.

As growth pressures rose in Boulder, strategies were devised to either put a cap on growth or to slow it and then mitigate its effects. Thus, groups such as PLAN-Boulder focused on trying to slow the rate of population and employment growth and on persuading the city to buy open space surrounding the city. The city council went so far as to say that no further attempts would be made to attract primary employment to the area.

In early 1971, the growth debates came to the forefront of Boulder politics when the local chapter of Zero Population Growth (ZPG) issued a report "Is Population Growth Good for Boulder Citizens?" (Johnson 1971). This report shifted the terms of debate from rather vague notions of growth that included economic changes to specific issues surrounding population increases; economic growth was not identified as a problem per se. Packed with charts and figures documenting increases in crime, pollution, and municipal debt associated with population growth, the ZPG report recommended limiting Boulder to 100,000 residents. When the City Council refused to consider a population cap, ZPG launched a successful campaign to place the issue on the fall ballot. This set off a flurry of activity and maneuvering by Council, the Chamber of Commerce, and PLAN-Boulder that resulted in a second measure being placed on the ballot.

While many members of PLAN-Boulder were sympathetic to the ZPG report, the group's official position was that a population cap was infeasible and that, in the absence of restrictions on where development could occur, a cap would not preserve sensitive environments. As such, PLAN-Boulder helped to write and then supported a second measure that called for a significantly lower (but unspecified) rate of growth in the future and a citizens' commission to study the best ways to limit and manage growth. The PLAN-Boulder measure passed, setting the stage for five more years of study, debate, and recommendations focused on identifying public aspirations for growth and the future of Boulder.

In retrospect, many in Boulder see this election as a change in the local regime that had ruled Boulder. The oligarchy identified by one PLAN-Boulder member was thrown out. Of the five incumbents who ran for reelection, four were defeated. This outcome is even more remarkable in light of Boulder's history of reelecting officials; in the preceding fifty years, only one incumbent had failed to win reelection. The new members had appealed to the eighteen year olds who voted for the first time in this election with platforms that were progressive in environmental and social terms. The new city council members were much younger than the men they defeated and were identified with a variety of countercultural, radical, feminist, and gay rights groups in town. It was after this election that the town gained its moniker the People's Republic of Boulder. This was also the first election in which a slate of candidates endorsed by PLAN-Boulder won and in which the values espoused by PLAN-Boulder members were legitimated.

GENDER RELATIONS, USE VALUES, AND THE GROWTH CONTROL DEBATE

As mentioned previously, the debates over growth in Boulder were expressed in terms of the ways in which population growth affected the environment, economy, and Boulder as a place to live. Members of PLAN-Boulder generally saw population growth as reducing the use values attributable to each (although they would not have expressed their opposition to growth in those terms). However, members were not united either in the specific ways in which they saw use values being reduced or in the relative importance that they placed on each. Significantly, the ways in which uses were evaluated by PLAN-Boulder members reflect gender relations in the home, the community, and American society. As such, the views of PLAN-Boulder members can provide a means of unpacking the gender-based dynamics at work in urban growth politics. In this section, I examine some of the ways in which women and men evaluated the impacts of growth and defined their goals for growth control. In the final section, I will argue that the ability of participants to act on their goals and the strategies they followed may have influenced the outcomes of growth control in Boulder and changed the political opportunity structure for women.

Before moving to that discussion, however, two cautions should be noted.

First, strict categorizations of values as applying only to women or only to men are not intended. Nor do I intend to argue that *all* women and men are motivated to act on these values. The historical record of Boulder's growth control movement demonstrates that both sexes were motivated to preserve their homes and environments. Rather, I argue that each of these values takes on special meanings for women and men in the context of gendered social relations.

Second, the interviews are used to illustrate the meanings these values assumed for women and men; they are not used to prove the salience of the categories in a positivist sense. The relatively small number of respondents means that no claims of universality could be made, even if such claims were a goal of the research. Further, the power relations inherent in an interview may lead people, particularly women, to offer explanations other than those offered in a different setting (Pred 1990a). For example, women tended to mention a greater number of reasons for their involvement in the growth control movement than did men. This may have been because women are more introspective (a common stereotype), or because women often feel the need to justify taking on "nontraditional" roles (Daniels 1988), or because these women view growth as connected to a greater number of community and environmental conditions. Alternatively, it may simply be a reflection of the longer, more leisurely interviews that I had with women. Thus, the comments made by respondents may have as much to do with the gender relations present in the interview as with the gender relations at work in the growth control movement. On the basis of these interviews, therefore, it is not possible to argue for a definitive set of motivations. Rather, the analysis presented here describes the interests these individuals believe they brought to the growth control movements as illustrative of the gendered nature of urban growth politics that was identified theoretically. With these understandings, it is now possible to evaluate use values critically.

Valuing the Environment

The primary set of use values that members wanted to preserve related to the environment. All of the members I interviewed mentioned their concern over the impacts of growth on the environment when I asked them why they became involved in PLAN-Boulder; it was the first reason provided by most of them. While there was a general sense that growth posed a threat to the environment, the ways in which their environmentalism was expressed varied greatly. Concerns ranged from specific environmental impacts (e.g., the effect of a development on flooding) to the role of the environment on the quality of life in Boulder to a sense of responsibility as stewards of the earth. Both the variety of responses and the distribution of responses were remarkable; they provide the first evidence of gender-associated dynamics and motives in the growth control movement in Boulder.

Three of the four men and two of the eight women named specific environmental issues as part of their motives for joining PLAN-Boulder. Two of these men were founders of the organization in 1959 when the group was formed to stop proposed developments on the Flatiron Mountains bordering the city. The third man became involved after PLAN-Boulder members learned of his expertise in floodplain management; his subsequent involvement in the organization was crucial in terms of the organization's ability to demonstrate the impacts of development on flooding. One of the women joined PLAN-Boulder after she was asked to run for office by members so they could fight a spot zoning ordinance (this was the woman who was not asked because of her environmentalism, but because of her image as a housewife). The other woman mentioned the impacts of fringe development on open space and what that meant for horseback riding.

Several people expressed their concern over the environmental impacts of growth in more general terms. Three women conceptualized the environmental impacts of growth in terms of fairness; they worried that the negative environmental impacts would be borne by middle- and lower-income families. One of these women is a historian with extensive knowledge of the mining history in the area. Among her concerns was development that was being proposed on top of old mines—several of which were in danger of collapse and several of which had extensive underground fires.

It is criminal that they were going to allow houses to be built [over the old mines]. They are toxic; they are on fire, they are going to collapse, they are a hazard. You can't build on land like that. . . . It is not right to sell land to people when they know it is over a coal mine. That will be someone's home and their biggest investment. If something happens, insurance will not cover it, because it is not an act of God. It is not fair to those young people who buy homes in the unincorporated areas, because they can't afford to build in the city. The people who can afford to build in a safer environment can protect themselves. These families have fewer options in a place like Boulder.

Thus her environmental concern was that affordable development was being channeled into areas that were not safe.

Another woman expressed her concern for environmental protection in terms of fairness, as well. She saw that with continued low-density development, people would have to go farther and farther away to get an open space and to see nature. She saw PLAN-Boulder's proposals for buying open space surrounding the town as the best way to ensure that everyone would have access to the mountains and to the grasslands. She said, "The open space is wonderful. It makes Boulder a wonderful and unique place to live, but also it is something that everyone can take advantage of. I can't imagine anything else that has made a bigger difference to more people. Some people think it's a good planning tool, that it helps to define the shape of the city, but I think that it is wonderful because everyone can use it. It is not like Aspen or Vail, or even the health clubs in town. It is free to any who want to use it." The environmental concern of these women was that growth was proceeding in ways that either put people at risk or that denied access to the environment to those who were less wealthy. One woman put the issue succinctly: "The environment belongs to everyone, but only a few people were making decisions. I thought it was important to give the people a chance to say what they wanted, and to say whether and how they wanted the environment used."

Two women expressed their environmentalism in spiritual terms. One woman felt her role as a Christian was to be a steward of the earth; she felt it was important for her to be active in efforts to preserve an environment in which "God's wonders are so clear." Another woman spoke of the spiritual connection she felt with the environment and wanted to be able to pass this along to her children: "I have sent my roots into the land, and its roots are in me. [Growth] was threatening to take this from me and from my children. I didn't know what would be left for them."

A final environmental concern expressed by the people with whom I spoke can be thought of as a 1960s version of thinking globally and acting locally. Three women were alarmed at global population growth and issues of environmental sustainability. They all traced their involvement in a growth control movement (as different from some other environmental protection activity) to their concern about population growth. One woman responded to my question about why she became involved in PLAN-Boulder by saying, "First and foremost, population growth is going to kill this planet." On the surface, involvement in a local organization attempting to limit growth in one small city does not seem like a very effective way to solve global population problems. Indeed, one man argued that PLAN-Boulder's attempts at growth control at the city level were "absurd. We have one city working with one county trying to preserve open space and limit growth. Yet we are on the fringe of a huge metropolitan area. It's a bit of a golden ghetto when the rest of the world is going to hell." This man did not see his involvement as contributing to anything larger than the problems faced in Boulder, yet the three women were sincere in the connection they saw between local political activity and the solution to global problems. It seemed that locally based groups were the kinds in which these women could become actively involved, given the constraints of their households and American society in the 1960s.

The distribution of these responses by gender is intriguing. The three men who cited the environment as the reason they became involved in PLAN-Boulder all cited very specific environmental issues (a specific development or a specific issue). While some of the women did this as well, many women provided reasons that reflected an abstract environmental ethic (e.g., fairness or spirituality) or concern for global environmental problems. The different ways in which environmental concerns were expressed might reflect either gendered ways of speaking or the personal styles of the individuals. For example, all three men were physical scientists at the university. The language they used may reflect training and personal proclivities toward precision. When I asked them why they became involved in PLAN-Boulder, they responded with specific issues. They might have responded very differently to a question of "What were the environmental issues posed by growth?'' As such, the very narrow answers they provided might not be reflective of narrow conceptualizations of the environment and of environmental use values.

That caution noted, however, the fact that many women (and no men) provided more general and abstract environmental concerns bears examination. The responses by these women suggest a need to reevaluate research that has argued that women are more likely to become involved in local-level environmental issues out of a concern for their homes and families (cf. Blocker and Eckberg 1989; Hamilton 1985). The responses by PLAN-Boulder women suggest that they became involved in a local organization but were not necessarily motivated by purely local issues. This distinction between the issue and the organization may be very important in evaluating the impact of activism on the empowerment of women. Women are generally seen as more effective political agents at local levels than at state and national levels (e.g., Flammang 1984; Regulska et al. 1991), but effectiveness is typically measured in terms of electoral success. If women are using local organizations to mount grass-roots challenges to problems that originate at higher scales, then local electoral success is not necessarily a sign of achieving their goals. As such, we should reconsider the constraints faced by women who enter local politics in response to problems that extend beyond their communities. On the one hand, they may face great difficulty in achieving meaningful, structural changes; on the other hand, their actions force recognition that women's political activism is more than municipal housekeeping.

Valuing the Economy

The debate over growth control was often framed as a debate between environmentalists and Chamber of Commerce supporters. Environmentalists generally, and PLAN-Boulder members specifically, were characterized in letters to the editor as people who would sacrifice jobs and property rights for open space. Letter writers pointed to the larger number of PLAN-Boulder members from the university or federal scientific communities as well as to the retirees in the organization. These people were argued either as not having a stake in the local economy (i.e., their livelihood did not depend on local growth) or as being able to afford their environmentalism due to their class position. On the other side, many environmentalists and PLAN-Boulder members charged that City Council members were mere puppets of the Chamber of Commerce. They debunked the economic growth argument claiming that ''growth causes unemployment'' and labeled claims that growth would pay for itself as ''municipal mythology'' (Bartlett 1986).

The ways in which the links (if any) between the economy and environment were conceptualized were critical to the goals many participants in the debates wanted to achieve; they shaped both their environmental outlook and hopes for the growth control movement in Boulder. The positions of the PLAN-Boulder members I interviewed fell into one of three categories[3]: giving absolute primacy to the economy over the environment; beliefs related to the ways in which property rights led to environmental degradation; and beliefs that a healthy environment necessarily included the availability of jobs for all residents.

The one person who argued that it was both possible and necessary to disregard economic concerns in environmental planning was a male. After twenty years, this man was still outraged by the threats to Boulder's environment posed by growth. He dismissed any suggestion that growth might provide some benefits, saying, "Growth never pays for itself. A lot of times you hear people say that we need to compromise between the environment and the economy. But that's bad, because it's always the environment that suffers. Maybe not as much as if there had been no compromise and developers had their way, but it adds up. Protecting the environment is the best thing you can do for the economy. Look at Boulder. We haven't been hurt by stopping growth. Even the realtors talk it up now." He concluded the interview by saying that "protecting the environment is an absolute necessity. Who cares about tax revenues—which wouldn't have come anyway—if you don't have a place to live?"

Two other people saw a connection between economic relations and environmental protection, but in ways that did not endear them to the progrowth faction any more than the aforementioned man did. One man and one woman thought that private property rights inhibited the abilities of local governments to protect the environment. Both of these people pointed to examples of community rights over land in Europe and argued that giving up some control of land is the most important step in protecting the environment. Many PLAN-Boulder members felt some sympathy with these ideas, but primarily when applied to large property holders or to property holders in sensitive environments. For example, the other four people who talked about the relation between the economy and the environment clearly struggled with the role of property rights in environmental protection efforts. At least two of them, however, concluded that the property rights were fundamental in the United States. One man said, "After all, one of the reasons I cared about growth was that it infringed on my property rights."

The final category was represented by those people who were uncomfortable either separating or prioritizing the economy and environment. These three women and one man seemed to argue for a definition of environment that included the economic environment. Property rights played some role in shaping this definition, but a concern for the availability of jobs was paramount. These people struggled to balance their concerns about the physical environment with concerns about the economy. One woman had been worried about a city council decision in the late 1960s to stop attempting to attract basic employment: "I was really nervous about that. The City had been drawing all these computer companies to town, and then just stopped trying to get new companies to move here. It seemed like a lot of eggs in the computer basket. What if they all went broke? I'm not so worried about that now, but I don't like to hear people say we can forget about jobs." Similarly, another woman wanted to ensure widespread availability of jobs. She argued, however, that the city needed to diversify its employment structure: "They were going to turn this into a rich man's town. Well, not everyone who lives here has a PhD, and they need jobs, too. That's as important to me as open space, even though I worked on the open space campaigns." Finally, in an intentional play on another's man's comments, one man said, "What good's a pristine environment if you can't live there?"[4]

In summary, while some PLAN-Boulder members gave primacy to physical environmental concerns, many others wanted to protect the economic environment as well. These people were concerned not just with Boulder's rate of growth, but also with the *way* it was growing. They argued that uncontrolled growth threatened the livelihood of many in Boulder by driving up housing prices and in the creation of highly skilled jobs and jobs in upscale retail and service establishments. Thus, they sought to preserve an economic environment—in addition to a natural environment—that allowed everyone to benefit. Significantly, the difference in outlooks did not seem to be associated with household socioeconomic status, since all of the people interviewed were from upper-middle-class households and all but one of the people who talked about the relationship between the environment and economy were from households associated with the university and scientific communities.

I am wary of interpreting these responses in strictly gendered terms. Many analysts have suggested that upper-middle-class women are more likely to be concerned with job availability since they occupy a more marginal economic position than do upper-middle-class men. Women are also more likely than men to come in contact with people of other classes, again making women more sensitive to the quantity and quality of jobs. However, because so many of the businesspeople who opposed prioritizing the environment over the economy were men, one should be cautious in attributing concerns for the use values provided by the economy only to gender relations. However, the economic concerns expressed by these women were integral to their concern over Boulder as a place to live and the quality of life it provided. It is in this category of use values that I think the effects of gender relations become most obvious.

Valuing Boulder as a Place to Live

The preceding discussion indicated that some PLAN-Boulder members used a very expansive definition of environment—one that included the human habitat. For these people, their environmentalism covered the economic, built, social, and physical environment. Their overarching goal in joining PLAN-Boulder was to maintain Boulder as a place to live and to raise their families. The use values they expressed were of two types: the value of Boulder as a small town in which children were raised, and the moral, social values to be found in Boulder.

Many people in Boulder were concerned that the town was losing its small-town status; letters to the editor and testimonials at city council hearings attest to the salience of this concern. Generally, people were afraid that Boulder was turning from a town where "you just knew that if you went down to Potter's drug store on Saturday, you would run into everyone you needed to see'' into a town that would become just another suburb of Denver. According to one woman, this concern was reinforced every time a resident drove into town. Boulder is in a bowl-shaped valley, and almost every approach to it provides scenic vistas. In the 1960s, the vistas provided the opportunity to see the effects of individual developments on the town as a whole. This has led to an appreciation for holistic, comprehensive planning to preserve the environment and to preserve the smallness of the town.

Almost everyone felt that the small-town character of the town was important in raising their children. Indeed, children in open space became some of the most potent images used to promote the growth control campaign. A famous advertisement that featured a picture of five children running hand in hand across a field with the Flatirons behind them was mentioned by several people I interviewed as being one of the most effective means of sparking conversations about growth and in conveying PLAN-Boulder's message. This was not just a message about environmental preservation; it was a message about preserving children. Two of the four men I interviewed were involved in the preparation of this advertisement and a third man's children were pictured in it. In what may be a reflection of gendered ways of speaking, all these men told me about the advertisement and its effectiveness as an image; the women spoke of advertisement in relation to their children or the need to preserve Boulder as a small town in which other children would be raised.

While men and women both spoke of preserving Boulder as a small town, six of the women and none of the men spoke explicitly about the quality of life in Boulder as it related to fairness and social justice. The concerns they held were expressed in a number of ways. For example, five women believed the city and county were trying to attract new residents and employers to Boulder but were doing little to plan or prepare the area for their arrival. One woman in particular was concerned that the city and county governments needed to work together to ensure that newcomers and long-time residents were both treated fairly and that animosity between the two groups did not arise as growth pressures mounted: ''After all, since the city and business groups worked so hard to attract them here, they had a responsibility to be sure that services were ready and that they didn't enter as villains.''

The issue of fairness arose in another context, as well. Two women noted that the growth Boulder experienced in the 1950s had driven up housing prices and reduced the availability of rental housing. As mentioned before, these women were also concerned that the type of jobs being attracted to Boulder were only going to employ people in white collar positions. They feared that Boulder would soon become too expensive for lower-income households and that the new firms would not employ local residents in need of jobs. In short, they believed that growth would not help lower-income residents, even though those residents would suffer disproportionately the costs.

Overall, six of the eight women and none of the men with whom I spoke said that the effects of growth on quality of life, fairness, and planning were important reasons for their involvement. For these women, growth pressures threatened the physical, built, and social environments as places to live and work. None of the women thought that preservation of the natural environment was an end in itself. In retrospect, many women spoke with sadness that Boulder seemed to have preserved riparian habitats better than the human habitat. As they look back on their efforts in the 1960s and 1970s, they cannot escape the irony that the growth management measures taken in Boulder are attributed by some to be the cause of high housing costs affordable only to upper- and middle-income households. Indeed, it is one of the most expensive communities in which to live in the Denver region; a single woman with one child, for instance, must earn over $10 per hour to support herself and family (Culkin et al. 1990). The women with whom I spoke expressed ambivalence about the intended and unintended consequences of their activism. They recognized that the fact of their participation in the growth control movement was not sufficient to ensure that all their concerns were heard and enacted.

In interpreting these concerns raised by women, however, it is important to remember the cautions I raised previously about gender and interpersonal relations present in interview settings that may also have been at work. For example, I have conversed with one man from the study in other settings, and my sense is that issues of fairness were very important to him. However, those sentiments have not been voiced to me—even with prodding. In addition, there were other men who were not associated with PLAN-Boulder who *have* expressed these concerns in other settings. Economist Kenneth Boulding, for example, testified before a city forum on growth that "it's not a privilege to live in Colorado—it's a right." He was concerned that growth limitations would make some people worse off, and he argued that "human betterment," not growth, should be the city's concern (Gruis 1973). However, his was one of a few masculine voices reported in local newspapers to raise that concern.

The reasons for this gender gap in the ways growth-related concerns were raised may in part be due to gendered languages, but it is also possible that growth pressures affected the women in PLAN-Boulder differently than they did males due to the influence of gender relations operating at household, community, urban, and societal scales. It is, perhaps, the different social locations of women and men that provided the basis for gendered political attitudes toward growth. In saying that women and men are socialized to particular interests and, by extension, use values, I do not intend to imply that any of these four values are the exclusive domain of women or men. Rather, I argue that for all the diversity of individuals related to family, class, race, ethnicity, and sexuality, the shared experience of being a woman or a man in a patriarchal society provides a basis for gendered political interests. I argue that these gendered interests are reflected in the reasons women and men become involved in debates over urban growth and potentially in the outcomes they wish to achieve. Thus, women and men joined PLAN-Boulder and the debates over growth in roughly equal numbers, but some of the concerns that motivated them reflected gender relations and the ways in which women's social locations shape political attitudes. It was not the case that women saw their roles in the organization as municipal mothers or housekeepers, for many women saw their activism as an escape or release from domestic chores. However, in speaking with PLAN-Boulder members, it was apparent that women and men expressed subtle differences in the use values they brought to the debate over growth that are shaped by the web of power relations—including gender relations—that structure U.S. society.

PLAN-BOULDER WOMEN AS POLITICAL AGENTS

If women brought different goals and use values to the growth control move-ment than did men, how effective were women as political agents? The answer to this question depends on whether success is measured in terms of achieving specific goals or in terms of the changed political opportunity structure these women helped to create.

Goal Attainment

In terms of the goals women brought to their involvement, the outcomes were mixed. One goal that many women mentioned but that has not been discussed was a simple desire to escape for a while from their houses and household identities. These women felt that their activities in this and in other organizations helped them create part of an identity or role for themselves that was separate from their roles and identities in their households. They all said that their activities as PLAN-Boulder members helped them escape—at least temporarily. Whether other people continued to view them as housewives did not diminish their new sense of personal identity. As one woman said, "I came to realize what the men on the City Council thought of me, but I also came to realize that it didn't matter. I got enormous personal satisfaction out of what I was able to do." Thus, these women came to a new sense of themselves as knowledgeable political agents. They knew they had expertise and skills that could be used to effect change. They also came to know their positions with respect to the other agents shaping the growth debates and the likely limits of their effectiveness.

If we measure the women's effectiveness in terms of achieving the planning goals or in preserving the use values they identified, we would have to conclude that they were less successful. PLAN-Boulder has been instrumental in passing growth limitation and open space ordinances, in encouraging a planning ethic in the town, and in electing environmental candidates to office. However, housing prices and the cost of living in Boulder have continued to rise. The desire to maintain a place in which people from all socioeconomic strata may live has not been realized. It seems that those who used a more expansive definition of environment—incorporating the built and social environments—were not suc-cessful in achieving their goals. This has been a factor in the decisions by four women to decrease their involvement in PLAN-Boulder and to become active in other organizations that are dedicated to the broader issues with which they are concerned; in these settings women appear to have been more successful in moving toward the public provision of social services and in working for privately provided services such as a safehouse for women and a free medical clinic. It appears that for all the openness of PLAN-Boulder's structure, these women were not able to transform the language of environmentalism to include housing, employment, and social issues. The idea sets of PLAN-Boulder's and the public's discourse, then, remained focused on the physical environment. When issues of fairness have been engaged in public debate, they have generally been raised by people not acting on behalf of PLAN-Boulder. While these women have learned from their experiences, it is not clear how much social learning has occurred. So at this level, the meaning of women's activism for their empowerment is mixed.

The Political Opportunity Structure for Women

At another level, however, the actions of PLAN-Boulder women have been significant in expanding the political opportunity structure for women in Boulder and in the state of Colorado. Many women in PLAN-Boulder have served as appointed members of planning, parks, open space, and urban renewal boards at the city and county levels; three of the women I interviewed have served in that capacity and two more were asked to, but declined. All of them believed that they were asked to serve as a result of their activities in PLAN-Boulder. In addition, several women have run for and some have been elected to public office after their involvement with the organization. Often the election is to city council, but Ruth Wright, the current minority leader in the Colorado House of Representatives, launched her political career in PLAN-Boulder. Several times since 1971 (the critical election in the growth debates), the majority of City Council members have been women. In fact, in the late 1970s a city charter provision requiring that appointed boards be not "all of the same sex" was invoked and a man had to be appointed to the planning board. Opening the political opportunity structure to women was not an explicit goal of the women interviewed, but it certainly was an important outcome. Significantly, it is an outcome that may make it possible (or at least easier) for women to achieve the results they desire through further activism and struggle.

CONCLUSION

Overall, it appears that the political activism of women is more complicated and more ambiguous than either the comments of individual activists or of urban political theorists might suggest. The stories of the activists recounted here suggest that ungendered analyses of use values in growth debates miss subtle yet significant differences in what women and men hoped to achieve through their activism. At a practical level, this has meant that much of the planning activity in Boulder was concerned solely with physical design issues. At a theoretical level, it has meant that the interests and values identified as relevant to growth politics are limited to those rooted in class relations. We would do well to understand that the full range of interests and values includes those created by the relations between women and men in the home, community, and, indeed, in the society as a whole.

These empirical findings also reflect on feminist and structurationist approaches to research on women and gender relations. The experiences and beliefs recounted here exemplify the ways in which some women attempt to shape public discourse and ideas through political activism and the intended and unintended consequences of their efforts. Proceeding from the social locations, or standpoints, of women in their households, communities, city, and society, it has been possible to explore gendered differences in political attitudes. At the same time, the structurationist perspective focuses attention on the varied ways in which women and women's social locations are mutually transformed through their actions. Taken together, this feminist and structurationist approach can help us open analyses to the full complexity of the ways in which women and men move through the web of power relations to effect social change.

NOTES

This research was supported with grants from the Hewlett Foundation to the Conflict Resolution Consortium and the Council for Research and Creative Work, both at the University of Colorado. I gratefully acknowledge the research assistance of Robin Leichenko and the comments of Susan Clarke, Meghan Cope, David Hodge, and Jim Huff.

1. PLAN-Boulder is the most prominent of the citizens' organizations that attempted to curtail population growth in Boulder. The PLAN stands for People's League for Action Now.

2. Data was acquired through open-ended interviews with an array of local actors in Boulder. Their identities are preserved in the study by mutual consent to ensure that responses were factual and accurate.

3. Three women and one man did not talk about the links between the environment and the economy, even when asked. The other participants brought up the topic in the conversations without prompting.

4. This man knew that the man who gave primacy to the environment had also been interviewed, and, as a long-time friend, had a good sense of what the other man had told me.

8

Discursive Limits to Agency

Joshua Van Lieu and John Paul Jones, III

Future judgments on the contemporary period may well mark it as the one that smiled least on the American working class. The collective organizations of workers has reached a new low, capital has proven resilient to various forms of state regulation, the engines that drive accumulation now operate at an international scale, and even to think about resisting these changes seems absurd. Given the metonymic relationship between knowledge and social reality, it is perhaps not so surprising that these same developments coincide with an explosion of theoretical tools that have sharpened our understanding of capitalism and of the structures that both limit and enable social action. Yet what remains ironic in the face of much current theorizing about agency is that, at present, the potential for praxis, for theoretically informed social action, seems more remote than ever.

Perhaps this state of affairs is a reflection of the fact that our knowledge of the complexities of structure exceeds that of its presumed duality. Recently, however, both movements have been supplemented by the increased recognition that social life must be conceptualized in grounded terms, that is, from a spatial perspective. A diverse collection of scholars have taken this position, offering that social life does not unfold on the head of a pin but intimately bound in spatial contexts at various scales, from the vast global operations of transnational corporations to everyday locally situated practices.[1] There remains faint optimism, therefore, that by examining the concrete nexus of these scales in particular circumstances we may discern clues to the limits to agency—certain to be a future marker of the contemporary period—such that we can deploy this knowledge for social and political change.

If there is some consensus on the theoretical importance of space, there is far less on how such theorizations should proceed. Particularly significant for the present chapter and, it seems, for theory in general is the divide between those who seek to concretize spatiality in traditional materialist terms and those who conceptualize space as a system of metaphors existing in discursive practices. To invoke materiality, as opposed to its presumed others—representations and discourse—is to ground one's investigations in concrete geographies and histories and to confine accounts of social life thereby embedded to a multiplicity of base and superstructure effects and consequences. In opposition to materiality is a no less geographic formulation that seeks to uncover the submerged spatiality of linguistic and other signifying practices that have the effects of marginalization, placement, and transport. As has been noted elsewhere (Natter and Jones 1993a, 1993b), however, viewing these perspectives as oppositions rests on an a priori dichotomy between the representation of social life and social life *as lived*, a distinction that fails to problematize the interrelationships between material conditions and their reproduction by, and consequences on, representations and discourse.

Overcoming this division is necessary we argue for theoretically informed social action. On the one hand, the material conditions of social life are rightly the locus of our investigations, but on the other hand these conditions do not exist independent of discursive practices. In other words, both material contexts and discourses are part of an interwoven matrix we might profitably call structure. By overcoming one-sided, aspatial accounts of each, would we not also enrich our understanding of structure's theoretical dual, agency?

This leads us to the frame of our account, which seeks to understand the limits to agency in terms that are both material and discursive. The empirical context is a familiar one by now, namely, a plant closure in a small community. The setting is Mount Sterling, Kentucky, a town of 5362 situated on the western edge of the Appalachian chain. In 1989 the Whirlpool corporation, Mount Sterling's largest employer, closed its dishwasher plant and relocated production, leaving 600 workers unemployed. Our task is to explain the passive acquiescence of these workers to the plant shutdown. They were, we argue, bound both materially and discursively. On the one hand, Mount Sterling is a small, conservative town whose local state is closely tied to dependent capital. On the other hand, these same conditions set the stage for the systematic exclusion of the workers by the discourse of local economic development. As a consequence, workers were doubly constrained: by the material contexts that made it seem futile to resist and by their exclusion from discussions over what should and could be done. The resultant web permits no heroes.

The remainder of this chapter is organized as follows. First, we briefly review

Whirlpool's decision to close its Mount Sterling KitchenAid facility.[2] Second, we discuss the concrete contingencies that supply one part of the limits to agency, the material context of Mount Sterling. In this section, the contrasting scales of firm and town are delineated and the relationships between labor, local capital, and the state are explored. Third, we examine the discourses of local economic development, with attention to the exclusionary practices limiting what could be thought, said, and done following the plant closure. In our conclusion, we consider whether the relations we mark between the material and the discursive provide a case for the inherent limits *of*, or the contingent limits *to*, agency.

THE WHIRLPOOL PLANT CLOSURE

On November 28, 1989, Whirlpool announced the commencement of a capacity study of three of its KitchenAid plants (*Mount Sterling Advocate*, hereafter *MSA*, November 30, 1989). The study was to consider manufacturing facilities in Findlay (Ohio), Oxford (Mississippi), and Mount Sterling. Whirlpool claimed that consolidation of its operations was of utmost necessity, as national production of dishwashers was outpacing demand by 2 million units annually. Whirlpool's options, it was said, were to close either the Oxford or Mount Sterling plant in anticipation of a transfer of production to the facilities in Ohio. Although Mount Sterling's plant was the only unionized one under study, Ken Porter, Manager for Human Resources for Whirlpool, was quick to assure the plant's workers that its union status was irrelevant to the corporation's decision. In his words, "we do not have problems with this union that they need to be concerned about," adding that "this is not a union/non-union issue" (*MSA*, November 30, 1989).

The closing of the plant would be no small event in Mount Sterling, as KitchenAid's workforce accounted for over one in every four manufacturing jobs in Montgomery County (Del White). Bob Teegarden, spokesperson for the United Auto Workers (UAW) Local 1562, sounded his concern but offered little in the way of optimism, noting that the workers "are taking it very seriously and they're concerned but they also realize they're helpless. This is a nationwide thing and corporations tend to consolidate" (*MSA*, November 30, 1989). Others, particularly representatives of local capital, were more optimistic. Del White, the county's Economic Development Director, averred that KitchenAid would stay because of the skill and high productivity of the Mount Sterling workers. White also cited the corporation's recent building improvements as an added incentive to maintain the Kentucky facility (*MSA*, November 30, 1989).[3]

Local government in Mount Sterling did not sit idly by while the study was underway. On February 8, 1990, an incentive package worth $7 million was presented to Whirlpool by city, county, and state governments and by private banks. The package consisted primarily of loans for equipment and infrastructure for the facility. One day after the tender of the state's offer, Kevin Cooney, Whirlpool's vice-president for manufacturing, announced the closing of the

Mount Sterling plant, noting that the $7 million incentive package was not enough to offset the excess capacity of the Ohio plant.

Whirlpool was quick to defuse blame following the announcement, denying that there was any connection between Mount Sterling closing and its union status (*MSA*, February 15, 1990). Indeed, the Mount Sterling workers received high praise for their accomplishments.[4] As Ken Kaminski, president of the North American appliance group, reported in an in-house publication: "I also want to assure the people of Mount Sterling plant that this decision in no way adversely reflects on their skills and dedication. They have produced the industry's most highly regarded dishwasher—and we fully expect to maintain the tradition that they have built over the years. In fact, we remain committed to strengthening our market leadership position for KitchenAid products and our ability to serve our customers in the marketplace" (*Employee Connection*, February 9, 1990).

Nor was the decision an easy one for the company, as Bill Marohn, executive vice-president of Whirlpool's North American appliance group, noted: "Clearly, these were not easy decisions to make since they affect a number of our people. Nonetheless, we very carefully considered all aspects of these moves, and we believe they are the right ones for Whirlpool's North American business over the long term" (*Employee Connection*, February 9, 1990).

In spite of these assurances, worker response to their evaporating livelihood was one of resentment and betrayal. In the words of one employee, Bob Teegarden:

I found [the closing] hard on me and I'm not an emotional person. I worked at that plant for twenty-two years. I gave them the best years of my life. I thought I done them a good job. In the nature of my job, we sometimes had machinery break down on lunch or during break. We'd leave break early or go during break to get a piece of machinery goin' . . . things you do just to contribute. When they closed it you feel like betrayal. You feel betrayed because of what you give them. It causes anger. It causes anxiety . . . there's a human factor that can't be measured . . . the human factor is very wide and very deep and it's really gonna hurt. There's just no way trying. It's a shame industry can't see the hurt they do when they do one of these plant closings.

Even after the announcement, many workers remained hopeful that a solution would be found and their jobs preserved. A former employee, Monford Greer, spoke of the last day of work before the plant closed. When the work was done, everyone was simply told to go home. Some remained in an attempt to prolong their employment as long as possible, while others wept despite consolation from their friends. For some, it was not until the final day on the job that the seriousness of their situations became apparent.

THE MATERIAL CONTEXT

A partial understanding of the events of Mount Sterling is provided by an interrogation of the complex intersection of scales surrounding the corporation's decision and the workers' response. At one level, no less manifest in the town, was a corporation bound to and by its international shareholders and competitors. At another level, no less significant for the corporation, was a town whose horizons were so insular as to make futile any resistance to global capital.

Cox and Mair's (1988) term, "locally dependent capital," captures well the problem between the firm and town. Whirlpool was, for a time, locally dependent on Mount Sterling's workers. Yet this dependence was increasingly diffused through the corporation's strategy of multilocationality, which intensified during the 1980s. The town, on the other hand, had no such remedy. Its local newspaper, retailers, banks, utilities, and workers were conjoined by previous *in situ* investments and situated practices that limited their range of options. In the aftermath of the plant closing, these dependent elements struggled over the definition of the locality—over how to project the tenuous alliance known as community. As noted earlier, the struggle took place discursively, but before it can be described we must first turn to the material contexts through which the intersecting scales of the corporation and the town may be better appreciated.

The Horizon of the Global

Whirlpool's acquisition of the Mount Sterling plant began in 1985 with its purchase of the KitchenAid line of appliances from Dart and Kraft, which was operating the already-unionized facility. The buyout was quickly contested in federal antitrust courts by two of Whirlpool's competitors, White Consolidated Industries and the Magic Chef corporation. In an effort to circumvent the antitrust suit, Whirlpool sold the KitchenAid plant to Emerson Electric Company, which then produced KitchenAid dishwashers for Whirlpool under a single contract agreement. In 1988, following Whirlpool's successful defense of the antitrust suit, the corporation terminated its arrangement with Emerson Electric by purchasing its Contract Division, thus giving Whirlpool complete ownership of the plant. The clash between the acquired factory and Whirlpool, a company committed to the flexibility demanded by the pressures of the international marketplace, could not have been greater. The workers were eager to please their new owners; Whirlpool, meanwhile, was embarking on a three-pronged restructuring in space, sector, and technology.

By Whirlpool's account, the times required shifts of unparalleled magnitude (Whirlpool *Annual Report*, various years), and the corporation rose to the challenge. Between 1980 and 1990 Whirlpool expanded its operations in Brazil, Italy, Mexico, India, and the Netherlands. Citing the "confluence of consumer lifestyles on a global scale" and the limited growth and high level of competition in the North American market, Whirlpool aimed to advance its position in both the European Community and in third world countries with substantial market potential. The global strategy was matched by rapid technological changes in the production process, culminating in the 1989 introduction of the "world washer'' whose design was flexible enough to be produced under a highly variable set of production and consumption conditions.

Sectoral restructuring was especially vigorous in North America, where by the mid-1980s subsidiaries were being bought and sold at an increasingly rapid pace. Eleven times from 1980 to 1990 the corporation discontinued major product lines or closed or sold plants. Lost in the process was its production of home heating and cooling equipment, electric organs, vacuum cleaners, and ice makers. The same period saw the corporation purchase or expand production at thirteen existing sites, considerably redrawing the map of the corporation's mainstay, appliance manufacturing. At no time during the 1980s, however, were any new plants constructed by Whirlpool. It is against this national and international restructuring that the story of the Mount Sterling closing unfolds.

The Horizon of the Local

Mount Sterling is the largest town and county seat of Montgomery County, which is situated at the border between the Bluegrass and Appalachian regions. The town might profitably boast a Rockwellian character, given its broad main street lined with turn of the century buildings and quaint neighborhoods. Yet behind this sanguine facade is the reality of chronic economic depression. Only 61 percent of the adult population is in the labor force, and the county's unemployment rates are among the highest in Kentucky, occasionally surpassing those of its more economically volatile, coal-dependent Appalachian neighbors to the east.

The pace of Whirlpool's globalization and North American restructuring must have appeared bewildering from the cultural setting of Mount Sterling, where the primary concern was the construction of a new elementary school and public library. Moreover, the plant's union, United Auto Workers Local 1562, was ill prepared for the changes awaiting it. In part this is due to Mount Sterling's location—midway between Lexington (population 225,000) and Appalachia. The town is too far from the Appalachian coalfields for its workers to have developed linkages with the more militant factions of the United Mine Workers,[5] while Lexington, a conservative city with a strong presence in the service sector, could provide few mimetic figures around which Mount Sterling might galvanize opposition.

The Mount Sterling union was hardly militant as a result. It staged only two walkouts in twenty-five years, and both of these considerably predated Whirlpool (in 1971 and 1978, see *MSA*, August 10, 1989). Moreover, under both Emerson and Whirlpool, management dominated labor negotiations and shopfloor activities. As former Whirlpool employee Larry Walters noted, ''at the last [contract negotiation], the union's hands was tied. They were there but that was it. That's what they would say, 'It's out of our hands.' It was in the contract. The company could do anything it wanted to as far as production. That was in our contract. Whatever they saw fit to do to get production out they could do. That was one of the things that was in our contract. If the company felt like business was dropping off and wanted to take a few people off the line they could do that. They would do that.''

Alongside this economic matrix of contrasting globality and locality arose a second effect, which was manifest in local politics. As Cox and Mair (1988) have demonstrated, forms of locally dependent capital often align themselves into a business coalition that seeks to protect fixed investments in the built environment. Yet what is unique about Mount Sterling's business coalition is its virtual inseparability from the local state. Whereas in larger localities one might encounter a triad of state, capital, and labor, in Mount Sterling the first two of these forms virtually collapse onto one another.

Our sketch of the town's business coalition commences with the Montgomery County Industrial Authority (MCIA). The MCIA is made up of six voting members and anywhere from four to six nonvoting members. The voting members are appointed in equal number by the county judge/executive and the mayor of Mount Sterling. All of the Authority's members, both voting and nonvoting, typically include real estate dealers, managers from local employers, retailers, developers, and representatives from all four local banks (Clifford Stilz).

The MCIA works closely with and serves as the governing board of another apparatus combining local capital and the state, the Economic Development Office (EDO). Formed specifically to deal with the problem of Mount Sterling's sagging economy, the EDO has been in operation since the mid-1980s and is funded through Mount Sterling's municipal government. The body coordinates incentive packages, finds potential investors, and engages in public relations promoting the area's business climate. A third player is the Mount Sterling Chamber of Commerce, and although it does not have the same official ties to the local state, it is closely related through common membership to the EDO and MCIA.

Thus, in this small-town setting, the local state shades directly into local capital, sharing funding and the appointment of members whose dual positions make it difficult to discern where capital ends and the state begins (see also Kirby 1985; Kleniewski 1987). Together, all three alliances formed a grid that seriously limited labor's role in local economic affairs. As we shall see later, this powerful coalition set the contours of economic development discourse in Mount Sterling that ultimately defined the town's crises in its own terms, ones that not only disciplined labor but that also had the effect of excluding it from contributing answers to the question of what was to be done.

ECONOMIC DEVELOPMENT DISCOURSE IN MOUNT STERLING

Discourse, as any reading of Foucault suggests, is more easily defined by what it is not, namely, a collection of words to describe events. For to focus on the "mere" assemblage of particular words would naturalize the social processes by which objects are named, given meaning, and interpreted. As Foucault notes, "discourses, in the form in which they can be heard and read, are not, as one might expect, a mere intersection of things and words: an obscure web of things, a manifest, visible, coloured chain of words . . . discourse is not a slender surface of contact, or confrontation, between a reality and a language, the intrication of a lexicon and experience" (1972a, 48). Instead, discourse provides a mediation of phenomena and consciousness, the purpose of which is to give meaning or order to the chaotic multiplicity of reality. Again, Foucault notes, "in analyzing discourses themselves, one sees the loosening of the embrace, apparently so tight, of words and things, and the emergence of a group of rules proper to discursive practice. These rules define not the dumb existence of reality, nor the canonical use of a vocabulary, but the ordering of objects" (1972a, 49).

To order objects is to provide a basis for their interpretation or, in other words, to constitute them socially. The consequent recognition—that material reality is defined discursively—suggests that to focus social investigation on discursive practices is not to deny materiality, but rather to question how some objects become central to discourse while others are excluded. Answers to such questions are found by interrogating the (spatial) material powers that define what is accessible, knowable, and within reason, on the one hand, and what is excluded, impossible, and irrational, on the other hand.

The foregoing considerations led Foucault (1980b) to reject universal Truth in favor of what he called the politics of truth. For Foucault, the discovery of Truth implies the existence of independent and objective facts that themselves do not rely on discursive regimes for interpretation. A politics of truth, by contrast, holds that facts do not exist in an asocial vacuum but are instead defined through systems of understanding that are always already socially determined. It is not too bold to suggest that, in the context of Mount Sterling, the business coalition and organized labor have spent the past few years haggling over the content of truth. What is at stake in this conflict is who shall set the rules for separating truth from fallacy through the construction and propagation of the discourse of local economic development. The winner in this struggle stands to gain the enviable ability to define the material community, while the losers must work to define their own identities in the face of their exclusion from the dominant discourse.

In the case of the economic development discourse under consideration here, the local state/capital alliance not only drew the contours of the discourse, but in so doing disciplined organized labor by its exclusionary and punitive character. Our account of these developments is organized by first considering the object of the business coalition's discourse. Second, we explore the modalities (particularly position and site) that enabled its propagation.

Constructing the Object

The case of Mount Sterling aptly demonstrates that the object of discourse is not pregiven, but is potentially subject to profound transformation. Whereas prior to the shutdown organized labor had itself captured the attention of various aspects of the coalition, the crisis of Mount Sterling initiated a profound shift. In the weeks following Whirlpool's announcement, the coalition turned to a new object, that of community. In this discursive shift, the coalition found a vehicle for eliding historic conflicts between business and labor as well as a propitious means for selling Mount Sterling to mobile capital.

To demonstrate this shift, we return to the walkouts of the 1970s, which by all accounts were indelibly marked into the town's collective memory. Elements of dependent capital, in tandem with KitchenAid, worked successfully to divide union members from other residents through disinformation campaigns that distorted the nature of contract disputes (Monford Greer, Larry Walters). The following excerpt from an interview with former KitchenAid employee Larry Walters illustrates how union disputes were received. It is worth quoting at length:

LW: A few times that we went on strike, the banks and a lot of the businesses didn't stand with the people. They stood with the company. They said, "You people are crazy. You make good money. Go back to work." A lot of the time it wasn't the money. It was benefits and other things. They said we had a bad reputation for striking. Other companies didn't want to come in on account of we went on strike so much. I disagree with that. I was in two strikes and they could have been settled without a strike, really. I don't know where it came from but it seemed that the company would play the union against the town. They would say things like "They don't want to work." Sometimes you'd go to the bank and they say, "You people are crazy. Go back to work." The funny thing about it is that the people saying this are making $45,000 a year and you're only making $16,000 . . . they'd say, "You're crazy. Y'all got a good job. You ought to keep it. Go back to work."[6]

JVL: Bank tellers would say this? Bankers?

LW: Yeah. Bank tellers, business people. There were a lot of hard feelings between the employees and the townspeople. The employees would say, "I'm not going to spend my money in Mount Sterling. I'm going somewhere else," on account of a situation like this. They played two parties against one another to try to get people to go back to work.

It is not surprising that organized labor could so easily be made an object of derision in Mount Sterling, given its exclusion from the state/capital coalition and its consequent inability to frame discussions. Interviews with members of the UAW local reveal the extent of this discursive exclusion. As the former president of the UAW local, Tom Reffit, expresses it, "They said there were problems between labor and management yet they never did invite either one of us, labor or management, to sit down and go over those things with them. As far as the union is concerned, we didn't have no problem doing anything like that, even with management present at those meetings. I've sit in on committees, we went to the local leadership in Montgomery County. If there's problems with labor, fine, come and talk to us." But the coalition preferred to operate without organized labor, without actually speaking with any of its representatives. Reffit continues: "I don't thing they want unions to get involved. They look at it like an eyesore. When a company is looking at a location you'll find that very few companies want a union around anyway. They'd like to put us on the back burner if there is any way possible. I would have to say that they wouldn't want us involved in it . . . except in maybe supporting their efforts or saying that we don't have problems."

Former UAW spokesman Bob Teegarden was able to engage the coalition, but only as the sole voice representing labor: "After I started writing letters to the editor [of the *MSA*] and making presentations to various groups, the county judge appointed me to the industrial board as a representative of organized labor. Up until that point labor had never been recognized. All the managers had been appointed or invited to be on boards and commissions but for some reason labor had never been included. The business community, the citizens at large, and everyone else had a voice in government but labor was never invited."

Teegarden's difficulties in the face of a hegemonic disdain for organized labor is reflected in a June 1989 meeting, held months before the announcement of the feasibility study. The Montgomery County EDO gathering featured remarks by a number of local business leaders. They accused unions of acting purely for their own benefit and of not thinking of the greater good of the county. Past strikes, it was offered, had labeled Montgomery as a problem county that discouraged potential investors. Teegarden responded that management was responsible for the strikes by providing poor working conditions. While not wanting labor to carry the entire burden of the region's poor economic performance, he nonetheless also noted that union labor was "willing to bend over backwards to project the type of image we want" (*MSA*, June 1, 1989).

With the word *we*, Teegarden purchased wholesale the soon-to-be-object of the coalition, community. For while labor was formerly a focus of derision, the crisis politics practiced after the plant closure required that labor be encompassed into the web of community. As Teegarden signals with his deference to the coalition, there is no alternative discourse operating outside of that practiced by the MCIA and EDO. Their objectives—the exculpation of capital and labor's full cooperation—were insured by the absence of a competing discourse. As a result, labor was quickly subsumed under the enveloping project of community.

In demonstrating the discursive transition, we turn to another meeting, this one held soon after the announcement of the closing. Larry Back, then a member of the MCIA, called for the creation of the Gateway Labor and Management Council as a vehicle for solving the economic woes of Mount Sterling (*MSA*, February 22, 1990). Back identified the root of the problem as poor labor relations and proposed that the council act as a liaison between business and labor. In this way the local state, through the MCIA and the council, would ease the supposedly tense relations between capital and labor in Mount Sterling. Under this model, labor and business could better understand the needs of the community, put aside their differences, and work for the common good. Back pointed out that this would be instrumental in erasing the county's scarred image.

Thus the crisis had set into motion the construction of a new object of discourse, that of community, which is so important to the image projection necessary to attract mobile capital. Acting as a veil of cooperation between capital and labor, community represents a new phase of the discourse, one designed for outside consumption. Whereas previously business and civic leaders openly offered that labor was too aggressive in its demands, the task of the new regime was the repression of any representation of capital-labor conflict. Thus the interests of capital were cast as the interests of all.

The effects of this shift were apparent within months of the shutdown. Then county judge/executive William Johnson, when asked about past labor problems in Montgomery County, offered the following enthusiastic and highly positive response:

We got the best work force in the country. There's people in this county that's got pride in what they do. They're good people. If someone was to come here and start a factory they'd tell you, just like Pat Irvine with the Plasti-drum. He's amazed at the people he's picked up here. Bob with Bob's Food Service said one time he'd like to take twelve people from Mount Sterling to Tampa, Florida and replace the twenty-five he's got down there. Nobody we ever brought in here has ever said, ''Well, you all lied to us about your work force.'' Everybody says, ''You told us you had a good work force and we believe it and we can vouch for it.'' That helps us now when we try to talk to [potential investors].

Conspicuously absent from Johnson's response is any mention of organized labor, which by then was thoroughly disciplined into the encirclement of com-munity—now the discursive base of the coalition's legitimacy. The weakness of organized labor arises from the fact that once the coalition was perceived to be working for the benefit of all, any chance of building an effective counter-discourse evaporated. Moreover, the successful alignment of the coalition with community and the legitimacy thereby bequeathed allowed it the flexibility to define the characteristics of community as well as to determine the real material conditions of Mount Sterling.

The coalition's success in disciplining labor is poignantly marked by mayor Bert May, whose comments betray both its discursive and material dimensions:

BM: I think the people who have lost their jobs at Whirlpool . . . have seen what [labor militancy] can do to you and I don't think it's going to be a problem.

JVL: It's not going to be a problem because they've seen what comes about because of strikes?

BM: Yeah. The [workers] understand that. They have had someone sit down and explain that to them, they understand it better, and I don't think they'll be as anxious to strike. They're gonna be a lot more thankful to have a job.

Though May's educated and thankful workers no longer pose a threat to the business coalition's project, that fact alone does not provide the grounds for the continued reproduction of Mount Sterling's economic development discourse. For this, May relies on a particularly instrumental program of discursive propagation: the Ambassadors Program. As he describes the project,

We need to work on the attitudes of our people. The Chamber [of Commerce] is starting an Ambassadors Program to educate people [so that] if somebody comes into the community these are people they can talk to. They can be versed in what they need to know. They can tell them that our daily supply of water is 1.8 million gallons or that our water treatment plant is capable of processing three million gallons a day, that our sewer system is capable of five million gallons a day. They can know things about the community and help sell the community. . . . It needs to be sold to the people so they can appreciate it. It's an education process to let people know what's happening and to get their attitudes positive.

The reproduction of coalition discourse thus requires the active shaping of attitudes such that Mount Sterling can be represented to mobile capital. May's words not only point to the power of discourse, they also raise questions over the modalities (Foucault 1972a) that would legitimate them. It is to this final question that we now turn.

Discursive Modalities: Position and Site

As we have seen, labor was not only unable to offer resistance to the coalition's discourse, its acquiescence rendered impossible the construction of a counterdiscourse. The result has been the discrediting, disempowerment, and virtual disappearance of organized labor in Mount Sterling. That such resistance did not take place is a testament to the power of who speaks the truth about Mount Sterling's future. We should not, however, fall victim to the implication that, in discussing the rights of individuals to speak, those without such credentials are described as operating under some sort of gag order. Rather, there are differences in the force of speaking, rooted in the modalities of the discursive matrix.

Two modalities are intertwined with the discursive regime established in Mount Sterling. The first, position, refers to the situated status that legitimates one's ability to speak. In Mount Sterling, those possessing the authority to construct and reproduce the economic development discourse are in elected or appointed positions in the business coalition. These positions include, but are not limited to, the mayor, the county judge/executive, the director of the EDO, and the chairperson of the MCIA. The state-legitimated validity of the coalition also extends to the institutional positions of its nonstate members, who, as noted earlier, are themselves appointed by local officials. Thus, the legitimacy of the state extends to both the MCIA and the EDO, either directly, through common membership, or indirectly, through the appointment process. Importantly, these actors have at their disposal a host of rights and resources they can draw on to join in the discourse. Perhaps most significantly for Mount Sterling is their ready access to the *MSA*. The paper was described by a former reporter, Steven Pyles, as being a champion of local capital. And indeed, the *MSA* repeatedly refused to publish articles about, or letters by, members of local unions (Bob Teegarden).

A second aspect of modality is that of site: What is the institutional site from which a person speaks and draws legitimacy? For elected officials site is usually a government office. For example, the judge/executive conducts business from the Montgomery County Court House, a large building located on the town's main square. The Court House's legitimacy stems not only from its impressive architecture and central location, but also from the institution that established it: the state. The state, in turn, gains its legitimacy from the ideology of representative democracy and through such instruments of power as the police and the legal apparatus.

Another site from which discourse emerges is the Bell House. An early nineteenth-century building that has been restored, the Bell House is home to the Chamber of Commerce, the EDO, the MCIA, and other smaller elements of the business coalition. Located on Main Street in downtown Mount Sterling, the Bell House shares in the light cast by the Court House's grand presence. The once decaying edifice now signals solidity, historicity, and continuity. The quasi-state groups it houses gain legitimacy through these signs, as well as from the restoration itself: arisen from the depths of decay, the Bell House stands as a landscape metaphor for the coalition's vision of Mount Sterling's future.

CONCLUSION

The past quarter century has witnessed major transformations in the capitalist world economy. The organization, methods, and geographies of production have undergone changes that have altered the economic fortunes of regions and countries around the world. In the United States, manufacturing operations have moved from traditional industrial areas in the northeast to southern states or third world countries in search of cheaper production costs and more friendly political environments. For many localities, competition between places for mobile capital has given way to growth politics, in which members of the local state and dependent capital cooperate to promote their areas to outside investors.

While the recognition of growth politics is not new, little attention has been devoted to the discourse of local economic development that has figured so prominently in and been so instrumental for the actions of business coalitions. In the case of Mount Sterling, the successful creation and implantation of a local economic development discourse by members of the business coalition was central to the construction of a political environment in which tensions between capital and organized labor were kept to a minimum. Through the discourse of community, the coalition was able to castigate oppositional forms that would question the harmonious identity it sought to create. What is more, labor in

Mount Sterling participated in this construction. Its ineffectiveness thus has everything to do with its position within the coalition's discourse.

Given that there is little if anything Mount Sterling unions could do to alter the course of either global restructuring or the strength of the local state-capital alliance, what might have been done to preserve some semblance of union autonomy? One option can be found in discursive interventions into the objects and modalities of discourse. For example, Mount Sterling's organized labor could have taken a more aggressive stance through the presentation of an alternative politics that emphasized redevelopment plans that did not reproduce conditions of dependency on mobile capital. Union leaders might also have attempted to recast the discursive object to include groups previously outside the coalition's definition of community. In fact, community could have been completely redefined such that economic development planning became a more democratic process. Such a strategy might have proceeded by pressing local officials to include more representatives from labor on the boards of the various development agencies.

In addition, labor might have simultaneously pursued another form of intervention focused on the sites of the coalition's discursive propagations. It is conceivable that the union could have obtained an office in the Bell House or in the downtown area near the Court House to take advantage of the legitimacy that these areas lend to statements made by the EDO, the mayor, or the county judge/executive. Unlike a redefinition of the discursive object, site intervention is limited in that it is largely reactive. But inasmuch as the coalition secured legitimacy from the ideological power vested in these sites, then interventions into those locations would constitute a form of spatial praxis.

On the other hand, such selected interventions may not be enough to overcome a much broader discourse, one that heralds the victory of capitalism at a global scale and requires localities to submit to capital's demands. Given this larger discourse, as well as the material limits faced by Mount Sterling's workers, is progressive social action an unrealizable goal? We think not, for though it may seem as if the current story binds hapless agents with the twin constraints of the discursive and the material, this does not imply that they together are inherently limiting qualities of agency. For to accept this would be to slide toward a model of human action stained by structural determinism, rendering resistance impossible.

Instead, we maintain that it is the recognition and deconstruction of discourse that currently holds the most promise for praxis. The identification of discourse immediately denaturalizes its material and ideational presuppositions, such that it becomes merely a contingently legitimated system of belief and communication whose power relies on its presentation as necessity. Yet in recognizing power discursively it is clear that discourse—despite its naturalization of social relations—is itself an unstable social construction that is dialectically embedded in equally unstable relations from which power diffuses. Thus a discursive limit is not a limit of agency but a contingency that can be constraining or enabling. It follows that an important task for praxis is to confront those seemingly transcendent constructions to expose their contingent limits to agency.

Those uncomfortable with the assertion that reality is defined through socially constructed discourse may counter that this formulation is one step away from discursive idealism. Such a charge rests on the assumption that one can exist in a position outside of discursive relations from which one can critique social life. This is most certainly not the case. Deconstruction itself is discursively produced and therefore never apolitical or independent of power. The process of deconstruction—of confronting a universalized and naturalized discursive system by unveiling its socially contingent character—therefore suggests the possibility of confronting one discourse with another.[7]

Finally, for those who would argue that deconstruction is merely ideational and therefore an ineffective form of resistance, we would offer instead the following: the emancipatory power of disassembling discourses comes not from the disassembly itself but rather from the *real* possibilities such activities produce. If deconstruction implies the construction of a new discourse, then it also implies a new space for social action. In this sense, the identification, deconstruction, and reconstruction of discourse is potentially a more effective means of resistance than discursive intervention. Reconstruction implies new rules for discursive relations, ones that overcome the limitations of the intervention model. Thus, labor in Mount Sterling would not have to acquire seats on appointed boards or obtain an office in the Bell House. It could, instead, use discourse against discourse in the goal of realizing its own self-identities.

NOTES

The authors extend thanks to Deborah Dixon, Wolfgang Natter, and Ted Schatzki for their helpful comments on this chapter.

1. Space prevents us from delineating in detail the various thinkers who, though differently, have come to argue this proposition. Any such listing, however, would include theorists such as de Certeau (1984), Foucault (1980a, 1986), Gregory (1993), Giddens (1984), Harvey (1989), Lefebvre (1979, 1991), Massey (1984, 1992), Pred (1984), Soja (1980, 1989), and Thrift (1981).

2. Interviewees in this analysis included: Monford Greer, former KitchenAid employee and member, UAW Local 1562; William Johnson, judge/executive, Montgomery County; Bert May, mayor, Mount Sterling; Steve Pyles, former reporter, *Mount Sterling Advocate*; Tom Reffit, former KitchenAid employee and president, UAW Local 1562; Clifford Stilz, local banker and member of Montgomery County Industrial Authority; Bob Teegarden, former KitchenAid employee and representative, UAW Local 1562; Larry Walters, former KitchenAid employee and member, UAW Local 1562; and Del White, director, Montgomery County Economic Development Office.

3. Discussions with local labor leaders called into question White's assertion of investment in the factory.

4. The corporation has a history of praising its workers, as the 1989 *Annual Report* essay titled "Responsibility," by CEO David Whitman, attests:

I would like to thank the entire Whirlpool family, the people who made this year possible. . . . I want to acknowledge the hard work and energy of our 39,000 employees worldwide and to thank each and every one of them for the dedication that has become a Whirlpool hallmark, from plant to plant and from continent to continent. . . . Because of the contribution, commitment and belief of all [our] people, Whirlpool enters the 1990's as a strong, energized competitor with a significant presence in the world economy. . . . The only possible source of true competitive advantage is our people. . . . We have a commitment to the enhancing of life . . . in plant communities. (Whirlpool *Annual Report* 1989)

5. For example, Harlan, in Eastern Kentucky—the site of Barbara Koppel's celebration of resistance by coal town women in her famous documentary film, *Harlan County, USA*—is over 120 miles from Mount Sterling.

6. In addition to highlighting the exclusionary character of the economic discourse prior to the plant's closing, Walters' quote also reveals the extent to which economic development discourses rely on a naturalized understanding of capitalism (Marx 1973; Smith 1990). As a result, the claims of labor are invalidated, as they are seen as inconsistent with reality. Workers therefore appear to be naive—if not irrational—for their reluctance to accept the natural conditions of their existence.

7. In Derrida's view, "what is called deconstruction" is the "effort to take this limitless context into account, to pay sharpest and broadest attention to context, and thus to an incessant movement of recontextualization" (1988, 136).

9

The Reproduction of Racial Differences in Educational Achievement: A Structurationist Analysis

Jeremy D. Browning

Across U.S. educational systems, African Americans and Latinos continue to produce lower test scores and grades when compared to white students (Hurn 1985, 140). Among the many types of supplementary programs that have been designed to help students excel in the classroom, few have had an impact on the proficiency levels of minority populations.[1] This ongoing reproduction of racial differences in educational achievement has confounded educators, in particular those in large urban school districts that contain significant concentrations of underachieving minority students (Louis and Miles 1990, 11).

In this chapter, I focus on the school district operating in the city of San Diego, California. This district, typical of many large urban school systems, has distinct racial disparities among students in terms of scholastic achievement. These achievement differences are pronounced throughout the various tiers of the school district but are particularly prominent at the elementary school level. My goal is to provide insight into the institutional forces that maintain these disparities. Specifically, I seek to comprehend how school district administrators interpreted persistent differences in educational achievement across races and how their explanations for this phenomenon were translated into policies that contributed to and reinforced the problem. Within the constraints of their job mandates, key institutional actors in the school district interpreted local educational problems to formulate strategies that affected the everyday educational experience of students. The emergence of educational strategies, I contend, reflected complex interconnections between structural constraints, human action, and local practices. These elements were recursively linked to forge a dynamic interdependency. At the core of my study is an important theoretic point: I contend that by examining these complex recursive interconnections, a substantial comprehension of the causal factors that reproduced differences in educational achievement across racial groups in San Diego can be obtained.

Anthony Giddens's theory of structuration provides the conceptual framework for this research. In his writing, Giddens (1981, 1984, 1985, 1991) develops this theory to investigate the recursive nature of human action and societal constraint. Unlike other perspectives that view structure and agency as essentially independent entities, structuration emphasizes their interconnections, or duality. Giddens (1984, 25) contends that "structural properties of social systems are both medium and outcome of the practices they recursively organize." Structures are viewed as rules and resources that actors draw on to (re)produce social action. At the same time, these structures are seen to constrain the type and amount of action possible by agents. This notion of structure as simultaneously constraining and enabling yields a sophisticated notion of causation, one that dissolves the artificial distinctions between micro and macro, society and agent that tend to be present in other theoretical perspectives (Giddens 1991, 204). For this study, local educators are presented as producing actions that affect educational strategies. Simultaneously, their organized actions are constrained by a variety of rules (e.g., the parameters within which they can function as employees of the school district). In the context of my case study analysis, this ceaseless tension between constraint and empowerment leads to distinct educational policies that critically affect achievement levels across races in the San Diego Unified School District.

BACKGROUND ON THE SAN DIEGO UNIFIED SCHOOL DISTRICT

The San Diego Unified School District has 107 elementary schools that have recently undergone a rapid ethnic transition. In 1976, 35.7 percent of elementary school students belonged to minority groups; by 1988, this had risen to 58.6 percent. Currently, the two largest ethnic groups are Latinos and African Americans, representing 23.4 percent and 17 percent of the total elementary school student enrollment, respectively (Community Relations and Integration Services Division 1988, A–4). The district is under a court order to mix racially its elementary schools, but there remains a distinct racial distribution to the student body (Map 9.1). There are fifteen schools where African American and Latino students represent 50 percent to 75 percent of the total enrollment; another nine schools have at least 76 percent African American and Latino students. All but one of these schools is clustered in the southeastern section of the school district. White students dominate most other schools, especially in the section of the

Map 9.1
**The Distribution of African American and Latino Students Attending Elementary
Schools in San Diego for Academic Year 1987–1988**

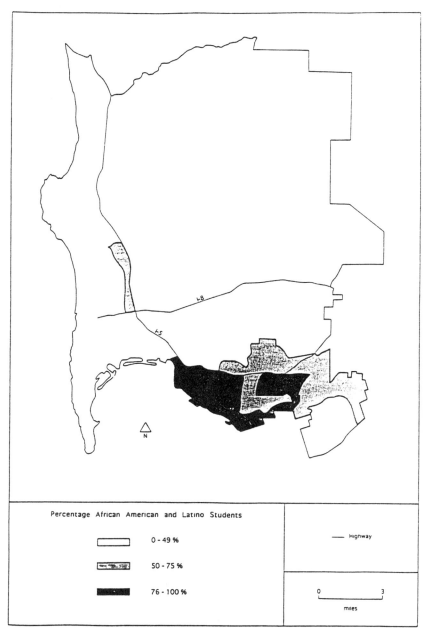

Source: Adapted from data in Community Relations and Integration Services Division,
1988 *Report of the San Diego Plan for Racial Integration 1987–88*, San Diego Unified
School District.

school district north of Interstate 8 (Community Relations and Integration Services Division 1988, A6–10).

Administrators in the San Diego Unified School District pride themselves on the uniformly high quality of education provided to schools in the system. The district is on record as being committed to increasing student achievement levels (Community Relations and Integration Services Division 1988). To accomplish this objective, administrators allocate more resources—supplies and funds—to schools with large enrollments and minority populations and operate a variety of educational programs. The cornerstone of these ameliorative programs was the Magnet School Program, a strategy begun in 1977 in response to a state court order mandating racial integration of schools in San Diego (Planning, Research, and Evaluation Division 1987). In this program, thirty-one racially imbalanced elementary schools were targeted with the intent of upgrading low scholastic achievement levels of minorities. These schools, predominantly African American and Latino, were concentrated in the less affluent neighborhoods of Southeastern San Diego. The goal was straightforward: to provide more personalized instruction for those with greatest need and to generate incentives for students to learn. These incentives consisted of making available role models for minority youth and incorporating high-technology tools—for example, computers—in the classroom (San Diego Schools 1987).

These programs have led to some improvement in test scores among elementary school students in the San Diego system. A majority now perform at or above the national norm in the Comprehensive Test of Basic Skills (CTBS) for reading, language, and math (Community Relations and Integration Services Division 1988, 40–41). However, the fact remains that elementary schools with high minority concentrations—in particular African Americans and Latinos—exhibited consistently below average achievement levels as measured by standardized tests throughout the 1980s. Conversely, elementary schools with predominantly white students achieved the highest test scores on the CTBS (Browning 1989, 70–74). These performance differentials between white and minority students indicate that efforts to reduce racial and ethnic disparities in achievement levels have been ineffective.[2]

A STRUCTURATIONIST FRAMEWORK IN THE REPRODUCTION OF RACIAL DIFFERENCES IN EDUCATIONAL ACHIEVEMENT

As numerous critics of structuration have suggested, applying structuration theory to the social world is a delicate enterprise (cf. Gregson 1987, 1989; Thrift 1983a). In my effort, I begin with a grounding of the duality of structure concept. Its two essential elements, recursively constructive of one another, are social structures and local agents. Social structures are the rules of, and resources for, education provided by federal, state, and local government to the San Diego Unified School District. Rules include policies mandating curricula and racial integration; guidelines for the operation of educational programs such as magnet schools; and plans for the long-range use of school facilities. Resources are the monies collected for the school district by a variety of sources, mainly state transfer payments and local property taxes (Community Relations and Integration Services Division 1988; Office of the Superintendent 1987). These rules and resources are the instantiated elements of everyday life that agents—educators and administrators in the San Diego school system—draw on to construct and implement educational programs. In this process, these instantiated elements both constrain and enable human action.

Local agents are a crucial part of the duality of structure. In this case study, they draw on a variety of rules and resources to (re)produce and transform school district practices. Local officials are empowered in their role as educational authorities by virtue of their employment in the school district's political and administrative hierarchy. By power, I mean the degree of control local educators have over the development of program guidelines, resource allocations, and the like. As knowledgeable agents, educators use this control to interpret educational needs and the appropriate system response. Simultaneously, however, these agents are constrained by the same rules and resources of the institution that gives them power. For example, jobs have clear mandates that define the limits to action. These forces that simultaneously constrain and enable key educators are a critical element of this analysis.

To break down the notion of agent power even further, I identify a power hierarchy in the local school district. The degree of control over educational decisions increases as an agent moves upward. At the top of the hierarchy are the school board members, constituting the political branch of the school system. They dictate the general ideology and management of the school district and are the least constrained of all agents. Below them on the hierarchy, in declining order of power, are the district superintendent, the assistant superintendents, and the area operation managers. These agents are part of the administrative branch of the school district. They have varying job powers and are answerable to those at the levels above them and, ultimately, the school board.

This notion of diminishing constraints imposed on actors situated higher up in this system does not imply that the school board members are constraint free. Rather, the school board is an operative unit whose function is most influenced by the operation of rules and resources that are externally imposed. For example, state mandates provide legal and ethical procedures that school systems incorporate into everyday practices. These mandates constrain the type and amount of practices available to school board members.

Giddens (1984, 28–34) suggests that actors draw on modalities of structuration in the process of reproducing systems of interaction. There are four modalities: symbolic, political, economic, and sanction. I view these modalities as the tangible elements of the educational system that local educators draw on to forward their interpretation of educational needs. In this study, the four modalities have distinct characteristics. The symbolic modality is the educational discourse of educators. By this, I mean that in everyday interaction, educators use carefully scripted rhetoric to indicate support of certain programs and financial allocations. The political modality is the various procedures and bylaws that local actors draw on to secure legislation that produces new education programs. The third modality—economic—is the budgetary appropriations allocated to programs by educators. Finally, the manner in which educators are able to control actions in the school district through procedures and meetings is an example of the sanction modality. I contend that these modalities are not mutually exclusive. They can be used simultaneously, for example, where educational rhetoric (symbolic) is used to secure new legislation (political). Often one modality is most substantially drawn on in any given circumstance. The modalities enable educators to express, justify, and control actions. Those educators higher in the power hierarchy, in general, have the greatest potential to use modalities to dictate interaction within the system, thereby advancing their educational philosophy.

METHODOLOGY

This case study of persistent racial and ethnic disparities in educational achievement scores in the San Diego school system is based on a series of interviews with school officials conducted in 1989 in conjunction with other published material pertaining to school district operations.[3] The interviewees were local educators—school board members, assistant superintendents, and area operation managers—who were responsible for all major decisions regarding educational problems and policy initiatives. There were five school board members, four assistant superintendents, and eight area operation managers. The interviews were performed by telephone, covering employment responsibilities of the officials, successes and failures of the district, and causal factors of interracial achievement disparities. School board members forwarded their political agendas through weekly meetings where policy decisions on racial integration, scholastic achievement, and other educational topics were made. Assistant superintendents and area operation managers implemented policy directives from the school board while simultaneously responding to the concerns of principals and teachers in the elementary schools (L. Villegas).

LOCAL INTERPRETATIONS OF RACIAL DIFFERENCES IN EDUCATIONAL ACHIEVEMENT

Within the San Diego Unified School District, the wide range of local educators across the school board hierarchy interpreted the reasons for the reproduction of racial differences in educational achievement. With these interpretations, they drew on guidelines for the operation of educational programs to implement policies that constitute solutions. In this manner, these agents have been instrumental in maintaining existing educational practices. In the San Diego case, agents at the top of the power hierarchy—school board members—were most crucial in setting an educational agenda that focused on the positive attributes of the school district. These politicians used educational rhetoric to express the notion that minority student underachievement was not a significant problem. In this process, these elected officials have tended to view achievement levels as good. "Test scores are not bad and are certainly better than the state average" (S. Davis). To this group of educators, racial differences in achievement levels were explainable by typical grade distributions: "People must accept that test scores will not be brilliant for all students" (A. Armstrong).

The ideology of these elected officials—deemphasizing racial differences in achievement levels—filtered down to administrators lower on the power hierarchy of the school board. In interviews with administrators, three of four assistant superintendents and six of eight area operation managers expressed opinions that students performed "very well in test scores" (J. Liddell). Many schools were categorized as "high-performance" (B. Hawthorne), while the district has "wonderful curricula and excellent outreach programs to families" (F. Callahan). These ideas were communicated in social interaction through the symbolic modality. Local educators used a discourse of positive educational rhetoric to express their belief that students attending the San Diego Unified School District had a bright future.

What did these local educators have to gain from denying the problem of minority underachievement? The members of the school board represented distinct political districts (Map 9.2). Board members Ann Armstrong, Jim Roache, Kay Davis, and Susan Davis served areas that were predominantly white. Of the twenty-four elementary schools that contain at least 50 percent Latino and African American Students (Map 9.1), only two were located in District C, while three were in District D. Districts A and B contain none of these schools. I contend that the parents of white students in these four districts were unlikely to favor new educational programs that focus on minority students primarily located in District E and funded perhaps by new taxes. Given this public opinion, I believe that these school board members minimized the significance of minority underachievement to reflect the attitudes of their constituents. However, as I now discuss, this problem was so apparent that these agents had to construct multiple lines of explanation to dominate the educational discourse in San Diego.

On delving further into the issue of interracial scholastic differences, local agents admitted to being aware that a core of African American and Latino students continue to underachieve relative to the rest of the school population. Their explanation, however, identified the students themselves as the source of the problem. These students were presented as "not prepared for school" (S. Davis) because they came from culturally deprived families. By culturally deprived, educators meant that these families were frequently single parent and were not interested in the positive role education could have on career opportunities. Local officials noted that only by changing the ideas of minority families and students could achievement levels be improved. In this perspective, minority

Map 9.2
Political Districts of the San Diego School Board

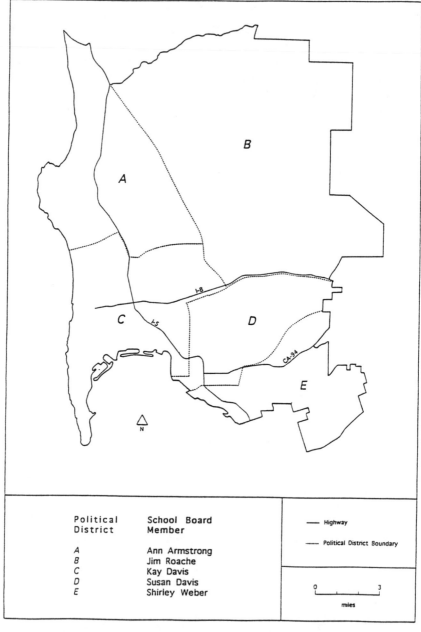

Political District	School Board Member
A	Ann Armstrong
B	Jim Roache
C	Kay Davis
D	Susan Davis
E	Shirley Weber

—— Highway

------ Political District Boundary

0 _____ 3
miles

Source: Adapted from data in Office of the Superintendent, 1987, *San Diego Unified School District: Statistical Report 1987–88*, San Diego Unified School District.

students needed to be taught "self-esteem and the importance of education" (R. Anderson) to make up for the "breakdown of family structure" (J. Liddell) and the "culture of minority families" (C. Hopper). The issue of scholastic underachievement, consequently, was not linked to society or the educational district; the problem as perceived by these educators was a set of cultural predilections that minority families embraced.

This interpretation was communicated in public forums throughout the school district. It represented a distinct ideology, one that blamed the victim's supposedly deficient cultural background. With this ideology of cultural deprivation, local officials argued that minority students came to school ill prepared and unable to cope with the rigors of the educational system. This explanation, I would contend, built on the original denial of the minority underachievement phenomenon. These educators were suggesting that even if there was a problem, it was not due to policies of the educational system. On the contrary, blame could be affixed to the students themselves. In this manner, the educators were absolved of any culpability.

This interpretation, however, was not without potential problems. Simply put, this ideology cast doubts on existing ameliorative programs whose effectiveness appeared to be minimal. To head off this perception, educators espoused the idea that new and innovative programs were necessary to offset the impact of culturally deprived backgrounds. It was through these programs that educators translated their interpretation of minority underachievement into policy. In so doing, they also reinforced the notion that their educational expertise was indispensable. They argued that by funding educational programs, the school district could be a safety net for minority students. To these educators, these programs needed to emphasize the importance of education and academic role models to compensate for cultural deprivation. There was widespread belief that "minority kids see academic role models with integration and try to copy them" (L. Kidd) and that "to solve problems we need to involve parents to emphasize to them the importance of education" (R. Anderson). With these programs, local agents emphasized their crucial role in educating children. In such a manner, both politicians and administrators justified their respective roles in the school district.

At the core of this educational corrective strategy was the Magnet School Program. The philosophy underpinning this program was the belief that white students, bussed in from other neighborhoods, would act as academic role models, enhancing the educational atmosphere of minority-dominated schools. Typically, these educators believed that "the District has a good magnet program that helps integration and standards (L. Kidd). This would supposedly galvanize minority students to produce higher test scores, thereby solving the underachievement problem.

The majority group of educators was able to implement this perspective through the Magnet School Program because they controlled the power relations in the school district. In particular, four of five school board members supported the ideology of cultural deprivation. These politicians used their power in two ways to influence the operational guidelines of Magnet Schools. First, they used educational rhetoric in speeches and interviews to emphasize to constituents that minority achievement levels would only increase if these students incorporated the educational values of whites. Second, school board members, by virtue of their place atop the educational hierarchy, had the greatest control of any agents over educational procedures. This authority enabled them to legitimate their educational philosophy of eradicating racial differences in educational achievement through the Magnet School Program. In doing so, these educators also reinforced the notion that their expertise in the field of education was essential to solving academic problems.

While the majority of local actors in the school district communicated the ideology of cultural deprivation, a handful attempted to counteract it. Of the seventeen local agents interviewed, four interpreted racial differences in scholastic achievement as the responsibility of the educational system. Dr. Shirley Weber is an African American member of the school board. She represents District E (Map 9.2), which contains nineteen elementary schools with at least 50 percent African American and Latino students. Unlike her colleagues, she believed that "we are not doing a great job. . . . Test scores are too low. . . . Kids are at-risk of failing" (S. Weber). This small group of agents argued that to give minority students a chance to achieve scholastic levels similar to whites, the learning system of the district must be transformed. By opening up the educational process to new styles of teaching and learning, minority students could reach their full potential. Information is not getting through to students. . . . We have to restructure curricula, both types of courses and the way we deliver them" (E. Cisnersos). "The system is still structured as it was in the 1950's and this needs change. We need to cater more to minority groups with varying modes of instruction such as lectures, one-on-one, and the like" (L. Villegas).

This small group of educators contested not only the interpretation of racial differences in achievement levels, but also the corrective strategy adopted by the dominant set of local officials. They were able to use their power as employees of the school district to argue that the educational philosophy of the Magnet School Program was part of a system inherently biased against minority students. "Kids do not want to learn. . . . Programs have poor institutional interfacing. . . . Kids do not bond with this school environment" (L. Villegas). Their negative perception of Magnet Schools was supported by available data on achievement levels for enrolled students. For example, at Encanto Elementary School, operating as a Magnet School since 1978, white students consistently achieved significantly higher grades in standardized tests for reading, language, and math than minority students. At the same time, there was no strong indication that minority student scores were improving over time (Planning, Research, and Evaluation Division 1987, 17–20). To many parents of minority students, academic role models had not worked in this school. While this small group of educators used these data to contest the prevailing ideology, their small numbers and relative lack of influence—only one school board member supported the minority opinion—prevented any modifications of the Magnet School Program's operational guidelines. As with the process of interpretation of achievement disparities across races, the lack of power in this group prevented their educational philosophy from being implemented. In the end, the Magnet School Program was reproduced to reflect the ideology of the majority group of educators.

CONCLUSIONS

In this chapter, I focused on the forces responsible for the reproduction of racial differences in educational achievement in the San Diego school system. Specifically, I analyzed the constantly evolving structuration process that recursively linked societal constraints, human action, and local practices to reproduce scholastic underachievement by a core of Latino and African American students. In this process, a majority of local educators advocated the ideology that minority underachievement was due to the students' culturally deprived background. This interpretation was used to advance a corrective strategy that placed the Magnet School Program at its core. This program was designed to use high-achieving white students as academic role models to galvanize minority children to produce higher test scores. Despite their efforts, a small group of local agents voicing the concerns of the African American and Latino communities were unable to modify this dominant interpretation of underachievement.

This division of beliefs between local educators was an example of locally based conflict, which Giddens contends is an integral feature of the structuration process (1981, 29). In the San Diego case, conflict was played out between two groups of educators. The majority group—in particular four of five school board members—used the symbolic modality to communicate through public meetings and published operational guidelines the rhetoric of cultural deprivation as the causal factor of minority educational underachievement. Those who disagreed with this perspective were too few in numbers and lacked sufficient power—especially at the school board level—to contest the dominant ideology.

However, I would contend that the majority group of local agents was not operating without any constraints during this ongoing process of interpretation. State mandates provided the legal and ethical procedures for the everyday governance of the school district. These mandates operated in two ways to constrain the dominant group of officials: they limited the amount of control over educational programs and provided the means for the minority group of educators to contest the prevailing ideology through participation in public meetings. While this minority group failed to transform this ideology, available rules of the school district enabled its contestation. If the minority group was able to modify the balance of power relations among local educators, its educational philosophy could be advanced. This would be an example of the recursive nature of the social world. Local actors would use their access to rules to transform them, critically affecting achievement levels. However, during the time period of this study, this did not occur.

In conclusion, structuration provided a good conceptual framework for eliciting the complexity of forces that reproduced racial differences in educational achievement. I suggest that the duality of structure concept enabled a sophisticated notion of causation to be unearthed. With the artificial distinction between structure and agency eradicated, I was able to reveal how human action and social structures conjoined in a ceaseless process of constraint and enablement to create a distinct social outcome. Integral to this explanation was the role of power (i.e., the degree of control local educators had over program guidelines and financial allocations). School board members had the most power and used it in social interaction to control the dialogue about, and policies toward, racial differences in educational achievement. Therefore, despite the thoughtful and well-documented concerns of research (cf. Gregson 1987, 1989; Thrift 1983a), the careful and critical adapting of structuration permitted fresh insight into a complex social phenomenon.

NOTES

1. Statistics compiled by the U.S. Department of Education indicate that educational programs have narrowed the learning gap between whites, African Americans, and Latinos. However, the minority groups continue to underachieve significantly relative to whites. For example, the percentage of fourth graders reading at the basic proficiency level in 1974–1975 was 69 percent for whites, 33 percent for African Americans, and 33 percent for Latinos. By 1987–1988, these percentages were 68 percent, 39 percent, and 47 percent, respectively. These racial disparities are reproduced in other subjects— for example, science, math, and history—and are maintained throughout the students' educational career (National Center for Education Statistics 1991, 112–121).

2. The elementary schools of the San Diego Unified School District contain significant numbers of African American and Latino students, as well as smaller concentrations of Asians, Indochinese, and Filipino children. The educational performance of these three smaller ethnic groups is relatively good. Therefore, when I discuss minority underachievement I am referring specifically to the educational problems of African American and Latino elementary school students in San Diego.

3. Interviewees who participated in this 1989 case study included: R. Anderson, Area Operations Manager, San Diego Unified School District; A. Armstrong, School Board member, San Diego Unified School District; F. Callahan, Area Operations Manager, San Diego Unified School District; E. Cisnersos, Assistant Superintendent, San Diego Unified School District; S. Davis, School Board member, San Diego Unified School District; B. Hawthorne, Area Operations Manager, San Diego Unified School District; C. Hopper, Assistant Superintendent, San Diego Unified School District; L. Kidd, Area Operations Manager, San Diego Unified School District; J. Liddell, Area Operations Manager, San Diego Unified School District; L. Villegas, Area Operations Manager, San Diego Unified School District; and S. Weber, School Board member, San Diego Unified School District.

10

A Critical Analysis of Gender-based Property Relations in Ghana

Cherub Antwi-Nsiah and James O. Huff

This is a story about the marginalization and the empowerment of women in Ghana. The story is neither linear in its development, nor is it the same for women who find themselves in very different locales and must begin their struggle within widely divergent social and economic circumstances. The story is therefore told in many voices, all unique in their personal circumstances and outcomes. Ghanaian women, however, are not alone in their struggle for identity, in their struggle to gain control over their lives. They are bound together and their lives are embedded within exploitive social systems based on rules, conventions, and beliefs that subordinate women. These macroforces operate to siphon off the life force of women in Ghana and relegate them to faceless and powerless anonymity.

The popular belief is that women have substantial power and influence in Ghana (Fiawoo 1978; Manu 1984)—a view reinforced by images presented by the media both in and outside Ghana (Bentsi-Enchill 1979; United Nations 1975). These images are myths. The media's view may be true for a small segment of the urban female population. The majority of Ghanaian women live in rural areas where they exist at subsistence levels, denied access to resources both by tradition and by recent changes in tradition.

Education is clearly an important resource that affects power relations in the workplace, in the job market, and within the household. Males currently have the educational advantage in every occupational category in Ghana, as shown

Table 10.1

Ghana: Percentage Distribution of Workers by Levels of Education in Selected Occupations, 1984

Occupation/Sex	Level of Education			
	None	Primary	Middle	Secondary & Above
Agriculture				
Male	57.2	9.2	30.9	2.7
Female	72.3	9.9	17.4	0.4
Sales Worker				
Male	36.3	4.5	42.2	17.1
Female	59.5	9.1	28.7	2.1
Production and Related Worker				
Male	27.0	8.1	57.5	7.4
Female	62.6	7.5	27.8	2.1
All Major Occupations				
Male	45.5	7.9	37.3	9.3
Female	64.3	9.1	23.3	3.3

Source: Based on the *1984 Population Census of Ghana: Demographic and Economic Characteristics, Total Country*, Ghana Statistical Service, Accra, 1987, Table 16, p. 73. Cited by National Council on Women and Development, "Non-formal Education for Women: Situational Analysis Indicators," Document I: GHA/85/006, National Council on Women and Development, Accra, 1990, Table 4.10, p. K–117.

in Table 10.1. This advantage becomes the basis for gender inequalities in power relations insofar as those with higher education are perceived to have more resources at their disposal and are accorded higher status.

This example, which could be augmented easily by data from other aspects of life, leaves little doubt that severe gender inequalities exist in Ghana. Our concern in this chapter is to look more closely at the social structures contributing to the perpetuation of the systematic subordination of women within Ghanaian society. We will present a familiar account of women who are defined in terms of their function and in terms of their subordinate position within a male-dominated culture. Within this scenario, however, there is evidence of a less familiar countertheme of women beginning to take greater control of their lives. The women we interviewed are tired of doing all the work and receiving little in return. They are converting their frustration into constructive action. In the empirical analysis that follows, we focus on the reproduction and the transformation of socially constructed rules giving males control over property, a decision that follows directly from Giddens's analysis of property relations within class-divided societies (Giddens 1981). Property relations in Ghana, as part of a class-divided society in a world increasingly dominated by capitalism, are at the very core of the Ghanaian social structure. Property, particularly in the form of land, serves as the material basis for the male-dominated power relations contributing to easily observed gender inequalities.

We begin our studies with a historical account of the changing nature of property relations in Ghana and the implications for women caught up in these changes. This material provides a critical contextual basis for understanding how Ghanaian women are taking control of their lives through the acquisition of personal property, actions that are not only transforming traditional inheritance systems, but the very fabric of the society itself.

The empirical analysis of property relations is based on data from a personally administered survey of the experiences, attitudes, and intentions of 104 women and 100 men. These heads of households are drawn from a cross section of kinship and class divisions in Ghanaian society and from a wide variety of rural and urban localities. Although every story is unique, the data show that women and men are beginning to circumvent traditional, male-dominated rules governing property transfer to gain increasing control over tangible assets. Structuration theory, augmented by closer attention to patterns of male domination, provides a useful vocabulary for understanding this significant social change.

THEORETICAL FOUNDATIONS

As with others who are drawn to structuration theory (Giddens 1981, 1984), we found that previous structural theories provided valuable insights into the influence of social structure on individual circumstances, but failed to capture the importance of individual action in the transformation of social institutions. Structuration theory provides a means of comprehending and analyzing this essential duality: "Analyzing the structuration of social systems means studying the modes in which such systems, grounded in the knowledgeable activities of situated actors who draw upon the rules and resources in the diversity of action contexts, are produced and reproduced in interaction" (Giddens 1981, 25).

The problem facing anyone interested in using structuration theory as a guide for empirical analysis is one of translating Giddens's general propositions into propositions that relate to specific social structures that mediate and are reproduced through particular kinds of situated practices. Our main concern in this chapter is to understand the reproduction of social structures of male domination

in Ghanaian society and more specifically to understand changing property relations and gender inequalities in access to and control over resources.

In *A Contemporary Critique of Historical Materialism*, Giddens (1981) makes
a number of insightful observations on the structuration of class-divided societies
that speak directly to the Ghanaian experience. A particularly important observation is that "in non-capitalist societies coordination of authoritative resources
forms the determining axis of societal integration and change" (Giddens 1981,
4). More specifically, "tradition and kinship continue to play a fundamental role
in societal integration" and are "of pervasive importance in the structuration of
social relationships" (Giddens 1981, 162).

This is not to say that allocative resources in the form of property play an
inconsequential role in the structuring of Ghanaian society. Property relations
are bound up with "the modes of organization of kinship and tradition that . . .
are the chief foundations of the dialectic of control in non-capitalist societies"
(Giddens 1981, 103). Two fundamental insights are that the "chief form of
private property in the means of production in class-divided societies is *land*"
(Giddens 1981, 113) and that a critical feature of land, relative to capital, is its
low alienability. Land is fixed in place, which reinforces the emergence of social
systems/communities with "high presence availability," low time-space distanciation, and high levels of social integration (Giddens 1981, 114).

Given the central importance of land as a resource in class-divided societies,
any change in accepted patterns of land transfer and control signal a major
deviation from traditional norms. In his analysis of capital-induced transformations of class-divided societies, Giddens identifies the "*commodification of
urban land*" as a fundamental transformation threatening the security of tradition
in class-divided societies (Giddens 1981, 152–153). These transformations in
property relations are the unacknowledged cause as well as the unintended consequences of changes in the actual transfer of properties within a class-divided
society like Ghana.

The irony is that Giddens could be so perceptive when it comes to a critical
analysis of the changing nature of property relations under the logic of capitalism
and so blind to the logic of patriarchy that dominates the structuration of traditional social structures based on kinship. While others have criticized Giddens
for his insensitivity to gender relations (see Murgatroyd 1989 for a critique of
Giddens in this regard), the larger failure is to ignore patriarchy as a fundamental
structural principle. This represents a serious omission that cannot be ignored
when analyzing the structuration of Ghanaian society. As shown in Figure 10.1,
a dynamic tension exists between Ghana's economic system, which is being
structured in accordance with the logic of capital, and Ghana's social system,
which is still heavily influenced by the logic of patriarchy.

Once patriarchy is added to the theoretical mix, several abstractions in Giddens's theory of structuration become much more accessible and useful in the
analysis of gender-based property relations in Ghana. The inherent contradiction
between the logic of patriarchy and the logic of capital moves to center stage in

Figure 10.1
Capitalism and Patriarchy in the Reproduction of Ghanaian Society

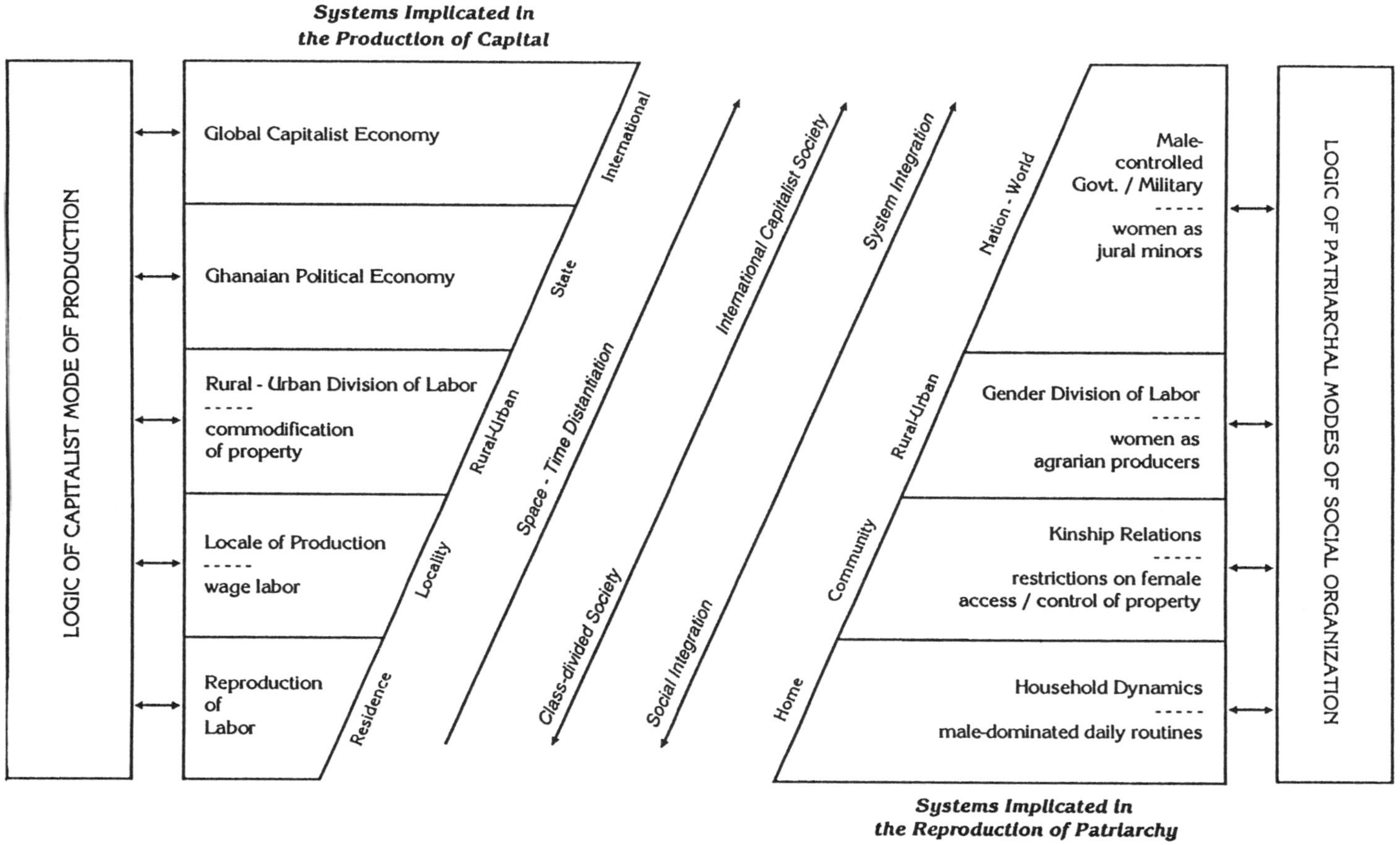

LOGIC OF PATRIARCHAL MODES OF SOCIAL ORGANIZATION

Systems Implicated in the Reproduction of Patriarchy

Male-controlled Govt. / Military
- - - -
women as jural minors

Gender Division of Labor
- - - -
women as agrarian producers

Kinship Relations
- - - -
restrictions on female access / control of property

Household Dynamics
- - - -
male-dominated daily routines

Nation - World

System Integration

Rural-Urban

Community

Home

International Capitalist Society

Social Integration

Class-divided Society

Systems Implicated in the Production of Capital

International

State

Rural-Urban

Locality

Residence

Space - Time Distanltation

Global Capitalist Economy

Ghanaian Political Economy

Rural - Urban Division of Labor
- - - -
commodification of property

Locale of Production
- - - -
wage labor

Reproduction of Labor

LOGIC OF CAPITALIST MODE OF PRODUCTION

the examination of structural change. These contradictions find their expression most clearly in the transformation of "land as property" relations as male-dominated rules of access and control are confronted by the commodification of land (particularly in urban areas).

Giddens's distinction between social integration involving "face-to-face interaction, a primary manifestation of time-space *presence* in social organization" and system integration "expressed as relations between collectivities" (Giddens 1981, 29) also comes into focus. The logic of patriarchy informs and is maintained by social integration, whereas the logic of capital is intertwined with system integration. The implication is that gender inequalities arising from the subordination of women in Ghanaian society are situated most clearly at the level of the household and in the durée of day-to-day experience. Within the local community, male-dominated rules governing the intergenerational transfer of property (i.e., kinship-based inheritance rules) are critical to the reproduction of gender inequality.

On the agency side, however, Ghanaian women as knowledgeable actors are endeavoring to gain increased control over their lives through the acquisition of property. The resulting structuration of property relations is facilitated by the dynamic tension between the logic of capital and the logic of patriarchy. The commodification of land is serving as a vital but largely unacknowledged condition for the acquisition of land by Ghanaian women. Women and men, through their actions, are challenging and changing the very structure of property relations. As women, in particular, become increasingly involved in the purchase and sale of property, an important, unanticipated consequence is the breakdown of traditional inheritance systems. Following Giddens, we argue that this breakdown is deeply implicated in the restructuring of Ghanaian society.

A HISTORY OF PROPERTY RELATIONS IN GHANA

An overview of the social organization of Ghanaian society is necessary to understand the basis for existing gender inequalities in access to and control over property. The social organization of the people, including property entitlement and transfer, is strongly influenced by the kinship system. There are two main systems in Ghana: matrilineal and patrilineal. The ethnic groups in Northern Ghana are patrilineal, and the Akan of Southern Ghana are matrilineal (see Map 10.1).

In the patrilineal societies, descent and inheritance are through the paternal line. The oldest son of the senior wife has first and major claim over his father's property upon the latter's death. Although the senior daughter gets the estate of her mother, she competes with maternal aunts and her female siblings, who also have claims (Robertson 1990, 145). Women with children therefore are better off regarding property rights because children inherit property and are required to take care of their mothers. Women in the patrilineal society do not inherit

Map 10.1
Patrilineal and Matrilineal Divisions in Ghana

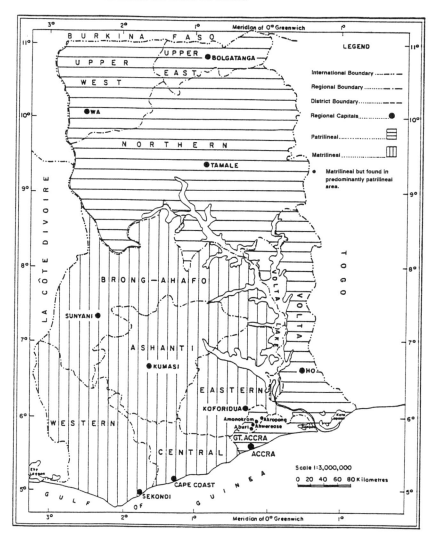

land, although they may have contributed to its acquisition. In cases where women have acquired land through gifts, they usually accept it in their sons' name (Bukh 1979; Robertson 1990).

In the matrilineal society, distribution of title is through females, but it is not necessarily for females. Descent and inheritance pass to males through the maternal line. Children are not members of their father's family. In fact, the natural or biological father is just the genitor rather than the social father or pater. The maternal uncle has the role of pater. In the matrilineal system, women hold property in trust for their sons. When the biological father dies, the wife's family has custody of the children while the man's family keeps the property. A matrilineal widow can be driven out of her home upon the death of the husband, from a home and property to which she may have contributed a significant amount of her time and money. Nor do a man's children inherit his property; the matrilineal descendants of his mother do. Therefore a man's successors are usually his brothers, or his sister's sons, not his wife or children. Generally, a woman's children and her matrikin inherit from her as the trustholder. In these societies women are able to acquire individual property, and they enjoy higher status and power than women in patrilineal systems. Because demands on their labor usually do not enable women to farm large plots, however, their holdings are usually much smaller than those of the men.

Precolonial Ghana

In the precolonial Ghanaian economy, land was the most important factor of production, and the system of land ownership determined the structure of the economy. Land was not held privately but was owned by the whole community. Members of lineages had only user rights over the land (Birmingham et al. 1967, 252).

In the predominantly Akan matrilineal societies, the leaders of the community were in charge of the land. The common view of Akan land tenure is a communal system in which the individual can never acquire more than a farming right or usufruct. In these societies, the *abusua* or lineage continued through its female members. The *Abusua Panyin*, the head of the linage, was the *asaasewura* or land custodian. This individual, usually male, was in charge of administering the lineage property, including the allocation of the *abusua asaase*, the family rights to use land, to lineage members. He also approved marriages and divorces of lineage members.

In the patrilineal societies, the priests were in charge of the land and performed rites to ensure fertility of the land. The priest or community leader was regarded as the owner or the caretaker of the land in whom was vested the right to make grants of land use. Access to a fair share of available land was the right of every member of the community. Since land was owned by the whole community, the possession of unsufructuary title was the highest form of land right an individual could have (Birmingham et al. 1967). This land policy was designed to protect against artificial scarcity and to ensure that land did not accumulate in the hands of only a few people (Hymer 1969, 3).

Although everyone had user (cultivation) rights to land, individual cultivators in both types of society held the land as if they were the owners. In cases where the individuals were the first to cultivate the *kwaei* or forest, they actually passed on the land to their heirs, even to the extent of giving land gifts to those who would normally not inherit from them such as wives and sons. There also were cases in which the land was sold outright (Vercruijsse 1988, 39). However, this type of ownership varies from present-day concepts about the ownership of private property in the sense that during the precolonial era, one had to be a subject of the chief, the *Omanhene*, to own land—outsiders were excluded. The sale of land also required the consent of the *Omanhene*, as well as the youngest member of the family, who had to perform a symbolic act to show consent. Possession of land also involved substantive obligations to the *abusua* and the *Omanhene*, in the form of military service, labor services, and taxes in kind or in money. Private property ownership in present-day Ghana does not have these restrictions, although services of different kinds are still expected.

On the legal level, the individual ownership of land, as with other immovable property, was limited to exceptional cases. This was ensured by the rule that upon the death intestate of a person, his self-acquired property would become family property. Thus individual property, in the absence of testamentary gifts to individuals, would forever become family property (Bentsi-Enchill 1964, 81 cited by Vercruijsse 1988, 44). In sum, the *abusua* in essence prevented the tenure security of individuals, although individuals continued their attempts to increase the security with which they held their lands.

Contrary to the popular belief that matrilineal women had sufficient access to land and other resources, as well as the right to pass on their accumulated resources to their children, women in both matrilineal and patrilineal societies had limited ownership and no control over any type of property in precolonial Ghana. Ownership of land was a male phenomenon. A woman's relationship to land during this time was simply as a user; she had cultivated rights but could not own land in her own right. Although wives contributed substantially to husbands' farms, they were aware that they were not working on joint enterprises, and they expected other compensation for their labor. Returns to investment in farm development could be in the form of food crops, cash, land, or other assistance for the establishment of separate properties; ultimately it could include the transfer of ownership of the farm following the death of the owner (Okali 1975).

Colonial and Postindependence Changes in Traditional Land Tenure

Ghana's first contact with Europeans was in 1471 (*Ghana Today* 1983, 5). Each European power that entered the Gold Coast—the Portuguese, French,

English, Swedes, Danes, and the Dutch—built forts and castles, with the exception of the French and English, who conducted their trade from ships (Hymer 1969, 11).

The actual process of incorporating Ghana into the sphere of exchange did not take place until the middle of the eighteenth century (Wallerstein 1976, 32–50), when the country began to trade gold, ivory, salt, palm oil, rubber, and coffee. Exchange and commerce set the stage for further development of merchant capital in Ghana. The basic change in the economy at this time was the change from production for use to production for exchange and the replacement of the barter system by monetary transactions; there was very little interference with the precapitalist mode of production (Howard 1978, 20).

Competition in international trade and the spread of the industrial revolution outside Great Britain increased the demand for raw materials. In Ghana, the response was an expansion in the production of palm oil, rubber, coffee, and gold. Palm oil continued to be the leading export crop until the fall of world market prices of palm oil in 1885 led to a search for new sources of export production. In addition, foreign mining companies started investing in mines (Birmingham et al. 1967, 257).

Cocoa was the most successful of the new crops introduced into the Gold Coast in the 1890s (Cambridge History of Africa 1985, 262). It was first grown on the Akwapim Ridge (Hill 1963, 167). Hard currency was introduced into the Ghanaian economy in 1913. The monetization of the economy facilitated trade in commodities. Coupled with the demand for land for cocoa production, the availability of currency also led to the sale of land previously not for sale.

The introduction of cocoa brought a significant change in the value of land. Land was sold for private use as farmers sought to expand cash crop production. Cocoa crop production was a predominantly male activity; women dealt with subsistence farming. The increase in the sale of land as more farmers cultivated cocoa, coupled with population growth, caused an exhaustion of local supplies of land on the Akwapim Ridge. In an attempt to regulate land sales, the Colonial government in 1894 proposed the Crown Land's Bill and a subsequent Land's Bill in 1897. These bills did not interfere with peasant user rights to land, but they attempted to regulate the rights of chiefs to make grants of land to foreigners (Vercruijsse 1988).

By the 1890s, an influx of migrants from the Gold Coast's northern territories and French West Africa provided much needed labor, particularly for Akan women, and the number of autonomous female farmers increased during this time. Mikell (1986, 71) states that "by keeping such property distinct from that of husbands and brothers, rural Ghanaian women acquired an autonomy unprecedented before or since that time." Unlike their matrilineal counterparts, however, patrilineal females faced restrictions in gaining access to land.[1] The result of the economic changes just described for these women was an increase in responsibilities both on and off farm with eroding access to resources.

The first shift in inheritance and transfer patterns among the Akan occurred when monies gained from operating profits from privately owned matrilineal farms, with the approval of the matrilineage, were used for the education of sons. Some of the farms were even passed on to sons (Hill 1963, 129). (All these transfers had to be made during the lifetime of the individual giving the gift. If a person died before actually handing over the land, it reverted to the linage.) During this period Akan women began to acquire small farms primarily as gifts from their husbands, although some were able to purchase their own farms (Okali 1983, 172). However, women, if married, were responsible for contributing a portion of their labor to the conjugal household by working on family food farms as well as their husband's cocoa farms. The inherent limits on their labor restricted women's ability to expand their own farms or acquire new ones.

The fall in the world market price of cocoa in 1929 lead to a depression in the Gold Coast, which was then dependent mainly on cocoa exports for revenue (Hill 1963; Prah 1976). During this period male profits from cocoa farming fell. In consequence, many men abandoned cocoa farming and migrated to the cities. Because there was thus less pressure on Akan women to contribute labor to men's cocoa farms, and they had greater access to land (Mikell 1990, 24), Akan women were able to expand existing farms and acquire new ones.

While many women had intended to transfer personal farms to their children, especially daughters, the implied transformation of male-dominated property relations did not happen. In fact, many of the gains that women had made prior to independence were lost in the period immediately following independence. Three reasons have been suggested for this situation. The first reason is that because of the condition and fragmented nature of women's farms, they were passed on as food farms, which by definition were family farms. Second, it has been suggested that as the economic decline deepened in the 1960s, the *abusua* or matrilineage may have appropriated private farms, if they were viable, and passed them on to brothers and sons, rather than the intended female heirs, because of the traditional emphasis of males as heirs to income-producing property (Mikell 1986, 74; 1990, 25). Another possible reason was the spate of bush fires that destroyed many cocoa farms in Ghana; unlike the men, women were unable to reinvest in their farms. In the end, women had few farms to pass on to their daughters. Their intentions were circumscribed by limitations on their resources.

More broadly, lack of education left all Ghanaian women with few viable alternatives to farming. Those with trading and marketing links abandoned rural areas and moved to the towns. However, women trading in urban areas were also affected by the economic collapse and had to depend more on their husbands (Mikell 1990, 25).

In short, the colonial era and early postindependence period saw development of private ownership that did not exist during traditional times, including ownership and control of land by women. Historical accounts show that some matrilineal men started giving land and proceeds of sales to their children, though the recipients were sons and not daughters (Vercruijsse 1988). Although female farms often were intended for female and male children, the data suggest that this transfer often was not accomplished (Vercruijsse 1988). It can be argued, therefore, that at the end of the colonial period there were individual or agency moves to overcome systemic constraints on female property ownership, but these were not very successful.

The Current Status of Property Relations

Presently, private property can be individual or lineage owned in Ghana. However, land is increasingly moving from lineage property to the government and to individuals as lineage heads continue the sale of lineage lands, particularly in Accra. The sale of land to the government has become a large source of income for lineage heads, priests, and other individuals. Since authority to manipulate land is vested in male lineage elders,[2] proceeds from the sale of lineage lands to the government and income from the rent of land and houses also go to men (Robertson 1990, 49). Property therefore tends to be used to the advantage of men and to the exclusion of women.

In addition to sales, lineage property also dwindles in size when members (invariably men) are given portions to farm or build on. Such land then becomes an individual entitlement rather than corporately owned. The individual acquires ownership rights in addition to cultivation rights. What this means is that there is less land for everybody's free use. The result for women is a loss of their cultivation rights without any compensation.

In contemporary Ghana, whether in a patrilineal or matrilineal system and regardless of the form of marriage, a wife is still not considered to be a member of her husband's lineage. This is because the family is defined as "the group of persons linearly descended from a common ancestor, exclusively through males in the patrilineal communities, or exclusively through females in the matrilineal communities, and within which succession to office and to property is based" (Manu 1984, 21). Thus, the concept of family ignores the spouse. In essence, customary law denies any concept of the conjugal family, a situation that now poses a problem for a society where it is obvious that the primary economic unit is increasingly moving toward the nuclear family rather than the extended family model.

The government's response to the plight of women and children regarding inheritance and property was to enact four laws that address social and family policies in 1985: the Intestate Succession Law (Provisional National Defence Committee Law [PNDCL] 111); the Customary Marriage and Divorce (Registration) Law (PNDCL 112); the Administration of Estate (Amendment) Law (PNDCL 113); and the Head of Family (Accountability) Law (PNDCL 114) (Tipple 1986, 179). These laws seek to bring the law of property succession into line with changes taking place within the increasingly nuclear family system. They also emphasize the interdependence of Ghanaian men and women.

The Intestate Succession Law (PNDCL 111), for example, stipulates that if a person dies intestate the surviving spouse and children are entitled to all household goods. The house (if more than one house is involved, the spouse and children can choose only one) and the rest of the estate are to be shared as follows: the surviving spouse takes three sixteenths of self-acquired property, children take nine sixteenths, with the remaining quarter divided between any surviving parent (one eighth) and the traditional family (one eighth). Where the estate is less than fifty thousand cedis,[3] the spouse and children are entitled to all of it. Throughout the law, spouse, child, and parent shares are to be shared by all spouses, children, and parents (Tipple 1986).

These laws are generally welcomed by Ghanaian women, although some critics argue that they have differential effects on women, depending on their class, marital status, and whether they have children (see Manu 1984; Mensah-Bonsu n.d., 231). For women who are married through the customary system and have no expectation of inheriting from the husband's estate, this law provides security because it confers a specific interest in their husband's estate. Since the law has a very liberal definition of children, anyone can come and claim that the deceased is the natural father of their child. This law is therefore also to the advantage of unmarried mothers, because it removes the anxiety that existed concerning the welfare of their child or children.

Unfortunately, the woman who has toiled with the man may be the loser under current succession law. The law appears to motivate women to acquire their own independent property instead of contributing to their husband's property. Childless women stand to lose the most from this law because husbands of childless women may have children outside the marriage. The childless woman gets only three sixteenths of the husband's property, while the husband is entitled to half of hers if she precedes him in death. As Mensah-Bonsu aptly puts it, "society could not have declared its contempt for childless women more loudly than it has under the law" (Mensah-Bonsu n.d., 233).

Another law of importance is the Customary Marriage and Divorce (Registration) Law (PNDCL 112), which recognizes all types of marriages, once registered, as legal. The PNDC Law 113 is an amendment to the Administration of Estates Act, 1963, to take account of the contents of the new succession law. Under this law, if the personal representative administering the estate deems it necessary, he or she may apply to the court for permission to convert "household chattel" to immovable property or the residue into money (Tipple 1986, 180). The Head of Family Accountability Law (PNDCL 114) ensures that no confusion arises between what is personal property and family or lineage property. People should therefore feel more secure in the knowledge that their personal property will go to the people to whom it has been designated. However, there are claims that because of the new law of inheritance, extended family members of the deceased are unwilling to take interest in the funeral arrangements of the man. The argument is that since the wife and children are going to inherit the man's property, they should bear the funeral expenses (Mensah-Bonsu n.d., 232). This places an extra burden on wives and children.

These laws certainly encourage women to take greater interest in the estates of their spouses and contribute more because they now have a stake in the benefits of their labor. Although men and women are more equal under current law, attempts to use laws and legislation to give women a fair share in property, access to resources, and to correct gender inequalities have not been too successful in practice. Many women are not aware of their legal rights because of lack of education, and many do not possess the economic means to exercise them. In the rural areas, despite acceptance of equality in the law, changes in attitudes and implementation of these laws will be slow because of fear of recriminations from the extended family. In the urban areas, there is more evidence of the new legal empowerment of women in the cases brought before the urban family tribunals (Mikell 1990, 25).

EVIDENCE OF CHANGING PROPERTY AND INHERITANCE RELATIONS

Description of the Property-Inheritance Survey

We now change the level of discourse and focus attention directly on the situated actions of Ghanaian women as they struggle for identity, equality, independence, and security within a male-dominated society. We are particularly interested in how women are taking control of their lives through the acquisition of personal property, thereby transforming the very fabric of traditional inheritance systems.

The data reported cover one aspect of a major research project in which 1600 Ghanaians were interviewed for approximately an hour each by the first author or by assistants she trained. This report on property ownership and transfer is based on the personal experiences of 204 of these individuals, who are self-identified as heads of household (104 women and 100 men) and who live in the Eastern Region of Ghana. The Eastern Region was chosen for two reasons. First, it was chosen for its heterogeneity. It is one of the two administrative regions in Ghana with both matrilineal and patrilineal sociocultural groups within its administrative boundaries. Second, the region has many ethnic groups as well as a large migrant population. In addition, it is the region where cocoa, a crop responsible for major structural changes in the Ghanaian economy, was first introduced in the nineteenth century.

The map of the study area (Map 10.1) identifies the eighteen localities included in the sample. The localities were selected to encompass a wide range of life changes. As such, they range from isolated rural communities (Akwadum, Amanase, Atibie, Jumapo, Nankese, Obomeng, Sawer, Sra), through peripheral localities of Accra (Abiriw, Ahwerease, Amanokrom, Obosomase), to free-standing urban settings (Aburi, Koforidua, Larteh, Nknawkaw, Nsawam, Somanya). The localities were also differentiated in terms of the prevailing kinship

Table 10.2
Distribution of Study Sample by Categories

Variable	Category	No.	Category	No.
Gender	Female	104	Male	100
Class	High	98	Low	106
Socioculture	Matrilineal	105	Patrilineal	99
Region	Urban	101	Rural	103

system (matrilineal or patrilineal) so the sample could be stratified not only along gender lines but also in terms of the household's kinship system, social class, and locale (rural/urban), as shown in Table 10.2.

Although information was collected on every member of the household, only the head of the household was interviewed, and the occupation of this particular individual defines the class of the household. The Ghanaian census definition of class was adopted for the purpose of selecting the households. The head of the household was chosen as the respondent because she or he is the person most likely to have information on all the other members of the household. In Ghana, this particular individual is usually the oldest person in the household. Since part of the survey is on social change and historical events, it was important to interview the person most likely to have lived through historic events and changes in the society.

Table 10.3 summarizes the basic questions asked in each interview that pertain to this study. Questions 1, 5, and 6 were designed to bring out the difference between ownership and control of property. Other questions provided demographic data and covered issues of education, consumption, household dynamics, and perceptions of social status.

In the rural areas, it was necessary to contact the chief, or *Odikro*, of the locality to inform him of the study's mission before starting the interviews. Ghanaian custom demands that one perform certain rites before gaining an audience with a chief. In each rural locality, a bottle of schnapps (local gin) was purchased to take to the meeting with the chief. The size of the bottle depended on the status of the chief. Custom demands one full-size bottle (about 1 liter) for a chief, and one small-size bottle (about 1/2 liter) for a subchief. In some cases the interviewer's manual was left for the chief to read through a few days before the meeting.

The purpose and objectives of the survey were explained through the *okyeame*,

Table 10.3
A General Overview of the Questions Asked

1.	Do you own any property?
2.	What type? -- property was classified into land for building, houses, businesses, stores, factories, fallow agricultural land and farms
3.	Where is the property located?
4.	What is the size of the property?
5.	Who owns this property? -- whether it belonged to the husband or wife, wife's family or husband's family
6.	If group ownership, who had usufruct rights?
7	How was it acquired? -- purchase, inheritance, or gift
8.	When was it acquired?
9.	Who was it acquired from?
10.	Who do you project to transfer the property to?
11.	What is the relationship of this individual to you?
12.	What is the reason for transfer to this individual? -- whether because of rules of inheritance, part ownership, or other reasons

the linguist or speaker for the chief. The description emphasized that the information collected would be treated as confidential. Having satisfied himself that the mission was not of a dubious nature, the chief through the *okyeame* passed on information about the survey to his subjects and asked for their cooperation. A fee of ¢200.00 (U.S. $0.57 in 1986) was typically charged for *dawuro*, or gong gong beating. At dawn of the next day, the town crier beat his *dawuro* to inform the people of the survey and ask that they give us their full cooperation.

In one particular instance, the chief, who had access to the interview book before the meeting, explained to the people that the study was just an academic exercise for writing a history book. He emphasized the importance of documenting historical events for the transfer of knowledge and customs to future generations. He asked them whether they would not be happy to know that they helped write history. The chief asked for the full cooperation of his subjects. He cautioned them that some of the questions would be sensitive and even irritating and so they should have patience. He said, ''If you have not had any food to eat the whole day and they come to ask you what kind of food you ate that day, please do not throw a knife at them.'' This statement was received with much laughter by the people.

In the urban localities, it was not necessary to go to the chief since the areas were too large for the town crier to beat his *dawuro*. In one large urban center, Koforidua, the first author and her research assistants went to the Ghana Broadcasting Corporation, where they were interviewed on a live local vernacular talk show. The discussion described the survey and the benefits that the citizens would derive from the dissemination of some of the findings of the survey. The announcer informed the listeners of the sections of the town to be covered by the survey, assured them of the confidentiality of their responses, and appealed to them to give the interviewers their full cooperation.

The data collected show that male-dominated property relations are continuing to affect adversely the lives and the life chances of women in Ghana. However, the survey also provides evidence that male domination through the control of property is changing; and women, in unprecedented numbers, are finding ways to gain control of private property. We are particularly interested in exploring the breakdown in traditional rules implied by present and prospective intergenerational patterns of property transfer, and at the end of the chapter we will summarize how women are leading the way in forging new rules governing property transfer.

Gender Differences in Access to and Control of Private Property

Of the 204 households sampled, 37 percent own no property. Fifty-one percent of all households own land, 30 percent own houses, and 10.8 percent own stores, factories, and other businesses. As expected, female-headed households in the sample exhibit lower ownership rates than male-headed households in all three categories of property surveyed. Taken as a whole, however, the ownership rates for female-headed households are surprisingly high; although significant inequalities are found to exist when households are differentiated on the basis of class, region, and culture.

Forty-nine percent of female-headed patrilineal households own no property, whereas only 32 percent of male-headed patrilineal households own no property. Female-headed households living in urban areas are at a significant disadvantage, with 50 percent owning no property, while 40 percent of male-headed urban households own no property. Female- and male-headed households in rural areas (70 percent and 73 percent of whom respectively own land) fare significantly better than their urban counterparts. Upper-class male heads of household are much more likely to be property owners than are lower-class male heads of household as well as female heads of household; however, class differences in ownership rates are minimal for female heads of household.

Although significant inequalities are found to exist between female- and male-headed households, the aforementioned results mask the degree to which women are subordinated within the household. Only 59 percent of the females who head households with property actually control the property—53 percent of the time the property is in the woman's name or owned jointly with the husband (6 percent). Property in the remainder of the cases is controlled either by the husband (30 percent) or relatives (11 percent). In contrast, male heads of household with property are in sole control of household property 83 percent of the time and jointly own the land 8 percent of the time. Wives in male-headed households are in sole control of property 3 percent of the time, with relatives controlling the remainder (6 percent). For example,

Question 1: *Wo wo adwapadee?* (Do you own property?)

Response: *Aane me wo asaase mmienu ene dan baako.* (Yes, I have two plots of land and a house.)

Question 5: *Hwan din na eda assase no so anaase Edan no hwan dea?* (Whose name is the land in or Who owns the house?)

Response: *Me kunu* or *Me kunu dea.* (My husband or It is for my husband.)

The "half empty" interpretation of the foregoing results is that women continue to be subordinated with respect to property relations even in those instances where women are the designated heads of household. This trend exists even after the enacting of gender-based legislation, as discussed earlier. The "half full" interpretation of these same results is that women have control over property to a much greater degree than is sanctioned under traditional rules governing the distribution and control of property. The implication is that women are finding ways to circumvent traditional modes of property transfer in their efforts to take control of their lives, and this activity is occurring under very diverse circumstances.

Property Acquisition

The foregoing data are cross-sectional in nature and as such cannot provide much insight into the actions that are creating significant changes in property relations. As a point of departure, what we want to know from the interviews is how property owners gained control over their property.

All of the four possible modes of acquisition (inheritance by rules, inheritance not following rules, purchase, and gifts) have the possibility of contributing to female/male property inequalities to a greater or lesser degree. As described earlier in this chapter, if traditional inheritance patterns were being maintained, all property would be transferred by rules (either patrilineal or matrilineal) and males would be in control of all property (except property held in trust for sons that are not yet of age). However, transactions involving the sale and purchase of property have weakened the influence of traditional rules governing the transfer of property. The lineage has no control over purchased property, and women in particular are empowered through purchase to establish their own rules governing the transfer of property. Even in those cases where property is acquired through inheritance, there is ample evidence that traditional rules are breaking down. The most striking deviation from rules is found for women in patrilineal kinship systems. These women cannot inherit property under traditional rules, and yet many of the women interviewed indicated that they inherited their property (see Figure 10.2).

There are a wide variety of ways to deviate from traditional rules of inheritance; in the interviews, however, we were especially interested in cases where females inherit. (It is important to remember that all inheritance from women is necessarily a deviation from traditional rules.) Figure 10.2 summarizes the evidence on current inheritance. What is striking about the property acquisition patterns summarized in this figure is that property transfers by rules represent a minority of all property transfers, and this is true for both males and females and across kinship systems. We conclude from these striking findings that the acquisition of property through purchase is clearly transforming and replacing traditional property relations.

As expected, the commodification of property is most evident in urban areas where land and housing markets are well established. Urban markets are particularly important as a means of acquiring property for women in patrilineal kinship systems and men in matrilineal kinship systems. Traditional rules governing the transfer of property hold nothing for women in patrilineal kinship systems, and the commodification of property (especially in urban areas) is both the means and the outcome of efforts to circumvent the male-dominated property relations.

Projected Modes of Property Transfer—Matrilineal and Patrilineal Men

The data summarized in the preceding section certainly point toward major structural changes in the modes of property transfer, with the commodification of property emerging as the primary cause and consequence of changing acquisition patterns. The interviews provide interesting evidence on the intergenerational implications of the continued changes in property relations. We are specifically interested in the degree to which property owners in our sample intend to adhere to traditional inheritance rules when they pass on their property to their heirs. A strict interpretation of traditional modes of transfer by rules

Figure 10.2
Pattern of Property Acquisition by Group (Sex by Socioculture by Region)

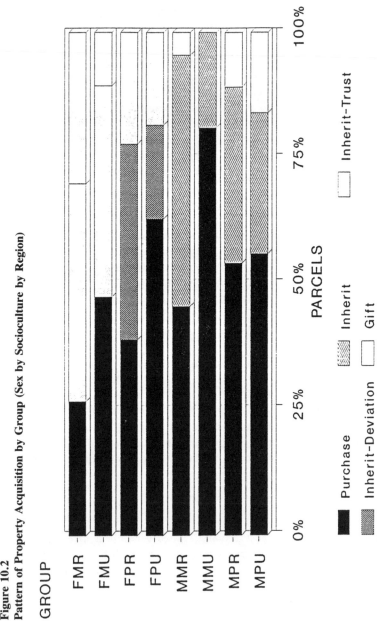

N = 196
Parcels

would require that a male expects to transfer property to his nephews (matrilineal) or to his eldest son or brother (patrilineal). Matrilineal men who were planing to transfer by rules would say, *"Yedi wofa adee,"* which is literally translated as, "we eat the uncle's property" and means "we follow the matrilineal rules of inheritance." For the patrilineal men, it was, *"Yedi egya adee,"* or "we eat father's property," meaning "we follow the patrilineal rules of inheritance."

Some men interviewed in this study could not conceive of any other way to transfer property and looked surprised when asked, "Why are you giving the property to that particular individual?" A typical state, was, *"Oye me wofaase"* or *"Oye me nua kuma/me ba,"* which translates as "He is my nephew" or "He is my younger brother/son."

What we found, however, is that those proposing to follow traditional inheritance rules were in a decided minority. Regardless of kinship system, most men and women who currently own property indicate that they plan to pass their property on to their children without regard to the sex of the child. Only 16 percent of the matrilineal men (who are property owners) intend to transfer property by rules. The discrepancy between rural and urban dwellers is particularly marked, with 31 percent in the rural areas intending to transfer by rules, whereas none of the matrilineal men in urban areas intend to transfer their property by rules. This breakdown in traditional rules appears to be a secondary consequence of the mode of property acquisition for matrilineal men. Recall that 80 percent of the property in urban areas was acquired through purchase (see Figure 10.2).

In most instances, matrilineal men recognize the traditional rules of inheritance, but they feel stronger obligations to the members of their nuclear family—their wives and their own children. For example, one respondent said, *"Nansa yi wiase aye den, woanhwe wo mma a, hwan na ebehwe won?"* This means, "These are tough times; if you do not look after your children, who will look after them?"

In short, the breakdown of traditional inheritance rules in the matrilineal social system appears to be nearly complete. The next generation can expect nothing from their urban matrikin. Even in rural areas, there is no assurance that a person's children will be taken care of by the matrikin.

Significant departures from traditional inheritance rules are also implied by the projected inheritance pattern for patrilineal males. Only 20 percent of all property is slated to be transferred by rules to the man's son or brother. As in the matrilineal case, the main deviation is associated with a transfer of obligation away from kinship ties and toward the members of the man's nuclear family. Children—daughters and sons—are now the intended beneficiaries for 80 percent of the patrilineal men in the sample.

Although traditional rules are clearly breaking down, the unequal and inferior status of women as wives of patrilineal men remains strong, in comparison to the changing status of women within matrilineal systems. Even when patrilineal men propose to deviate from traditional inheritance rules, in this sample they never designated their wives as prospective heirs to property, whereas matrilineal men expect to transfer 24 percent of all property to their wives.

In summary, men in Ghana are actively choosing to deviate from traditional rules. There is a feeling of power to act as one wishes. Tired of being pushed around by the rules of inheritance, people are doing something about it. They are taking control. As one matrilineal man said, "*Adwapadee no ye me dea, na mederema me yere ne me mma,*" which means, "The property is mine and I am giving it to my wife and children."

Projected Modes of Property Transfer—Matrilineal and Patrilineal Women

In traditional inheritance systems, matrilineal women are passive agents in the intergenerational transfer of property. Women hold property in trust for their sons: "*Eye abusua asaase/adwapadee,*" or "It is family land/property." Our survey data show that 45 percent of all property currently held by matrilineal women is held in trust under traditional rules, and yet matrilineal women expect to transfer only 8 percent of their property in accordance with traditional rules. In other words, these women propose to become active agents in the transfer of 92 percent of all property currently in their possession—active agents in the process of making their own rules.

Matrilineal women in rural areas in particular are in the process of actualizing their own mother-daughter inheritance rules—new rules that are growing in strength as the old male-dominated rules are swept aside. Who would have expected to find that 40 percent of all rural property held by matrilineal women is projected to pass to their daughters?

In the patrilineal society, under traditional rules, women have no place in the inheritance system; and yet 49 percent of the patrilineal women in our study own property and 30 percent of that property was inherited—an impossibility under traditional inheritance rules. Women who have inherited property also have the power to pass it on. For these women the old rules of inheritance were broken when they inherited the property, and therefore they have been empowered to pass on the property as they wish. All of the property passed on by these women will be transferred outside the dictates of traditional rules.

The transfer of property as a gift has always been a very important means of circumventing inheritance rules. Traditionally, property as a gift was in appreciation for services rendered. Men designated property as gifts to their wives to get around the problem that property transferred to women in the form of inheritance often reverted to the lineage. For patrilineal women, the transfer of property as gifts meant that they could escape the bonds of tradition and could have control over the disposal of their property. In fact, many women who have purchased properties are in turn circumventing inheritance rules by designating the property as gifts:

"Eye mea me adwapadee enti mede bema obira mepe."
"It is my personal property and therefore I can give it to whoever I please."
"Mmanye no akyedee a, abusua no befa."
"If I don't designate it as a gift, the extended family will take it."

The projected inheritance patterns of patrilineal women actually differ little from the projected patterns for patrilineal males. It is interesting that some women who have purchased their property or received property as gifts consider their actions and intentions to be consistent with tradition. They legitimate their actions by redefining the rules. An interesting case in point is that of the woman in the sample with the most property—eight pieces. This woman had purchased seven parcels of land and had received a house as a gift. She is not bound by any traditional rules of inheritance because all her property is personal property. In patrilineal societies only men inherit; the rules then specify that property be passed on to the eldest son of the senior wife and a senior brother. The property holder interviewed appeared to be very powerful, and clearly she is making her own rules. Nevertheless, she says she will pass her property on to family members (sex and relationship not specified) because "the rules of inheritance demand it."

A FORMAL SUMMARY OF THE GHANAIAN EXPERIENCE

The historical account of property relations in Ghana points up the existence and the long-term persistence of gender inequalities and the associated male-dominated power relations that women in Ghanaian society experience on a daily basis. The dual structural principles of patriarchy and capitalism converge to create and mediate a web of exploitive property relations that drain the creative and productive potentialities of Ghanaian women. The picture that emerges supports but clarifies Giddens's characterization of a class-divided society experiencing the disorienting and the dislocating effects of colonialism as the logic of capital penetrates and transforms the fabric of traditional society.

Although the main theme in the historical account is one of exploitation and male domination, an important counter theme begins to emerge from the contradictions created by the collision of patriarchy and capitalism. The cracks and contradictions in the structure of Ghanaian society create possibilities for women that were denied under traditional rules. Of particular interest in the empirical study is the fact that male-dominated property relations are implicated in and are transformed by the actions of Ghanaian women and men as they attempt to gain control of their lives through the acquisition, selective transfer, and control of property.

The data show that Ghanaian women remain at a significant disadvantage in terms of property ownership and control. Even in cases where women are the designated heads of household, male members of the household frequently remain in control of the household's property; whereas women in male-headed households rarely retain control of the household's property.

The other side of the coin is that female heads of household control the household's property in the majority of the cases surveyed. In light of traditional inheritance rules denying women any ownership rights, this finding is truly amazing and is an important indication that traditional modes of property transfer are breaking down. This breakdown is directly linked to the purchase and sale of property as the primary means of transferring ownership of property. Women are clearly becoming active agents in the commodification of property; and the trend is particularly evident in urban areas, as illustrated in Figure 10.2.

An equally startling finding from the survey involves projected property transfers. Inheritance rules governing the intergenerational transfer of property are the very core of male-dominated property relations. Our survey indicates that the overwhelming majority of Ghanaian property owners intend to deviate from traditional inheritance rules when they pass their property on to those in the next generation. Most men and almost all women plan to pass property on to their children without regard to the sex of the child. The basic social and economic unit is fast becoming the nuclear family, particularly in urban areas (see Figure 10.2).

These empirical results support specific propositions pertaining to the structuration of gender-based property relations in Ghana, propositions that state in much more explicit terms the basic propositions of Giddens's theory of structuration (Giddens 1981, 26–29). Each proposition serves as a summary of the actual experiences of Ghanaian women and men—experiences structured by male-dominated property relations as well as experiences contributing to significant changes in property relations.

Proposition 1. Gender divisions are social constructions that justify the subordination of women. The social system in Ghana continues to be divided along gender lines. Ghanaian women are placed at a material disadvantage based solely on their sex. Patriarchy resulting in the social construction of gender divisions and the sanctioning of male domination is made explicit in both matrilineal and patrilineal kinship systems, which remain the structural bases for observed gender inequalities in employment, education, and in the control of property.

Proposition 2. Socially sanctioned limitations on women's access to and control over property are deeply implicated in the perpetuation of male-dominated power relations within Ghanaian society. Culturally defined rules governing property entitlements and modes of transfer place women in a subordinate position within Ghanaian society. Women work the land but men control the land; women are jural minors under traditional kinship rules. The male-dominated property relations are reproduced and reinforced with each transfer of property from a male to a male in accordance with traditional rules.

Proposition 3. Growing contradiction is arising between the property relations sanctioned within traditional kinship/descent systems rooted in patriarchy and the commodification of property occurring under the logic of capitalism. The contradiction centers on the rules governing ownership and the transfer of property—transfers based on kinship relations versus transfers based on transactions within a market. The contradictions are most evident in the changing nature of property transfers in urban areas. These are the "time-space edges" where the traditional Ghanaian social system collides with the agents of international capital (Giddens 1981, 168). The contraditions between traditional male-dominated society and the capitalist system are creating "cracks in the social pavement" that are openings for women where none had existed before (see Figure 10.3).

Proposition 4. Ghanaian women are knowledgeable actors; and they are finding practical ways to circumvent the male-dominated land tenure and inheritance system. The extent of Ghanaian women's success in the acquisition and control of property is historically contingent and inextricably bound up in and with the localities in which these women live their lives (see Figure 10.3). More women in Ghana than ever before have access to and control over property; women living in urban areas and within matrilineal kinship systems have been more successful in their efforts to gain control of property than their rural, patrilineal sisters.

Proposition 5. The accelerating commodifcation of property is at the heart of the structuration of male-dominated property relations, in that commodification is an essential, though unacknowledged, condition for and a direct and largely unanticipated consequence of the rate at which women are gaining control of property (see Figure 10.3). The majority of the households in our survey acquired their property through purchase. The obligation of traditional kinship relations is nullified once property becomes a commodity to be bought and sold. Women can and do become active agents in the acquisition of property once property becomes a commodity.

Proposition 6. Ghanaian women are empowered by their successful efforts to gain control of private property. Heyzer defines empowerment as "having control and gaining greater control over our own lives; having a voice and being listened to; and being able to define and create from the perspective of women; being able to influence the social choices that affect the whole society, not only the areas of society recognized as women's place; having the contributions of women recognized and valued; having access to responsibilities and opportunities" (cited in Everett 1990, 25). Ghanaian women are struggling to gain control of their lives, and they are using the control of property as one important way to improve their material condition and that of their children (see Figure 10.3).

CONCLUSION

Ghanaian women are becoming increasingly aware of the injustices of a social system built on property relations that exploit them, and they are finding ways to exploit the contradictions inherent in the property relations of Ghanaian society to enhance their material position. They are becoming active and knowledgeable

Figure 10.3
Structuration of Gender-based Property Relations in Ghanaian Society

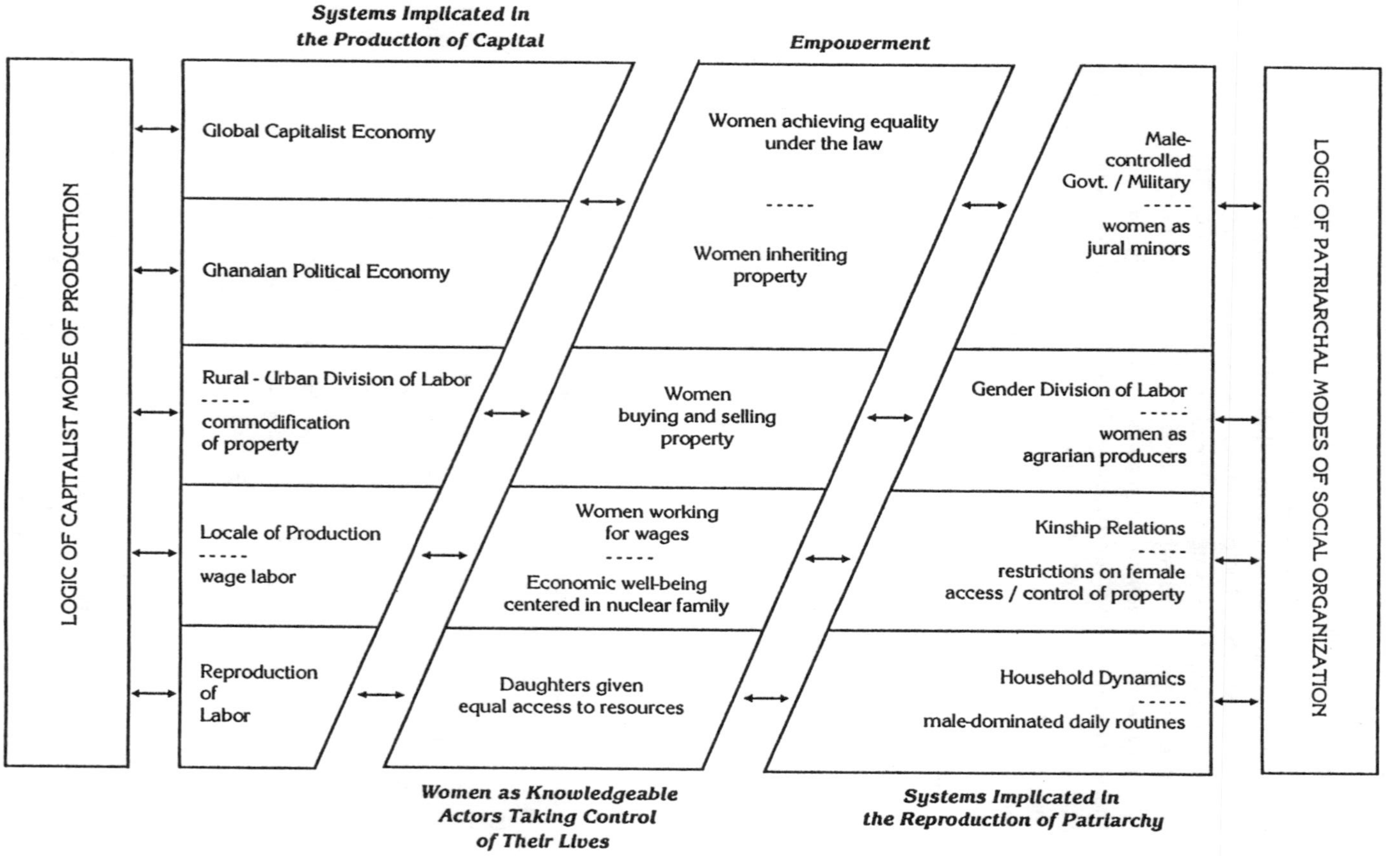

LOGIC OF PATRIARCHAL MODES OF SOCIAL ORGANIZATION

Systems Implicated in the Production of Capital

Empowerment

Systems Implicated in the Reproduction of Patriarchy

Male-controlled Govt. / Military
-----
women as jural minors

Gender Division of Labor
-----
women as agrarian producers

Kinship Relations
-----
restrictions on female access / control of property

Household Dynamics
-----
male-dominated daily routines

Women achieving equality under the law

Women inheriting property

Women buying and selling property

Women working for wages

Economic well-being centered in nuclear family

Daughters given equal access to resources

Women as Knowledgeable Actors Taking Control of Their Lives

Global Capitalist Economy

Ghanaian Political Economy

Rural - Urban Division of Labor
-----
commodification of property

Locale of Production
-----
wage labor

Reproduction of Labor

LOGIC OF CAPITALIST MODE OF PRODUCTION

architects of new inheritance rules that break the historical patterns of male domination. The advantage of self-acquired or personal property for women is that they can pass it on to individuals of their choice. Through their actions and intentions as knowledgeable agents involved in the acquisition and transfer of property, Ghanaian women (and men) are recasting the very structure of male-dominated inheritance relations to create a better, more equal future for their children.

The stories that we have told in this study cannot and should not be abstracted from the unique historical and geographic context that is Ghanaian society; and yet we find the basic themes summarized in these formal propositions hauntingly familiar. They are themes that speak to women in every society. The story of gender inequalities permeating every aspect of daily life in Ghana is no less important to tell because of its universality. It is essential that we continue to voice the injustice of a society that subordinates the life chances of women to those of men. It is not right that Ghanaian women are relegated to lower status and lower-paying jobs. It is not right that Ghanaian girls are denied the same educational opportunities as their male counterparts. It is not right that women make improvements on the land only to see the land appropriated and sold by men. Ghanaian women need to know that their voices have been heard and they are not alone in their resolve to take control of their lives and to make it right for themselves and their daughters.

"Empower women to transform structures or transform structures to empower women," advises Capeling-Alakaja (Everett 1990, 33). Ghanaian women are empowered by their successful efforts to gain control of private property. Their efforts are indeed transforming the social structures of Ghanaian society.

NOTES

1. Bukh (1979) gives a detailed account of cocoa development among the Ewes, a patrilineal group, in *The Village Women in Ghana*.

2. Women rarely become lineage heads. The few that do, however, are only allowed authority over other women and are not allowed to take part in the land transactions.

3. The Ghanaian currency is cedis and pesewas. The mid-1993 exchange rate was about 600 cedis to a dollar.

Concluding Remarks: "The Giddens Phenomenon"—Fuzzy Theory and Empirical Cutting Edges

Eliza K. Ellis Husband

The chapters in this volume were written with the purpose of bringing together, conceptually and empirically, structuration theory and geographical research. I imagine that others, like myself, have had a pervasive awareness of discussion on the subject of structuration accompanied by a persistent query, a vagueness, as to geographical practice guided by the theory. How extensively, and effectively, has structuration theory been applied by geographers? What limitations of the theory have been revealed by geographical applications? This volume brings into conjunction a set of studies that succeed in suggesting the range of responses to this reciprocating pair of questions.

The topical focus is "structurationist theory and methodology as a means of examining the geographic causes and consequences of subordination, isolation, and marginalization" (Wilson and Huff, this volume). The fact that a single volume contains chapters by researchers on this topic who come from both humanist and structuralist intellectual perspectives is illustrative of the eclectic and wide-ranging reach of structuration theory. Such an ideological spread is also helpful, in and of itself, in assessing structuration and its applicability within geography.

Most of my own research is within the area of social-equity issues. My formative years as a geographer and planner spanned the exciting and confusing decade during which geographers most actively sought new ways to address social-equity issues head on in their research. The experiences I had are for the most part summarized in Wilson and Huff's introduction in this volume. My perspective was dominated, first, by an awareness of social inequality and, second, by an interest in cultural phenomena approached historically. I felt the two to be somehow relevant to each other and was dissatisfied with the classificatory approaches that prevailed in cultural geography. I knew that neither classification nor the "frozen geometries" (Wilson and Huff, this volume) of spatial analysis would ever furnish a language in which I, at least, could talk about society and space.

From a student perspective, both geographical discussion and departmental politics seemed nearly obsessed with the theme of disciplinary unity and the erection of a theoretical banner under which all could, or would have to, march. I felt I was supposed to be seeking The Answer, and I tested theoretical alternatives one after another. Just as Eyles described in Chapter 5, each theory contributed to my development as a researcher, but none seemed complete. Behavioralism did not really address society's formative influence; phenomenology and other forms of humanism did not discuss power relationships; critical theory seemed lacking in the areas of culture and historical contingency.

The only stop I missed from Wilson and Huff's intellectual travelogue, I think, is Weberian managerialism. I found too much of the poet and historian in Max Weber to accept the managerialist reduction of his complex, even tragic vision of emergent, bureaucratically dominated societies (Jaspers 1965; Wolin 1981; see also Giddens 1972). Through my sense of his complexity and the contradictions with which he struggled, the very timely themes such as irrationality that he embraced, Weber was my entree into postmodernism. To Weber I joined Foucault, and the Heidegger of *Being and Time* for his revolutionary discussion of space. These three have formed a kind of larger than life committee for theory to whom I shall long report; and I shall refer to their contributions in evaluating the role and applicability of structuration to social-spatial research.

Whatever the shortcomings of the postmodernist discussion to date, I am obviously not the only one to have welcomed it with relief, for it has given voice to scholarly promptings once intellectually and politically marginalized into incoherence or silence. I place Giddens's structuration theory, in spite of its failure to thematize discourse, as one of a range of postmodern syntheses. Embracing a pluralist and revisionist agenda, structuration attempts to combine critical social theory with an interactionist, culture-and-locality-sensitive emphasis on social process. The present volume is an example of the way in which Giddens's theoretical program, both for its positive contributions and for its very limitations, has enabled broad-based discussion of, and the beginnings of empirical work in, geographical topic areas heretofore inchoate or contentious.

STRUCTURATION THEORY AS A PERMEABLE SYNTHESIS

"Structure and agency [are] dualities that recursively produce one another in ceaseless interplay" (Moos and Dear 1986, 30). The use of rules and resources structures systems, which (contrary to the position of neoclassicists and other voluntarists) condition or situate the decisions of individuals. But only the individual as agent can make use of these rules and resources for perpetuation or change; therein (contrary to the position of structuralists and other determinists) is the sole demonstrable existence of structure. Giddens emphasizes that social reproduction, the sedimentation of practices in systems, is continually related and rerelated to the constructive role in everyday life, the decisions of individuals who live it, and the locales where life is lived.

In one stroke, this formulation presents a way around the structure-agency dichotomy, calls attention to the processual nature of social interaction and the negotiated quality of resource distribution, and specifies a theoretical role for space-time as the enabling context of all social processes. In Chapter 5, Eyles aptly termed the response to this deft synthesis the ''Giddens phenomenon.'' Although one could readily point to other theoretical sources to establish any one of Giddens's points, even two, no other theoretical schema brings all of these together. Further, within the context of disciplinary politics, where researchers have sometimes been marginalized through labeling as phenomenologists, Marxists, and so on, structuration as a synthesis avoids the disadvantage of being associated with any one historical theorist.

Finally, as this volume amply illustrates, the fact that Giddens and his followers have offered structuration theory as a sensitizing device rather than a complete and exclusive account of the world has left critically important free zones for scholarly thought and action. One account of a complex situation does not logically exclude another (Wollheim 1970, 577); but the unsupportedly global and unitary conceptualizations of various positivist frameworks, including classical Marxism, have diverted considerable energy toward competing claims to theoretical purity, authority, and comprehensiveness.

As I noted earlier in respect to various ''isms'' that have contributed to my own intellectual development, each theoretical perspective, in shedding light on certain issues, inevitably casts others into shadow. Further, the notion of theory as a sensitizing device composed of somewhat loosely connected, unequally developed concepts reflects the need for theoretical revision and recombination. Our theoretical formulations are like ourselves, inherently perspectival because situated in time and space. So too the objects of social theorization: as products of intentionality, they are moving targets, It may be that what survives best in any body of theory is a set of separately applicable sensitizing concepts, such as the Marxian ideas of alienation, commodification, and the opposition of use value and exchange value. Arguably, it is through isolation and development of various of these concepts (as in Bourdieu's cultural capital), rather than through the totalizing revisions of practitioners such as Althusser, that Marxism has remained relevant. To the extent that structuration continues to be useful, it may be so largely because it allows researchers both to incorporate other theoretical content in a flexible way and to pick and choose among structuration's own axioms.

I take as a mark of maturation in social theory that we have begun to admit the unlikelihood of establishing foundational knowledge, but have not fallen back on a relativist refusal to seek criteria (J. Smith 1993). In other words, we have begun to accept ongoing responsibility for the quality of a conversation that has no inherent culmination in the discovery of a final truth. The chapters in this volume are best viewed, I believe, as a moment in the conversation and an invitation to continue it. This I shall now begin to do, considering several issues in the development and use of structuration theory that the chapters have raised.

THE PROBLEMATIC OF INEQUALITY STUDIES

As Wilson notes in his critical review, structuration has particular relevance to studies of inequality. Classical social theory, preoccupied with modernity and its salient industrial-capitalist face, separated systems effects from intentional acts. One body of theory examined the former: Durkheim's mechanical versus organic solidarity, Marx's capitalism, Weber's instrumental rationality; another theoretical body examined the latter, in terms of experience, meaning, and the life world. Giddens's project has been to bring together these two halves of the world of presenting structures not as the invariant producer of systems effects but as tools for use by knowledgeable agents.

Wilson makes the point, however, that empirical applications of structuration simply do not support Giddens's schema. In whatever way structure is construed, individual and system are not implicitly or potentially equal in causal force. Rather, "structures emerge as creatively generated rules and resources that are produced under the local circumstance of *guiding capitalist impulses and imperatives*" (Wilson, this volume; emphasis added). Effects of the commodity production system retain causal primacy both in the empirical studies Wilson discusses and in empirical studies within the present volume.

I believe that two points need to be noted in applying this state of affairs to structuration theory. First, a certain amount of confusion easily arises over the possible roles of Giddens's agent and system. They tend to be identified, respectively, with innovation and the status quo. Marx himself helped foster these common associations, sketching out a strong role for the agent as innovator, set against a broader powerful materialist regime. Marx believed that the political activity of organized individuals was to lead to a new world order. The failure of this event to materialize should suggest that individual agency is not necessarily innovative. At the same time, of course, it is systematization through the rules and resources of structure that renders innovation effectual, as in Warf's striking case for the influence of telecommunications. Warf's study seems to posit a mechanism for determinacy that does link agent and system, when it suggests that systems effects may in fact be the unintended consequences created by individual actors bent knowledgeably on maximizing profit.

Underlying this ready conflatability of roles between agent and system is a

Foucauldian theme that I take to be the central problematic of inequality studies: the incrementally revealed fact of *complicity* within the determinative nature of capitalist modernity. Inequality studies are often conceived as an emancipatory project. However, it must be asked what emancipation can consist of when most individuals, not only owners of the means of production, appear to identify their interests with the commodity production system. This state of affairs reveals the insights that Marxist theory provides us. On the other hand, it must be noted that this complicity is constantly negotiated in different ways across places, is an unstable situation in its ongoing need for ideological support, and is acted out in different ways as capitalism perilously pushes itself forward.

In the long run, this identification may be rightly describable as false consciousness. But a short-term calculus of self-interest suggests to most of us that we are unlikely to survive, much less prosper, outside of the economic-political system whose essence permeates every life condition. Nor do many individuals feel able to devote their lives to attempts at change. The commodity production system, no matter how contingent and locally variant, retains by default both causal and motivational primacy. In terms of theory, scholars of social inequality are left with the two interpretive poles, meaning and exigency, no closer together than before.

However, this analysis can be said to apply to the economic rather than the political system, distinct under capitalism in the way that Giddens has characterized them (1981). Within polities, distribution of both allocative and authoritative resources is affected by individual acts, such as the initiatives of praxis that Marx advocated, as well as by systems effects such as the outcomes of technology. Marginalization of certain groups within the polity is obviously a subject for inequality studies, and there are clear connections at this level between meaning and exigency (for instance, Weber's point that exigent resource distribution systems also contribute to status hierarchies, and thus serve the meaning-related "problem of order").

STRUCTURATION AS METHODOLOGY

Structuration affords hints for bringing together structuralist and humanist research foci, then, by bringing agent, structure, and system into theoretical relationship. The methodological force of this point is illustrated in Rogers's study of Rifle, Colorado after the 1980s oil shale bust, a study that uses Pred's place- and agent-oriented development of structuration theory. Rogers shows how structures—that is, rules and resources—were developed by local actors during the boom and bust years under systems effects dictated by the externally based oil industry, then afterward appropriated as managerial experience in the service of local community building. One community goal is the creation of new, locally controlled systems effects; and residents as knowledgeable actors clearly conceive such effects as an intersection of the economic (greater tax base, more local employment) and the experiential (community spirit). Rogers's process-oriented investigation, using historical narrative and the analysis of informants' perceptions in their own words (Staeheli, this volume), allows the structure-driven interpenetration of agent and system to emerge.

The broadening of geographic techniques to include ethnography, then, is facilitated by structuration's theoretical focus on *process*. This process orientation has been derided for its incompleteness, notably the lack of a body of substantive propositions. Underlying such attacks (e.g., Gregson and others in Held and Thompson 1989) is, I believe, a positivistic assumption that cause-effect study for the ultimate purpose of prediction constitutes the beginning and end of theoretical legitimacy. Prediction assumes a theory that is consistent and complete, a kind of Universal Transverse Mercator System for the social world.

However, "theory covers a multiplicity of endeavors," as Giddens has observed (1989, 295). The failure of prediction-centered research to effect striking change in the social world, I believe, has stimulated a consideration of process in relationship to the analysis of power. If there can be intervention in situations of social inequality, intervention must be based on knowing how the inequality is created and maintained. In my view, the orientation to process has encouraged observation of the political world, of negotiation and learning under conditions of power inequality, to move toward the center of inequality studies where it belongs.

Finally, in the context of appreciating Giddens's work, I would like to be able to say that the process orientation of structuration has contributed to the awareness that theory, empirical study, and the relationship between them exist in a social context. Staeheli, in her structurationist study in women's involvement in the Boulder, Colorado anti-growth movement, felt it important to choose "a research strategy that was consistent with the beliefs of at least some of the participants in the study"; she also focused considerable attention on research effects (see Chapter 7). However, sensitivity to process, in this piece of otherwise structurationist work, leads me to notice that structuration's process concerns have not extended to a theoretical basis for self-monitoring of the research act. Both Warf and Van Lieu and Jones cite the lack of deconstructionism, and the broader concern with discourse that it implies, as structuration's great shortcoming. I agree.

If there could be only one direction of development for structuration theory, I would wish this to be an escape from literalness. Such a program would most certainly include Browning's, Van Lieu and Jones's, and Warf's emphasis on discourse analysis within the research design; and it would also include a reexamination of the way in which we "write up" research (Richardson 1990), a fuller realization that the act of wording is necessary and integral to interpretation.

METAPHOR, VALUES, AND THE CONCEPTUALIZATION OF SPACE AND PLACE

I have begun to suspect that many of the theoretical concepts we like to apply with solemn literalness have survived most usefully not as blueprints of a social-economic process but as metaphors. An example is capitalism itself, standing in as it does for that Juggernaut of innovation to which Warf refers, in all its conceptual complexity, dynamic energy, and ability to evoke our fearful and half-guilty fascination. It is time that we formally and systemically incorporate such realities of analysis into our theorizing. Theory has among its purposes the energizing of thought and the capturing of what, among theorists, goes by the sadly pedestrian title of multivocality—which means that meanings are not variables, stable, static, and neatly bounded.

Giddens's observations on space and place are "commonplace," as Saunders justly observes (1989, 230); and the sentiment is echoed by several contributors to the present volume. Saunders resolutely sets his face against any consideration of the symbolic force of spatiality, but I believed Giddens's problem is exactly the lack of multivocality in the meaning of space that Giddens inherits from time-geography. Sayer (1984) has alluded to philosophy as a useful if not sufficient ingredient in explanatory social theory, and I would like to point to the spatial ontology of Heidegger in *Being and Time* simply as an example of how spatiality can be conceptualized multivocally for a greater explanatory reach.

Our everyday being, which for phenomenologists like Heidegger is ontologically prior to the objective mode, has the salient and defining characteristic of unselfconscious involvement in a network of relationships. Involvement or care is our very means of spatial apprehension, the means by which we locate everything, including ourselves, within the world. (In this way Heidegger hints at a discursive function for spatiality, but the point remains undeveloped and is better dealt with by Mead [1934] and Blumer [1969].) In Heidegger's example, the glasses on one's nose, the pavement under one's feet, may be "discovered," or located, as remote compared to the friend sighted 20 feet away, because we are attending to the friend and not to glasses or to pavement (1962, 141–142).

Space, then, is not a thing or a relation; rather, it is *the disclosure of location on the basis of significance* (1962, 145). Further, the quality of spatiality as an attribute of relational cobeing gives rise to what we may call instituitonalized space, the Heideggerian *place* or *region*. The region, a less literal version of geography's functional region, is the location of a totality of referents necessary to carrying out a task. Heidegger interprets task and its implements across levels both of scale and concreteness; a task can range from opening one's mail to putting through an antigrowth initiative or relocating a factory. Perhaps, as in Eyles's study, the task is identity, and place is the totality of social and physical-environmental proximities needed to know who one is.

One implication of the Heideggerian region is that space in its perceptual character—"how individual human beings have conceptualized their worlds," as Jakle (this volume) says—is always the space of places. Everything we know, we know as local, even if localness is metaphorically created by telephone or television. However, *causally* and often invisibly, space is very much Warf's space of flows. Extrapolating from Heidegger to a social analysis that he does not engage, relational proximity is determinative, based on motive (strategic intentionality) and the ability to enforce motive (e.g., through technological innovations). Spatiality thus conceived becomes a link between everyday life and systems effects. Such a formulation also suggests space's conceptual diversity in the usage of geographers, and the importance to us of that diversity (Foote 1993).

Heidegger concludes his analysis with a rather sinister characterization of spatiality as the very condition of our obliviousness, our everyday state of amorality (1962, 163–168). Cumulatively, our trait of "bringing things near" on the basis of involvement traps us in a perspectiveless here and now. We must oppose this condition with a resolute consciousness, says Heidegger, if we are to exist as moral beings.

I bring up Heidegger's conclusion partly for its suggestiveness to the theorization of social and cultural geography in general. Space as region or place is "normalizing" (Husband 1992). As Jakle demonstrates in the case of manipulated place meanings based on the historical built environment, place is capable of establishing a meaning quite independent of, even contrary to, its personal past and actual social-economic circumstances. More than one of the studies in this volume demonstrates that the ideology of place belongs to whoever holds the balance of power. However, complicity in the formation of "place normality" is suggested by Eyles's observation that place is also an object of the desire *to* normalize, in the interests of "coping," so that even a tire dump becomes "simply part of the landscape" to those who must endure the dump's menace (Eyles, this volume). Ontologically, then, place is a region created by discourse; and this discourse is made up of both verbal and environmental voices (Van Lieu and Jones, this volume; Husband 1992).

Heidegger's conclusion also commands our attention for the moral position it stakes out, similar to Jakle's, on a basis of authenticity or awareness of the real. Van Lieu and Jones describe how, in the relocating of a Kentucky factory, representatives of mobile capital, local power brokers, and the union members who stood to lose most all cooperated to create, through the discourse of community, an expeditious place-reality that was both economically and ethically destructive. Most, if not all, of the contributors to this volume have staked out a moral position on one ground or another. Usually the position is implicitly developed through lengthy exposition; by contrast, Antwi-Nsiah and Huff (this volume) cry, with great directness, "It is not right!" that gender inequality in property ownership circumscribes the life chances and undermines the labor of Ghanaian women. Heidegger's morally weighted analysis is to me a demonstration of the way in which social theory can more integrally and defensibly adopt these moral positions, and must adopt them with the same reasoned care that it adopts other analytic stances.

This step toward an articulated ethics is particularly incumbent on scholars of social inequality, since the very thematization of social inequality embodies a moral assumption. Many of us, in the tradition of Max Weber, may not be able to get past our discomfort with the concept of explicitly reasoned and defended value judgments as a part of our analyses. However, both contributors to this volume such as Van Lieu and Jones and Staeheli, and researchers such as John Forester (1989) in planning, have begun to demonstrate the feasibility of moral argument in empirical work.

Beyond feasibility, I would argue that the tacit status we presently accord to our ethical positions prevents a necessary appreciation of ethical complexity, of multivocality and equivocality. These characteristics are brought out by most, if not all, of the studies in this volume, with their empircally varied but conceptually unitary theme of the redistribution of resources. Redistribution inevitably creates not only new winners but new losers; and structuration theory itself, with its emphasis on creative agency and unintended consequences, has made the assumption of pure good and pure evil somewhat less adequately informing for inequality research than it once appeared.

References

Abler, R. 1977. The telephone and the evolution of the American metropolitan system. In *The social impact of the telephone*, ed. de S. Pool, 318–341. Cambridge, MA: MIT Press.

Abu, C. 1983. The separateness of the spouses: Conjugal resources in an Ashanti village. In *Female and male in West Africa*, ed. Christine Oppong, 156–168. London: George Allen and Unwin.

Ackelsberg, M., and M. Breitbart. 1987/1988. Terrains of protest: Striking city women. *Our Generation* 19:151–175.

Adams, P. 1971. *Lenin and philosophy and other essays*. London: New Left.

——. 1992. Television as gathering place. *Annals of the Association of American Geographers* 82:117–135.

Afonja, S. 1990. Changing patterns of gender stratification in West Africa. In *Persistent inequalities: Women and world development*, ed. Irene Tinker, 198–209. New York: Oxford University Press.

Africa Report. 1989. Cecelia Johnson: A woman's place. An interview with Cecilia Johnson, acting general secretary, Ghana's 31st December Women's Movement. 34:61–64, March–April.

Agyeman-Badu, Y., and O. H. Kwame. 1982. *The political economy of instability: Colonial legacy and political instability in Ghana*. Third World Monograph Series. Lawrenceville, VA: Brunswick.

Althusser, L. 1965. *For Marx*. New York: Pantheon.

Anderson, K. 1988. Cultural hegemony and the race-definition process in Chinatown, Vancouver: 1880–1980. *Environment and Planning D* 6:127–147.

Anderson, S. 1992. Voters approve Expo, Parachute real estate tax. *The Citizen Telegram* (Rifle, CO) September 30:1.

———. 1993. Expo Center group begins to shift gears: Initiatives grant puts Expo Center into motion. *The Citizen Telegram* (Rifle, CO) January 20:1, 4.

Antwi-Nsiah, C. 1991. *Analysis of the problem of gender, class, and regional inequalities in peripheral states: A case study of Ghana*. Unpublished Ph.D. dissertation. Urbana: University of Illinois, Department of Geography.

Appleton, J. 1975. *The experience of landscape*. London: Wiley.

Aries, P. 1978. The family and the city. *Daedalus* 106:227–235.

Babalola, S. O., and C. Dennis. 1988. Returns to women's labour in cash crop production: Tobacco in Oyo State, Nigeria. In *Agriculture, women, and land: The African experience*, ed. Jean Davis, 79–89. Boulder, CO: Westview Press.

Bagnell, K. 1989. *Canadese*. Toronto: Macmillan.

Baird, B.N.R. 1986. Tolerance for environmental health risks. *Risk Analysis* 6:425–435.

Barnes, T. J. 1984. *Theories of economic value and structure and agency in economic geography*. Paper presented at the Canadian Association of Geographers annual meeting, Nanaimo, British Columbia.

Bartlett, D. 1986. Municipal mythology. In *Highlights of PLAN-Boulder County, 1959–1986*, ed. J. Robertson, 21–26. Boulder, CO: PLAN-Boulder County.

Bastide, S., J. Moath, and J. Pages. 1989. Risk perception and social acceptability of technologies. *Risk Analysis* 9:215–223.

Baudrillard, J. 1983. The ecstasy of communication. In *The anti-aesthetic: Essays on post-modern culture*, 16–39. Port Townsend, WA: Bay Press.

Bauman, Z. 1989. Hermeneutics and modern social theory. In *Social theory of modern societies: Anthony Giddens and his critics*, eds. D. Held and J. Thompson, 34–55. Cambridge: Cambridge University Press.

Baxter, J. et al. 1992. The Hagersville tire fire. *Qualitative Health Research* 2:208–237.

Bentsi-Enchill, K. 1964. *Ghana land law*. London: Sweet and Maxwell.

Bentsi-Enchill, N. 1979. Losing illusions at Makola Market. *West Africa* 3742:1589–1592.

Berger, P. 1963. *Invitation to sociology*. Harmondsworth: Penguin.

Berger, P., and T. Luckmann. 1967. *The social construction of reality*. London: Allen Lane.

Berman, M. 1982. *All that is solid melts into air*. New York: Penguin.

Berry, B., and W. Garrison. 1958. The functional bases of central place theory. *Economic Geography* 34:145–154.

Berry, S. S. 1975. *Cocoa, custom and socio-economic change in rural western Nigeria*. Oxford: Clarendon Press.

———. 1984. *Fathers work for their sons*. Berkeley: University of California Press.

———. 1986a. Macro-policy implications of research on rural households and farming systems. In *Understanding African rural households and farming systems*, ed. Joyce Lewinger Moock. Boulder, CO: Westview Press.

———. 1986b. *Property rights and rural resource management: The case of tree crops in West Africa*. Working papers in African studies, no. 122. Boston: Boston University.

Bhaskar, R. 1979. *The possibility of naturalism*. Brighton: Harvester.

Birmingham, W., I. Neustaudt, and E. N. Omaboe, eds. 1967. *A study of contemporary Ghana*. Vols. I & II. London: George Allen and Unwin.

Blocker, T., and D. Eckberg. 1989. Environmental issues and women's issues: General concerns and local hazards. *Social Science Quarterly* 70:588–593.

Bluestone, B., and B. Harrison 1982. *The deindustrialization of America: Plant closings, community abandonment, and the dismantling of basic industry*. New York: Basic Books.

Blumer, H. 1969. *Symbolic Interaction*. Englewood Cliffs, NJ: Prentice Hall.

Boal, F. 1976. Ethnic residential segregation. In *Social areas in cities*, vol. 1, eds. D. T. Herbert and R. J. Johnson, 51–95. Chichester: Wiley.

Boateng, E. O, K. Ewusi, R. Kanbur, and A. Mackay. 1990. *A poverty profile for Ghana, 1987–88. Social Dimensions of Adjustment in Sub-Saharan Africa*. Working paper no. 5, Policy Analysis. Washington: The World Bank.

Boorstin, D. 1961. *The image: A guide to pseudo-events in America*. New York: Harper Colophon.

Boserup, E. 1970. *Women's role in economic development*. London: George Allen and Unwin.

Boulding, E. 1981. Integration into what? In *Women and technological change in developing countries*, eds. Roslyn Dauber and Melinda L. Cain, 9–30. AAAS Selected Symposia Series. Boulder, CO: Westview Press.

Bourdieu, P. 1977. *Outline of a theory of practice*. Cambridge: Cambridge University Press.

———. 1984. *Distinction*. Cambridge, MA: Harvard University Press.

Breton, R., W. W. Isajiw, W. E. Kalbach, and J. G. Reitz. 1990. *Ethnic identity and equality*. Toronto: University of Toronto Press.

Brokensha, D. 1966. *Social change in Larteh, Ghana*. Oxford: Clarendon Press.

———. 1981. Indicators of rural inequality. In *Development advisory team (DAT) training program manual*, 65–73. Washington: USAID.

Bromet, B. J. et al. 1982. Reactions of psychiatric patients to the Three Mile Island accident. *Archives of General Psychiatry* 39:725–730.

Brown, C. K. 1983. Social structure and rural poverty in Ghana. *Rural Africana* 17:19–30.

Browning, J. D. 1989. *An investigation into the spatial distribution of elementary educational resources and educational attainment levels in San Diego*. Masters thesis, Department of Geography, San Diego State University.

Brownlee, C., and B. Jones. 1990. Addendum to *Highlights of PLAN-Boulder County*, ed. J. Robertson. Boulder, CO: PLAN-Boulder County.

Brunn, B., and T. Leinbach, eds. 1991. *Collapsing space and time*. London: HarperCollins.

Bryant, C.G.A. and D. Jary, eds. 1991. *Giddens's theory of structuration: A critical appreciation*. London: Routledge.

Brydon, L. 1987. Women in the family: Cultural change in Avatime, Ghana, 1900–80. *Development and Change* (Netherlands), 18:251–269.

Bukh, J. 1979. *The village woman in Ghana*. Uppsala: Scandinavian Institute of African Studies.

Bullock, C. and S. MacManus. 1987. *Municipal electoral structure and the election of councilwomen*. Paper presented to the Southern Political Science Association Meetings, Atlanta.

Bulmer, M., and D. P. Warwick, eds. 1983. *Social research in developing countries: Surveys and censuses in the third world*. Bath, Avon: The Pitman Press Ltd.

Buvinic, M., M. Lycette, and W. P. McGreevy, eds. 1983. *Women and poverty in the third world*. Baltimore: The Johns Hopkins University Press.

Buvinic, M., and S. W. Yudelman. 1989. *Women, poverty and progress in the third world*. Headline Series, no. 289. New York: Foreign Policy Association.

Cadwallader, M. 1988. Urban geography and social theory. *Urban Geography* 9:12–26.

Cain, M. L. 1981. Women and technology—resources for the future. In *Women and technological change in developing countries*, eds. Roslyn Dauber and Melinda Cain, 243–240. AAAS Selected Symposia Series. Boulder, CO: Westview Press.

Caldwell, J. C. 1969. *African rural-urban migration: The movement to Ghana's towns*. Canberra: Australian National University Press.

Carney, J. 1988. Struggles over land and crops in an irrigated rice system in the Gambia. In *Agriculture, women, and land: The African experience*, ed. Jean Davison, 59–78. Boulder, CO: Westview Press.

Castells, M. 1989. *The informational city*. Oxford: Basil Blackwell.

Caughey, J. 1959. Toward an understanding of the West. *Utah Historical Quarterly* 27:7–24.

Central Bureau of Statistics. 1979. *Summary Report on Household Economic Survey, 1974–75*. Accra: Central Bureau of Statistics.

Chodorow, N. 1985. Mothering, male dominance and capitalism. In *Capitalist patriarchy and the case for socialist feminism*, ed. Zillah R. Eisenstein, 83–106. New York: Monthly Review Press.

Chouinard, V., and R. Fincher. 1983. A critique of "Structural Marxism and Human Geography." *Annals of the Association of American Geographers* 73:137–146.

Clark, G. L., and M. J. Dear. 1984. *State apparatus: Structures and language of legitimacy*. Winchester, MA: George Allen and Unwin.

Clegg, S. 1992. How to become an internationally famous British social theorist. *Sociological Review* 38:576–598.

Cloke, P., C. Philo, and D. Sadler. 1991. *Approaching human geography: An introduction to contemporary theoretical debates*. New York: Guilford Press.

Cloud, K., and J. Knowles. 1988. Where do we go from here? Recommendations for action. In *Agriculture, women, and land: The African experience*, ed. Jean Davison, 250–264. Boulder, CO: Westview Press.

Cobb, S. 1976. Social support as a moderator of life stress. *Psychosomatic Medicine* 38:300–314.

Cohen, A. P. 1980. Drama and politics in the development of a London carnival. *Man* 15:65–87.

Cohen, D. L., and J. Daniel. 1981. *The political economy of Africa*. London: Longman.

Cohen, I. J. 1987. Structuration theory and social praxis. In *Social theory today*, eds. Anthony Giddens and Jonathon Turner, 273–308. Stanford: Stanford University Press.

———. 1989. *Structuration theory: Anthony Giddens and the constitution of social life*. London: Macmillan.

Cohen, R. 1976. From peasants to workers in Africa. In *Political economy of contemporary Africa*, eds., Peter Gutkind and Immanual Wallerstein, 155–168. Beverly Hills: Sage.

Cohen, S., and L. Taylor. 1976. *Escape attempts*. Harmondsworth: Penguin.

Collins, J. J. 1978. Marshall falls short, but town in Michigan can boast about its fine collection of 19th century architecture. *American Preservation* 1:9–20.

Colorado Department of Local Affairs.1979. *Population estimates.* Colorado Population Reports, Series CP–26, No. 79C–1. Denver: Colorado Department of Local Affairs, Division of Planning.

————. 1989. *Colorado municipal population estimates 1981 to 1988.* Denver: Colorado Department of Local Affairs, Division of Local Government.

————. Annual. *Local government financial compendium.* Denver: Colorado Department of Local Affairs, Division of Local Government.

Community Relations and Integration Services Division. 1988. *Report of the San Diego plan for racial integration, 1987–1988.* San Diego: San Diego Unified School District.

Cooper, C. 1974. The house as symbol of the self. In *Designing for human behaviour,* eds. J. Lang, C. Burnette, W. Moleski, and D. Vachon, 130–146. Stroudsberg: Dowden, Hutchinson and Ross.

Cox, K., and A. Mair. 1988. Locality and community in the politics of local economic development. *Annals of the Association of American Geographers* 78:307–325.

Crompton, R., and M. Mann., eds. 1986. *Gender stratification.* Cambridge: Polity Press.

Crowell, T. 1982. 1,000 at Colony get layoffs, last checks. *The Daily Sentinel* (Grand Junction, CO) May 4:1A.

Culkin, M., J. Morris, and S. Helburn. 1990. Subsidies and the true cost of child care. *Proceedings, Second Annual Women's Policy Research Conference,* 6–12.

Curry, M. 1991. Postmodernism, language, and the strains of modernism. *Annals of the Association of American Geographers* 81(2):210–228.

Daniels, A. 1988. *Invisible careers: Women civil leaders from the volunteer world.* Chicago: University of Chicago Press.

Data-Bah, E. 1982. *Sex inequalities in an African urban labour market: The case-study of Accra-Tema.* Geneva: International Labour Office.

Davidson, O. G. 1990. *Broken heartland: The rise of America's rural ghetto.* New York: Free Press.

Davison, J., ed. 1988. *Agriculture, women, and land: The African experience.* Boulder, CO: Westview Press.

Day, A., and J. V. Day. 1977. A review of the current state of negotiated order theory. *Sociological Quarterly* 18:126–142.

Dear, M. 1986. Postmodernism and planning. *Environment and Planning D: Society and Space* 4(3):367–384.

de Certeau, M. 1984. *The practice of everyday life.* Trans. S. Rendell. Berkeley: University of California Press.

Denzin, N. K. 1988. *Limited Inc.* Trans. S. Weber. Evanston: Northwestern University Press.

————. 1992. *Symbolic interactionism and cultural studies: The politics of interpretation.* Oxford: Blackwell.

Derrida, J. 1988. *Limited Inc.* Trans. S. Weber. Evanston, IL: Northwestern University Press.

Devos, G. and Romanucci-Ross, L. 1975. *Ethnic identity.* Palo Alto: Mayfield.

Dohrenwend, B. P. et al. 1981. Stress in the community. *Annals, New York Academy of Science* 107:159–174.

Dondis, D. A. 1973. *A primer of visual literacy.* Cambridge, MA: MIT Press.

Douglas, M., and H. Wildavsky. 1982. *Risk and culture*. Berkeley: University of California Press.

Dovey, K. 1985. Home and homelessness. In *Home environments*, eds. I. Altman and C. M. Werner. New York: Plenum Press.

Dumor, E. 1983. Women in rural development in Ghana. *Rural Africana* 17:69–82.

Duncan, J., and D. Ley. 1982. Structural Marxism and human geography: A critical assessment. *Annals of the Association of American Geographers* 72:30–59.

Duncan, J. S. 1980. The superorganic in American cultural geography. *Annals, Association of American Geographers* 70:181–198.

———. 1983. Comment in reply. *Annals of the Association of American Geographers* 73:146–150.

Duncan, S. S. 1981. Housing policy, the methodology of levels, and urban research: The case of Castells'. *International Journal of Urban and Regional Research* 5:231–254.

Durrell, L. 1969. *Spirit of place: Letters and essays of travel*, edited by Allan G. Thomas. New York: Dutton.

Earle, C. 1987. Review of *Place, practice and structure* by Allan Pred. *Economic Geography* 63:273–274.

Edelstein, M. R. 1988. *Contaminated communities*. Boulder, CO: Westview Press.

Edwards, R., and J. Ribbens. 1991. Meanderings around 'strategy.'; *Sociology* 25:477–489.

Eisenstein, Z. R., ed. 1979. *Capitalist patriarchy and the case for socialist feminism*. New York: Monthly Review Press.

Elkin, S. 1987. *City and regime in the American republic*. Chicago: University of Chicago Press.

Employee Connection, February 9, 1990.

Entrikin, N. 1976. Contemporary humanism in geography. *Annals, Association of American Geographers* 66:615–632.

———. 1991. *The betweenness of place: Towards a geography of modernity*. Baltimore: Johns Hopkins University Press.

Epson, B. 1992. Ten years of the PNDC: A revolutionary decade of unity, stability and development? *West Africa* (U.K.) 3876:2138–2149.

Evans, D. 1987. Social interaction and conflict over residential growth: A structurationist perspective. In *Qualitative geography*, ed. J. Eyles, 61–70. London: McGraw-Hill.

Everett, J. 1990. *The global empowerment of women*. Summary report of the Fourth International Conference, Development Challenge for the 1990s: The Global Empowerment of Women, organized by the Association of Women in Development (AWID), November 17–19, 1989, Washington.

Ewusi, K. 1977. *Economic inequality in Ghana*. Accra: New Times Press.

Eyles, J. 1981a. Ideology, contradiction and struggle: An exploratory discussion. *Antipode* 13:39–46.

———. 1981b. Why geography cannot be Marxist. *Environment and Planning A* 13:1371–1388.

———. 1985. *Senses of place*. Warrington: Silverbrook Press.

———. 1989. The geography of everyday life. In *Horizons in human geography*, eds. D. Gregory and R. Walford. London: Macmillan.

————. 1990. Who defines and manages the environment? *Geography Research Reform* 10:29–36.

Eyles, J., and E. Perri. 1993. Life history as method. *Canadian Geographer* 37(2):104–119.

———— et al. 1992. Risk and anxiety in a rural population. In *La geografia medica e gli ecosistemi*, eds. C. Palagiano et al. Perugia: Edizioni Rux.

———— et al. 1993. The social construction of risk in a rural community. *Risk Analysis* 13:281–290.

Fendley, K., and J. Christenson. 1989. Rural reflation: An idea for community development. *Journal of the Community Development Society* 20:103–115.

Fiawoo, D. 1978. *Women and customs in Ghana*. Background paper for seminar on Ghanaian Women in Development. Accra: National Council on Women and Development (NCWD).

Fitchen, J. M. et al. 1987. Risk perception in a community context. In *The social and cultural construction of risk*, eds., B. B. Johnson and V. T. Covello. Dordrecht: D. Reidel.

Fitzgerald, J., and P. Meyer. 1986. Recognizing constraints to local economic development. *Journal of the Community Development Society* 17:115–126.

Flammang, J. 1984. Filling the party vacuum: Women at the grassroots level in local politics. In *Political women: Current roles in state and local government*, ed. J. Flammang, 87–113. Beverly Hills: Sage.

Foote, K. E. 1993. Review of *A question of place: Exploring the practice of human geography* by Ronald J. Johnston. *Annals of the Association of American Geographers* 83:381–383.

Forester, J. 1989. *Planning in the face of power*. Berkeley: University of California Press.

Foster, H. 1985. *Postmodern culture*. London: Pluto Press.

Foucault, J. 1972a. *Archaeology of knowledge*. New York: Pantheon.

————. 1972b. *Power/knowledge*. New York: Pantheon.

————. 1979. *Discipline and punish: The birth of the prison*. New York: Vintage Books.

————. 1980a. Questions on geography. In *Power/knowledge*, ed. C. Gordon, 63–77. New York: Pantheon.

————. 1980b. Truth and power. In *Power/knowledge*, ed. C. Gordon, 109–133. New York: Pantheon.

————. 1986. Of other spaces. *Diacritics* 16:22–7.

Freund, B. 1984. *The making of contemporary Africa: The development of African society since 1800*. Bloomington: Indiana University Press.

Fried, M. 1966. Grieving for a lost home. In *Urban renewal*, ed. J. Q. Wilson, 359–379. Cambridge: MIT Press.

Gallagher, E. 1976. Lines of reconstruction and extension in the Parsonian sociology of illness. *Social Science and Medicine* 10:207–218.

Garfield County Capital Improvements, Inc. (GCCI). 1992. *Harness the future, be pro Expo*. Promotional brochure. Rifle, CO: Garfield County Capital Improvements, Inc.

Garnham, N. 1990. *Capitalism and communication: Global culture and the economics of information*. Beverly Hills: Sage.

George, B. S. 1976. *Education in Ghana*. Office of Education, U.S. Department of Health, Education, and Welfare. Washington: USAID.

Gerhardt, U. 1989. *Ideas about illness*. London: Macmillan.

Ghana Information Services. 1983. *Ghana today.* Accra: Ghana Information Service.

Gibson, E. 1978. Understanding the subjective meaning of places. In *Humanistic geography: Prospects and problems*, eds. D. Ley and M. Samuels, 138–154. Chicago: Maaroufa Press.

Gibson, K. D., and R. J. Horvath. 1983. Aspects of a theory of transition within the capitalist mode of production. *Environment and Planning D: Society and Space* 1:121–138.

Giddens, A. 1971. *Capitalism and modern social theory: An analysis of the writings of Marx, Durkheim and Max Weber.* Cambridge: Cambridge University Press.

———. 1972. *Politics and sociology in the thought of Max Weber.* New York: Macmillan.

———. 1976. *New rules of sociological method: A positive critique of interpretative sociologies.* New York: Basic Books.

———. 1977. *Studies in social and political theory.* New York: Basic Books.

———. 1979. *Central problems in social theory.* London: Macmillan.

———. 1981. *A contemporary critique of historical materialism.* Berkeley: University of California Press.

———. 1982a. Labour and interaction. In *Habermas: Critical debates*, eds. J. Thompson and E. Held, 149–161. Cambridge, MA: MIT Press.

———. 1982b. On the relation of sociology to philosophy. In *Explaining human behavior: Consciousness, human action and social structures*, ed. P. Secord, 175–187. Beverly Hills: Sage.

———. 1982c. *Profiles and critiques in social theory.* Berkeley: University of California Press.

———. 1983. Comments on the theory of structuration. *Journal of the Theory of Social Behavior* 13:5–80.

———. 1984. *The constitution of society: Outline of the theory of structuration.* Berkeley: University of California Press.

———. 1985. Time, space and regionalisation. In *Social relations and spatial structures*, ed. D. Gregory and J. Urry, 265–295. London: Macmillan.

———. 1987. *The nation-state and violence.* Berkeley: University of California Press.

———. 1989. A reply to my critics. In *Social theory of modern societies*, eds. D. Held and J. B. Thompson, 249–301. Cambridge: Cambridge University Press.

———. 1990. *The Consequences of Modernity.* Cambridge: Polity.

———. 1991. Structuration theory: Past, present, and future. In *Giddens' theory of structuration: A critical appreciation*, eds. C.G.A. Bryant and D. Jary, 201–221. London: Routledge.

Gillespie, A., and H. Williams. 1988. Telecommunications and the reconstruction of comparative advantage. *Environment and Planning A* 20:1311–1321.

Glanz, W. 1991a. Ad hoc committee hosts officials, businessmen on trip to view indoor arena in Vernal, UT. *The Citizen Telegram* (Rifle, CO) July 10:3.

———. 1991b. Expo proponents ask county to help plant seed. *The Citizen Telegram* (Rifle, CO) August 28:1.

———. 1991c. Selling the pavilion—more than just another horse barn. *The Citizen Telegram* (Rifle, CO) June 19:3.

———. 1992. Manager urges construction of Garfield Expo Center. *The Citizen Telegram* (Rifle, CO) February 5:1,9.

Godelier, M. 1981. Origins of male dominance. *New Left Review* 127:3–17.

Goffman, E. 1959. *The presentation of self in everyday life*. New York: Doubleday.

Goldthorpe, J. H. 1977. The relevance of history to sociology. In *Sociological Research Methods: An Introduction*, ed. M. Bulmer, 177–191. London: Macmillan.

Golledge, R. G. 1981. Misconceptions, misinterpretations and misrepresentations of behavioral approaches in human geography. *Environment and Planning A* 13:1325–1344.

Goody, J. 1976. *Production, reproduction*. Cambridge: Cambridge University Press.

Goody, J., and S. J. Tambiah. 1973. *Bridewealth and dowry*. Cambridge: Cambridge University Press.

Gorelick, S. 1991. Contradictions of feminist methodology. *Gender and Society* 5:459–477.

Gottdiener, M. 1985. *The social production of urban space*. Austin: University of Texas Press.

———. 1987. *The decline of urban politics: Political theory and the crisis of the local state*. Beverly Hills: Sage.

Gottdiener, M., and M. Neiman. 1981. Characteristics of support for local growth control. *Urban Affairs Quarterly* 17:55–73.

Gough, K. 1961. The modern disintegration of matrilineal descent groups. In *Matrilineal kinship*, eds. David M. Schneider and Kathleen Gough. Berkeley: University of California Press.

———. 1975. The origin of the family. In *Towards an anthropology of women*, ed. Rayna R. Reiter, 51–76. New York: Monthly Review Press.

Gould, P. 1984. *The structure of television*. London: Pion.

Gregory, D. 1978. *Ideology, science and human geography*. New York: St. Martin's Press.

———. 1980. The ideology of control: Systems theory and geography. *Tijdschrift voor Economische en Social Geografie* 71:327–342.

———. 1981. Human agency and human geography. *Transactions of the Institution of British Geographers* 6:1–18.

———. 1982a. *Regional transformation and industrial revolution: A geography of the Yorkshire woolen industry*. Minneapolis: University of Minnesota Press.

———. 1982b. Solid Geometry: Notes on the recovery of spatial structure. In *A search for common ground*, eds., P. Gould and G. Olsson, 187–219. London: Pion.

———. 1984. Space, time, and politics in social theory: An interview with Anthony Giddens. *Environment and Planning D: Society and Space* 2:123–132.

———. 1985. Suspended animation: The stasis of diffusion theory. In *Social relations and spatial structures*, eds. D. Gregory and J. Urry, 296–336. New York: St. Martin's Press.

———. 1989. Presences and absences: Time-space relations and structuration theory. In *Social theory of modern societies: Anthony Giddens and his critics*, eds. D. Held and J. Thompson, 185–214. Cambridge: Cambridge University Press.

———. 1993. *Geographical imaginations*. Oxford: Basil Blackwell.

Gregson, N. 1986. On duality and dualism. *Progress in Human Geography* 10:184–205.

———. 1987. Structuration theory: Some thoughts on the possibilities for empirical research. *Environment and Planning D: Society and Space* 5:73–91.

———. 1989. On the (ir)relevance of structuration theory. In *Social theory of modern societies*, eds. D. Held and J. B. Thompson, 235–248. Cambridge: Cambridge University Press.

Grimes, W. 1991. A small town in grand style. *New York Times* June 23:xx,15–19.

Gruis, P. 1973. Optimum size termed wrong goal. *Daily Camera* September 13:28.

Gulliford, A. 1989. *Boomtown blues: Colorado oil shale, 1885–1985.* Niwot: University Press of Colorado.

Habermas, J. 1979. *Communication and the evolution of society.* Boston: Beacon Press.

Hagerstrand, T. 1970. What about people in regional science? *Papers of the Regional Science Association* 24:7–21.

———. 1984. Presences and absences. *Regional Studies* 18:373–380.

Håkansson, T. 1986. *Landless Gusii women: A result of customary land law and modern marriage patterns.* Working papers in African studies, no. 29. African Studies Programme, Department of Cultural Anthropology. Uppsala: University of Uppsala.

———. 1988. *Bridewealth, women and land: Social change among the Gusii of Kenya.* Uppsala studies in cultural anthropology, no. 10. Stockholm: Almqvist and Wiskell International.

Hakim, C. 1982. *Secondary analysis in social research: A guide to data sources and methods with examples.* Hempstead: George Allen and Unwin.

Halford, S. 1989. Spatial divisions and women's initiatives in British local government. *Geoforum* 20:161–174.

Hall, P., and P. Preston. 1988. *The carrier wave: New information technology and the geography of innovation, 1846–2003.* London: Unwin Hyman.

Hall, P. M. and Spencer-Hall, D. A. 1982. The social conditions of the negotiated order. *Urban Life* 11:328–349.

Hamilton, L. 1985. Concern about toxic wastes: Three demographic predictors. *Sociological Perspectives* 28:463–486.

Hamilton, R. 1978. *The liberation of women: A study of patriarchy and capitalism.* London: George Allen and Unwin.

Hance, B. J. et al. 1989. Setting a context for explaining risk. *Risk Analysis* 9:113–117.

Hansis, B. 1975. The struggle for land: A center of production in Chile. *Antipode* 7(2): 38–41.

Harding, S. 1991. *Whose science? Whose knowledge?* Ithaca: Cornell University Press.

Harris, O. 1981. Households as natural units. In *Of marriage and the market*, eds. Kate Young, Carol Wolkowitz, and Roslyn McCallagh, 49–68. London: CSE Books.

Hart, K. 1973. Informal income opportunities and urban employment in Ghana. *Journal of African Studies* 20(1):61–89.

Hartman, H. 1983. Capitalism, patriarchy, and job segregation by sex. In *The signs reader: Women, gender and scholarship*, eds. Elizabeth Abel and Emily K. Abel, 193–226. Chicago: The University of Chicago Press.

Harvey, D. 1973. *Social justice and the city.* London: Arnold.

———. 1974. Class-monopoly rent, finance capital and the urban revolution. *Regional Studies* 8:239–255.

———. 1975. Discussion. In *Proceedings of the Conference on Urban Change and Conflict*, 219–232. York: Centre for Environmental Studies.

———. 1976. The Marxist theory of the state. *Antipode* 8(2):80–89.

———. 1979. Monument and myth. *Annals of the Association of American Geographers* 69:312–381.

———. 1981. The urban process under capitalism: A framework for analysis. In *Urbanization and urban planning in capitalist society*, 91–123. London: Methuen.

———. 1989. *The condition of postmodernity*. Oxford: Basil Blackwell.

———. 1990. Between space and time: Reflections on the geographical imagination. *Annals of the Association of American Geographers* 80:418–434.

Hay, M. J., and S. Sticher, eds. 1984. *African women south of the Sahara*. London: Longman.

Heidegger, M. 1962. *Being and time*. Trans. J. Macquarrie and E. Robinson. New York: Harper and Row.

Held, D., and J. B. Thompson. 1989. *Social theory of modern societies: Anthony Giddens and his critics*. Cambridge: Cambridge University Press.

Hepworth, M. 1986. The geography of technological change in the information economy. *Regional Studies* 20:407–424.

Hilfer, A. C. 1969. *The revolt from the village*. Chapel Hill: University of North Carolina Press.

Hill, P. 1963. *The migrant cocoa farmers of southern Ghana*. Cambridge: Cambridge University Press.

Hirschon, R. 1984. Introduction: Property, power and gender relations. In *Women and property, women as property*, ed. Renée Hirschon, 1–22. London: Croom Helm.

Hodge, G. D., and M. A. Qadeer. 1983. *Towns and villages in Canada*. Toronto: Butterworth.

Horkheimer, M., and T. Adorno. 1972. The culture industry: Enlightenment as mass deception. In *The dialects of enlightenment*, eds., M. Horkheimer and T. Adorno, 116–139. New York: Seabury Press.

Hosmer, C. B., Jr. 1981. *Preservation comes of age*. Charlottesville: University of Virginia Press.

Howard, R. 1978. *Colonization and the underdevelopment in Ghana*. New York: Africana.

———. 1980. Formation and stratification of the peasantry in colonial Ghana. *Journal of Peasant Studies* 8(1):61–80.

Hudson, B. 1977. The new geography and the new imperialism. *Antipode* 9(2):12–19.

Hunt, G. 1987. The impact of oil price fluctuations on the economies of energy producing states. *Review of Regional Studies* 17:60–78.

Hurn, C. J. 1985. *The limits and possibilities of schooling*. Boston: Allyn and Bacon.

Husband, E.K.E. 1992. *The social and experiential role of the environment*. Person-environment theory series, Center for Environmental Design Research, University of California, Berkeley.

Hymer, S. 1969. *Economic forms in pre-colonial Ghana*. Economic Growth Center discussion paper no. 79. New Haven: Yale University Press.

Isenberg, J. 1984. Colony manager to county: "We are here. We are real people." *Rifle Tribune* (Rifle, CO) May 16:1.

Jackson, J. B. 1980. *The necessity for ruins and other topics*. Amherst: University of Massachusetts Press.

———. 1984. *Discovering the vernacular landscape*. New Haven: Yale University Press.

Jakle, J. A. 1982. *The American small town: Twentieth century place images*. Hamden, CT: Anchor Books.

———. 1985. *The tourist: Travel in twentieth century North America*. Lincoln: University of Nebraska Press.

———. 1986. Childhood on the middle border: Remembered small town America. *Journal of Geography* 85:159–163.

————. 1987. *The visual elements of landscape*. Amherst: University of Massachusetts Press.

————. 1990. Social stereotypes and place images: People on the trans-Appalachian frontier as viewed by travelers. In *Place images in media: Portrayal, experience and meaning*, ed. Leo Zonn, 83–103. Savage, MD: Rowman and Littlefield.

Janelle, D. 1969. Spatial reorganization: A model and concept. *Annals of the Association of American Geographers* 58:348–364.

Jansen, C. J. 1981. *Education and social mobility of immigrants*. Vancouver: Institute for Behavioral Research.

Jary, D. 1991. Society as time traveller: Giddens on historical change, historical materialism and the nation state in world society. In *Giddens' structuration theory: A critical appreciation*, eds. C. A. Bryant and D. Jary, 116–159. London: Routledge.

Jaspers, K. 1965. *Leonardo, Descartes, Max Weber*. Trans. R. Mannheim. London: Routledge and Kegan Paul.

Jiagge, A. 1975. *Enhancing African women's role in development*. Paper prepared for the African Development Bank. Abidjan: African Development Bank.

Johnson, E. 1971. *Is population growth good for Boulder citizens?* Boulder, CO: Boulder Zero Population Growth.

Johnston, R. J. 1991. *Geography and geographers*. London: Edward Arnold.

Kahneman, D. et al. 1982. *Judgement under uncertainty*. Cambridge: Cambridge University Press.

Karnig, A., and S. Welch. 1979. Sex and ethnic differences in municipal representation. *Social Science Quarterly* 60:465–481.

Kasperson, R. E. 1971. The post-behavioral revolution in geography. *British Columbia Geographical Series* 12:5–20.

Kasperson, R. E. et al. 1988. The social amplification of risk. *Risk analysis* 8:177–187.

Kellerman, A. 1987. Structuration theory and attempts at integration in human geography. *Professional Geographer* 39:267–274.

Kelly-Gadol, J. 1976. The social relations of the sexes: Methodological implications of women's history. In *The signs reader: Women, gender and scholarship*, eds. Elizabeth Abel and Emily Abel, 11–26. Chicago: The University of Chicago Press.

Kennedy, P. 1988. *African capitalism: The struggle for ascendency*. New York: Cambridge University Press.

Kern, S. 1983. *The culture of time and space 1880–1918*. Cambridge, MA: Harvard University Press.

Kessler, R. C. 1982. A disaggregation of the relationship between socio-economic status and psychological stress. *American Sociological Review* 47:752–764.

———— and Cleary, P. D. 1980. Social class and psychological distress. *American Sociological Review* 45:463–478.

Killick, T. 1978. *Development economics in action: A study of economic policies in Ghana*. London: Heineman.

Kirby, A. 1985. Nine fallacies of local economic change. *Urban Affairs Quarterly* 21(2):207–220.

Kleniewski, N. 1987. Local business leaders and urban policy: A case study. *The Insurgent Sociologist* 14(1):33–56.

Kubey, R. and Csikszentmihalyi, M. 1990. *Television and the quality of life: How viewing shapes everyday experience*. Hillsdale, NJ: Erlbaum.

Kuper, A. 1992. Introduction. In *Conceptualizing society*, ed. A. Kuper. London: Routledge.

Lakatos, I. 1978. Falsification and the methodology of scientific research programmes. In *The methodology of scientific research programmes, philosophical papers*, eds. J. Worrall and G. Currie, 8–101. Cambridge: Cambridge University Press.

Lamm, R., and M. McCarthy. 1982. *The angry west: A vulnerable land and its future*. Boston: Houghton Mifflin.

Langdale, J. 1985. Electronic funds transfer and the internationalisation of the banking and finance industry. *Geoforum* 16:1–13.

———. 1989. The geography of international business telecommunications: The role of leased networks. *Annals of the Association of American Geographers* 79:501–522.

Layder, D. 1981. *Structure, interaction and social theory*. London: Routledge and Kegan Paul.

———. 1991. The empirical correlates of action and structure. *Sociology* 25:447–464.

Lazarus, R., and S. Folkman. 1984. *Stress, appraisal and coping*. New York: Springer.

Lefebvre, H. 1974 (English translation 1991). *The production of space*. London: Blackwell.

———. 1979. Space: Social product and use value. In *Critical sociology*, ed. J. W. Freiberg, 285–295. New York: Irvington.

———. 1991. *The production of space*. trans. D. Nicholson-Smith. Oxford: Basil Blackwell.

Levine, A. G., and R. A. Stone. 1986. Threats to people and what they value. In *Advances in environmental psychology*, vol. 6, eds. A. H. Lebovitz, A. Baum, and J. Singer, 109–130. New Brunswick: Erlbaum.

Lewis. B. 1984. The impact of development policies on women. In *African women south of the Sahara*, eds. Margaret J. Hay and Sharon Sticther, 170–194. London: Longman.

Lewis, D. K. 1983. A response to inequality: Black women, racism, and sexism. In *The signs reader: Women, gender and scholarship*, eds. Elizabeth Abel and Emily Abel, 169–192. Chicago: University of Chicago Press.

Ley, D. 1980. *Geography without man: A humanistic critique*. Oxford: School of Geography, University of Oxford.

———. 1981. Behavioral geography and the philosophies of meaning. In *Behavioral problems in geography revisited*, eds. K. R. Cox and R. G. Golledge, 209–230. London: Methuen.

Lindsday, B., ed. 1980. *Comparative perspectives of third world women: The impact of race, sex, and class*. New York: Praeger.

Logan, J., and H. Molotch. 1987. *Urban fortunes: The political economy of place*. Berkeley: University of California Press.

Louis, K. S., and M. B. Miles. 1990. *Improving the urban high school: What works and why*. New York: Teachers College Press.

Lowenthal, David. 1966. The American way of history. *Columbia University Forum* 19:27–32.

———. 1985. *The past is a foreign country*. Cambridge: Cambridge University Press.

Luke, T. 1991. Touring hyperreality: Critical theory confronts informational society. In *Critical theory now*, ed. P. Wexler, 1–26. London: Falmer Press.

McDowell, L. 1988. Coming in from the dark: Feminist research in geography. In *Research in human geography*, ed. J. Eyles, 155–173. Oxford: Basil Blackwell.

Mackenzie, S. 1988. Balancing our space and time: The impact of women's organisation on the British city, 1920–1980. In *Women in cities: Gender and the urban environment*, eds. J. Little, L. Peake, and P. Richardson, 41–60. New York: New York University Press.

Mackinnon, C. A. 1983. Feminism, Marxism, method and the state: An agenda for theory. In *The signs reader: Women, gender and scholarship*, eds. Elizabeth Abel and Emily Abel, 227–256. Chicago: University of Chicago Press.

McLennan, G. 1990. Interchange: McLennan replies to Pred. In *Anthony Giddens: Consensus and controversy*, eds. J. Clark, C. Mogdil, and S. Mogdil, 141–142. London: Falmer Press.

McLuhan, M. 1964. *Understanding media: The extension of man*. New York: McGraw Hill.

Maher, V. 1974. *Women and property in Morrocco*. Cambridge: Cambridge University Press.

Mann, M. 1986. *The sources of social power, volume I: A history of power from the beginning to A.D. 1760*. Cambridge: Cambridge University Press.

Manu, T. 1984. *Law and the status of women in Ghana*. African Training and Research Centre for Women Research Series. Addis Ababa: United Nations Economic Commission for Africa.

Marchand, R. 1985. *Advertising and the American dream: Making way for modernity, 1920–1940*. Berkeley: University of California Press.

Marcuse, H. 1964. *One dimensional man*. Boston: Beacon.

Mark-Lawson, J., M. Savage, and A. Warde. 1985. Gender and local politics: Struggles over welfare policies, 1918–1939. In *Localities, class and gender*, eds. L. Murgatroyd, M. Savage, D. Shapiro, J. Urry, S. Walby, A. Warde, and J. Mark-Lawson, 195–215. 195–231. London: Pion.

Martin, M. 1991. Communication and social forms: The development of the telephone 1876–1920. *Antipode* 23:307–333.

Marvin, C. 1988. *When old technologies were new: Thinking about electric communication in the late nineteenth century*. Oxford: Oxford University Press.

Marx, K. 1973. *Grundrisse*. New York: Vintage.

Massey, D. 1983. Industrial restructuring as class restructuring: Production decentralization and local uniqueness. *Regional Studies* 17:73–89.

———. 1984. *Spatial divisions of labor*. New York: Methuen.

———. 1992. Politics and space/time. *New Left Review* 196:65–84.

Mayer, C., and G. Riley. 1985. *Public domain, private dominion: A history of public mineral policy in America*. San Francisco: Sierra Club Books.

Mead, G. 1934. *Mind, self, and society*. Chicago: University of Chicago Press.

Mehls, S. 1988. *The valley of opportunity: A history of west-central Colorado*. Colorado resource series, no. 12. Denver: U.S. Bureau of Land Management.

Mensah-Bonsu, H.J.A.N. n.d. *The subtle effects of legislature on women and childbearing*. Paper presented at the National Conference on Population and National Reconstruction held at the University of Ghana. *Conference Proceedings*, vol. II, contributed papers, pp. 229–237.

Messer-Davidow, E. 1991. Telling stories: The construction of women's agency. In

(En)gendering Knowledge: Feminists in Academe, eds. J. Hartman and E. Messer-Davidow, 11–34. Knoxville: University of Tennessee Press.

Meyrowitz, J. 1985. *No sense of place: The impact of electronic media on social behavior*. New York: Oxford University Press.

Mikell, G. 1986. Ghanaian females, rural economy and national stability. *African Studies Review* 29(3):67–88.

———. 1990. Women and economic development in Ghana: Fluctuating fortunes. *Sage* VII(1):224-227.

Mingione, E. 1985. *Social conflict and the city*. Oxford: Blackwell.

Moock, J. L., ed. 1986. *Understanding African rural households and farming systems*. Boulder, CO: Westview Press.

Moos, A., and M. Dear. 1986. Structuration theory in urban analysis: 1. Theoretical exegesis. *Environment and Planning A* 18:231–252.

Moore, H. L. 1988. *Feminism and anthropology*. Minneapolis: University of Minnesota Press.

Morna, C. L., J. Araka, M. Safo, Ouattara, S. B. Mbalaka, and S. Wainaina. 1991. Women seek control of the land. *African farmer: The key to Africa's future*. No. 6, 29–33. New York: The Hunger Project.

Moss, M. 1987. Telecommunications, world cities, and urban policy. *Urban Studies* 24:534–546.

Moss, M., and A. Dunau. 1986. Offices, information technology, and locational trends. In *The changing office workplace*, eds. J. Black, K. Roark, and L. Schwartz, 171–182. Washington: Urban Land Institute.

Mount Sterling Advocate. Various dates.

Murgatroyd, L. 1989. Only half the story: Some blinkering effects of "malestream" sociology. In *Social theory of modern societies: Anthony Giddens and his critics*, eds. D. Held and J. Thompson, 147–161. Cambridge: Cambridge University Press.

Nafziger, E. W. 1988. *Inequality in Africa: Political elites, proletariat, peasants and the poor*. Cambridge: Cambridge University Press.

National Center for Education Statistics. 1991. *Digest of Education Statistics*. Washington: U.S. Department of Education.

National Council on Women and Development. 1990. *Non-formal education for women: Situational analysis indicators*. Document I. GHA/85/005. Accra: National Council on Women and Development.

Natter, W., and J. P. Jones. 1993a. Pets or meat: Class, ideology, and space in *Roger and me*. *Antipode* 25(2):140–158.

———. 1993b. Signposts toward a poststructuralist geography. In *Postmodern contentions*, eds. J. P. Jones, W. Natter, and T. Schatzki, 165–203. New York: Guilford.

Nelson, B. 1984. Women's poverty and women's citizenship: Some political consequences of economic marginality. *Signs* 10:209–231.

Nelson, K. 1986. Labor demand, labor supply and the suburbanization of low-wage office work. In *Production, work, territory*, eds. A. Scott and M. Storper, 149–171. Boston: Allen Unwin.

Nicol, L. 1985. Communications technology: Economic and spatial impacts. In *High technology, space, and society*, ed. M. Castells, 191–209. Beverly Hills: Sage.

Norberg-Schulz, C. 1980. *Genius-loci: Towards a phenomenology of architecture*. New York: Rizzoli.

230 References

Office of the Superintendent. 1987. *San Diego Unified School District: Statistical report 1987–88.* San Diego: San Diego Unified School District.

Okali, C. 1975. *Dominase, a mobile cocoa farming community in Brong-Ahafo.* Technical publication series no. 35. Legon: Institute for Social, Statistical and Economic Research.

———. 1983. Kinship and cocoa farming in Ghana. In *Female and male in West Africa,* ed. Christine Oppong, 169–178. London: George Allen and Unwin.

Oliver, R., and G. N. Sanderson. eds. 1985. *Cambridge History of Africa: 1870–1905.* London: Cambridge University Press.

Ong, W. 1982. *Orality and literacy: The technologizing of the word.* London: Methuen.

Oppong, C., ed. 1983. *Female and male in West Africa.* London: George Allen and Unwin.

———. 1987. *Sex roles, population and development in West Africa: Policy related studies on demographic issues.* Geneva: ILO.

Oppong, C., and K. Abu. 1987. *Seven roles of women: Impact of education, migration and employment on Ghanaian mothers.* Women, work, and development series, no. 13. Geneva, ILO.

Overholt, A., K. Cloud, and J. E. Austin, eds. 1985. *Gender roles in development projects: A case book.* West Hartford, CT: Kumarian Press.

Pahl, R. E. 1984. *Divisions of labour.* Oxford: Blackwell.

Palmer, I. 1981. Seasonal dimensions of women's roles. In *Seasonal dimensions of rural poverty,* eds. Robert Chambers, R. Longhurst, and H. Pacey, 195–201. London: Francis Pinter.

Pankhurst, D., and S. Jacobs. 1988. Land tenure, gender relations and agricultural production: The case of Zimbabwe's peasantry. In *Agriculture, women, and land: The African experience,* ed. Jean Davison, 202–227. Boulder, CO: Westview Press.

Pardo, M. 1990. Mexican American women grassroots community activists: "Mothers of East Los Angeles." *Frontiers* 11:1–7.

Parker, C., and C. Bernhardt. 1991. Letter to the editor: Committee searching for broad based representation. *The Citizen Telegram* (Rifle, CO) August 7:5.

Parsons, T. 1951. *The social system.* Glencoe: Free Press.

Perri, E. 1990. *The Italian-Canadian experience in a changing Hamilton.* Unpublished M.A. thesis, McMaster University, Department of Geography.

Personal Narratives Group, ed. 1989. *Interpreting women's lives: Feminist theory and personal narratives.* Bloomington: Indiana University Press.

Planning, Research, and Evaluation Division. 1987. *Encanto elementary school magnet evaluation report.* San Diego: San Diego Unified School District.

Porteous, J. D. 1976. Home. *Geographical Review* 66:383–390.

Poster, M. 1990. *The mode of information: Poststructuralism and social context.* Chicago: University of Chicago Press.

Postman, N. 1985. *Amusing ourselves to death.* New York: Penguin.

Prah, K. K., ed. 1989. *Essays on African society and history.* Accra: Ghana Universities Press.

Pratt, G. 1981. The house as an expression of social worlds. In *Housing and identity,* ed. J. S. Duncan, 135–180. London: Croom Helm.

Pred, A. 1977. *City-systems in advanced economies.* New York: John Wiley and Sons.

———. 1981a. Power, everyday practice and the discipline of human geography. In

Space and time in geography: Essays dedicated to Torsten Hägerstrand, 30–55. Lund: Gleerup.

———. 1981b. Social reproduction and the time-geography of everyday life. *Geografiska Annaler B* 63:5–22.

———. 1982. Social reproduction and the time-geography of everyday life. In *A search for common ground*, eds. P. Gould and G. Olsson, 157–186. London: Pion.

———. 1983. Structuration and place: On the becoming of sense of place and structure of feeling. *Journal for the Theory of Social Behavior* 13:45–68.

———. 1984. Place as historically contingent process: Structuration and the time-geography of becoming places. *Annals of the Association of American Geographers* 74:279–297.

———. 1985. The social becomes the spatial, the spatial becomes the social: Enclosures, social change, and the becoming of places in the Swedish province of Skäne. In *Social relations and spatial structures*, eds. D. Gregory and J. Urry, 337–365. New York: St. Martin's Press.

———. 1986. *Place, practice and structure: Social and spatial transformation in southern Sweden*. Totowa, NJ: Barnes and Noble.

———. 1990a. In other wor(l)ds: Fragmented and integrated observations on gendered languages, gendered spaces and local transformation. *Antipode* 22:33–52.

———. 1990b. *Making histories and constructing human geographies: The local transformation of practice, power relations, and consciousness*. Boulder, CO: Westview Press.

Reading Club of Rifle, Colorado. 1973. *Rifle shots: The story of Rifle, Colorado*. Rifle, CO: Reading Club of Rifle.

Regulska, J., S. Fried, and J. Tiefenbacher. 1991. Women, politics and place: Spatial patterns of representation in New Jersey. *Geoforum* 22:203–221.

Relph, E. 1976. *Place and placelessness*. London: Pion.

———. 1981. *Humanistic geography and rational landscapes*. London: Croom Helm.

Remy, D. 1985. Underdevelopment and the experience of women: A Nigerian case study. In *Towards an anthropology of women*, ed. Rayna R. Reiter, 358–371. New York: Monthly Review Press.

Richardson, L. 1990. *Writing strategies: Reaching diverse audiences*. Newbury Park, CA: Sage.

Robben, A. C. 1989. Habits of the home. *American Anthropologist* 91:570–588.

Robertson, C. C. 1990. *Sharing the same bowl: A socioeconomic history of women and class in Accra, Ghana*. Ann Arbor: University of Michigan Press.

Robertson, C. C. and Berg, I., eds. 1975. *Women and class in Africa*. New York: Africana.

Robertson, J. 1986. *Highlights of PLAN-Boulder County, 1959–1986*. Boulder, CO: PLAN-Boulder County.

Rogers, S. C. 1975. Female forms of power and the myth of male dominance: A model of female/male interaction in peasant societies. *American Ethnologist* 2:727–757.

Rose, L. 1988. A woman is like a field: Women's strategies for land access in Swaziland. In *Agriculture, women, and land: The African experience*, ed. Jean Davison, 177–201. Boulder, CO: Westview Press.

Ross, M. D. 1972. Jacksonville. *Historic Preservation* 24:26–29.

Ryan, V. 1988. The significance of community development to rural economic development initiatives. In *Rural economic development in the 1980s: Proposals for the future,* eds. D. Brown et al., 359–375. Washington: U.S. Department of Agriculture, Economic Research Service.

Rybczynski, W. 1987. *Home.* New York: Penguin.

Sabbah, F. 1985. The new media. In *High technology, space, and society,* ed. M. Castells, 210–225. Beverly Hills, CA: Sage.

Sacks, K. 1975. Engels revisited: Women, the organization of production, and private property. In *Towards an anthropology of women,* ed. Rayna Reiter, 211–234. New York: Monthly Review Press.

Salamon, S. 1985. Ethnic communities and the structures of agriculture. *Rural Sociology* 50:323–340.

San Diego City Schools. 1987. *Magnet programs.* San Diego: San Diego Unified School District.

Sauer, Carl O. 1925. The morphology of landscape. *University of California Publications in Geography* 2(2):19–54; reprinted in John Leighly, ed., *Land and life: A selection from the writings of Carl Ortwein Sauer.* Berkeley: University of California Press, 1963.

Saunders, P. 1981. *Social theory and the urban question.* London: Hutchinson.

———. 1989. Space, urbanism, and the created environment. In *Social theory of modern societies: Anthony Giddens and his critics,* eds. David Held and John B. Thompson, 215–234. Cambridge: Cambridge University Press.

Sayer, A. 1982. Explanation in economic geography. *Progress in Human Geography* 6:68–88.

———. 1983. Review of *A contemporary critique of historical materialism* by A. Giddens. *Environment and Planning D: Society and Space* 1:109–114.

———. 1984. *Method in social science: A realist approach.* London: Hutchinson.

Schantz, J. and H. Perry. 1978. Oil shale—a new set of uncertainties. *Natural Resources Journal* 18:275–285.

Sen, A. A. 1990. Gender and cooperative conflict. In *Persistent inequalities: Women and world development,* ed. Irene Tinker, 123–149. New York: Oxford University Press.

Sennett, R. 1977. *The fall of public man.* New York: Norton.

Sewell, W. H. 1992. A theory of structure. *American Journal of Sociology* 98:1–29.

Sharma, K., H. Sahba, and S. Archana. 1984. *Women in focus: A community in search of equal roles.* Hyderabad: Sangam.

Sharma, U. 1984. Dowry in India: Its consequences for women. In *Women and property, women as property,* ed. Renée Hirschon, 62–74. London: Croom Helm.

Sheppard, E. 1988. The search for flexible social theory: Comments on Cadwallader. *Urban Geography* 9:255–264.

Sheth, J. N. 1978. *Household decision making: An exploratory study.* Faculty working papers, no. 525. College of Commerce and Business Administration. Urbana-Champaign: University of Illinois.

Short, J. F. 1984. The social fabric of risk. *American Sociological Review* 49:711–725.

Sivard, R. L. 1985. *Women . . . a world survey.* Washington: World Priorities.

Slovic, P. 1987. Perception of risk. *Science* 236:280–285.

———. et al. 1991. Risk perception, trust and nuclear waste. *Environment* 33(3):7–11, 28–30.

Smith, C. 1975. Being mentally ill—in the asylum or the ghetto. *Antipode* 7(2):53–59.

————. 1983. Structuration theory: The case of the pure bred beef industry. *Journal of the Theory of Social Behavior* 13:12–31.

Smith, J. M. 1993. Review of *Paradigms regained: Pluralism and the Practice of Criticism*, by James L. Battersby. *Annals of the Association of American Geographers* 83:371–33.

Smith, N. 1979a. Geography, science and post-positivist modes of explanation. *Progress in Human Geography* 3:356–382.

————. 1979b. Towards a theory of gentrification: A back-to-the-city movement by capital, not people. *Journal of the American Planning Association* 45:538–548.

————. 1982. Gentrification and uneven development. *Economic Geography* 58:139–155.

————. 1984. *Uneven development*. Oxford: Basil Blackwell.

————. 1990. *Uneven development*, 2nd ed. Oxford: Basil Blackwell.

Smith, P. 1981. *A look at Boulder: From settlement to city*. Boulder, CO: Pruett Publishing Company.

Smith, S. 1988. Political interpretations of "racial segregation" in Britain. *Environment and Planning D* 6:423–444.

Smythe, D. 1977. Communications: Blindspot of western Marxism. *Canadian Journal of Political and Social Theory* 1:1–27.

Soja, E. W. 1980. The socio-spatial dialectic. *Annals of the Association of American Geographers* 70:207–225.

————. 1983. Redoubling the helix: Space-time and the critical social theory of Anthony Giddens. *Environment and Planning A* 15:1267–1272.

————. 1985. The spatiality of social life: Towards a transformative retheorization. In *Social relations and spatial structures*, eds. D. Gregory and J. Urry, 90–127. New York: St. Martins.

————. 1989. *Postmodern geographies: The reassertion of space in critical social theory*. London: Verso.

Staeheli, L., and S. Clarke. 1994. Gender, place, and politics. In *Gender in Urban Research*, eds. J. Garber and R. Turner. Newbury Park, CA: Sage.

Stallen, P.J.M., and A. Tomas. 1988. Public concern about individual hazards. *Risk Analysis* 8:237–245.

Staudt, K. 1979. Class and sex in the politics of women farmers. *Journal of Politics* 41(1):492–512.

————. 1984. *Women's politics and capitalist transformation in sub-Saharan Africa*. Working paper, no. 54. East Lansing: Michigan State University.

Staudt, K., and Gluckman, H., eds. 1989. Beyond Nairobi: Women's politics and policies in Africa revisited. *Issue: A Journal of Opinion* 12(2):4–6.

Steel, W. F. 1954. Female and small-scale employment under modernization in Ghana. *Economic Development and Cultural Change* 3(1)153–167.

Stone, C. 1987. The study of the politics of urban development. In *The Politics of Urban Development*, eds. C. Stone and H. Sanders, 3–22. Lawrence: The University Press of Kansas.

Storper, M. and R. Walker. 1989. *The capitalist imperative: Territory, technology, and industrial growth*. New York: Basil Blackwell.

Strathern, M. 1984. Subject or object? Women and the circulation of valuables in Highlands, New Guinea. In *Women and property, women as property*, ed. Renée Hirschon, 158–175. London: Croom Helm.

Strauss, A. 1978. *Negotiations*. San Francisco: Jossey-Bass.

Strauss, A. et al. 1964. *Psychiatric institutions and ideologies*. Glencoe: Free Press.

Strobel, M. 1982. African women. *Signs* 8(1)109–131.

Sturino, F. 1978. Family and kin cohesion among north Italian immigrants in Toronto. In *The Italian immigrant women in North America*, eds. B. Caroli et al. Toronto: Multicultural History Society of Ontario.

Sullivan, N. 1983. Shale country—past to present. *Shale Country* 5(1)6–9.

Swinth, R., and A. Alexander. 1990. Power and dependence between the core and rural communities: Participating with major actors in solving local problems. *Journal of the Community Development Society* 21:71–82.

Swyngedouw, E. 1989. The heart of the place: The resurrection of locality in an age of hyperspace. *Geografiska Annaler* 71:31–42.

Tadria, H.M.K. 1985. *Changing economic and gender patterns among the peasants of Ndejje and Sseguku in Uganda*. Unpublished Ph.D. dissertation, University of Minnesota.

Taylor, G., and L. Mumby, eds., 1982. *Colorado energy statistical abstract*. Lakewood: Colorado Energy Research Institute.

Taylor, O., ed. 1987. *Oil shale, water resources, and valuable minerals of the Piceance Basin, Colorado: The challenge and choice of development*. U.S. Geological Survey professional paper 1310. Washington: U.S. Department of the Interior, U.S. Geological Survey.

Taylor, S. M. et al. 1993. *Psychosocial impacts in populations exposed to solid waste facilities*. Report to Ontario Ministry of Environment. Hamilton: McMaster University.

Thompson, J. B. 1989. The theory of structuration. In *Social theory of modern societies*, eds. D. Held and J. B. Thompson, 56–76. Cambridge: Cambridge University Press.

Thrift, N. J. 1987. The fixers: The urban geography of international commercial capital. In *Global restructuring and territorial development*, eds. J. Henderson and M. Castells, 203–233. Beverly Hills, CA: Sage.

———. 1981. Owners' time and own time: The making of a capitalist time consciousness, 1300–1880. In *Space and time in geography: Essays dedicated to Torsten Hägerstrand*, 56–84. Lund: Gleerup.

———. 1982. Editorial. Towards a human geography. *Environment and Planning A* 14:1280–1282.

———. 1983a. On the determination of social action in space and time. *Environment and Planning D: Society and Space* 1:23–57.

———. 1983b. Editorial. The politics of context. *Environment and Planning D: Society and Space* I:371–376.

———. 1986. Bear & mouse or bear & tree? Anthony Giddens's reconstitution of social theory. *Sociology* 19:609–623.

Tinker, I., ed. 1990. *Persistent inequalities: Women and world development*. New York: Oxford University Press.

Tipple, A. G. 1986. Revolution in property rights. *West Africa* 3569:179–180.

Tremblay, M. A. and W. J. Anderson. 1970. *Rural Canada in transition*. Ottawa: Agricultural Economics Research Council.

Tuan, Y. 1975. Place: An experiential perspective. *Geographical Review* 65:151–165.

———. 1977. *Space and place: The perspective of experience*. Minneapolis: University of Minnesota Press.

United Nations. 1975. *Fear woman*. Produced and directed by United Nations. 28 min. Filmstrip. New York: United Nations.

———. 1976. *Report of the World Conference of the International Women's Year*. Mexico City, June 19–July 2, 1975. New York: United Nations.

———. 1980. *World plan of action for the decade on women*. New York: United Nations.

Urdang, S. 1975. *Fighting two colonialisms: Women in Guinea Bissau*. New York: Monthly Review Press.

USAID. 1982. *Women in development policy paper*. Bureau for Program and Policy Coordination. Washington: United States Agency for International Development.

Vellenga, D. D. 1977a. Differentiation among women farmers in two rural areas. *Labour and Society* II(2)197–208.

———. 1977b. Who is a wife? Legal heterosexual conflicts in Ghana. In *Female and male in West Africa*, ed. Christine Oppong, 144–155. London: George Allen and Unwin.

———. 1985. Women, households and food commodity chains in southern Ghana: Contradictions between the search for profit and the struggle for survival. *Review* 8(3):293–318.

Vercruijsse, E.V.W. 1988. *The political economy of peasant farming in Ghana*. The Hague, The Institute of Social Studies.

Wallerstein, I. 1976. Three stages of African involvement in the world economy. In *Political economy of contemporary Africa*, eds. P.C.W. Gutkind and I. Wallerstein. London: Sage.

Ward, K. B. 1990. *Women in the world-system: Its impact on status and fertility*. New York: Praeger.

Warde, A. 1987. Review of *Place, practice, and structure* by Allan Pred. *Annals of the Association of American Geographers* 77:484–486.

Warf, B. 1986. Ideology, everyday life, and emancipatory phenomenology. *Antipode* 18:268–283.

———. 1988. Regional transformation, everyday life, and Pacific Northwest lumber production. *Annals of the Association of American Geographers* 78:326–347.

———. 1989. Telecommunications and the globalization of financial services. *Professional Geographer* 31:257–271.

Warner, K., and H. Molotch. 1990. *Growth management in three areas: Use and exchange values in political practice*. Paper presented to the Western Political Science Meetings, Newport Beach, California.

Webb, W. 1937. *Divided we stand: The crisis of a frontierless democracy*. New York: Farrar and Rinehart.

Weber, M. 1978. *Economy and society*. Berkeley: University of California Press.

Weiss, R. S. 1966. Alternatives in the study of complex situations. *Human Organization* 25:198–205.

Westwood, S. 1984. Fear woman: Property and modes of production in urban Ghana. In *Women and property, women as property*, ed. Renée Hirschon, 140–157. London: Croom Helm.

Whirlpool Corporation. *Annual Report*. Various years.

Whitehead, A. 1981. I'm hungry, Mum: The politics of domestic budgeting. In *Of marriage and the market*, eds. Kale Young, Carol Wolkowitz, and Rosyln McCallagh, 88–111. London: CSE Books.

———. 1984a. Men and women, kinship and property: Some general issues. In *Women and property, women as property*, ed. Renée Hirschon, 176–192. London: Croom Helm.

———, ed. 1984b. *Women and property, women as property*. London: Croom Helm.

Wilk, R., and E. J. Arnould, eds. 1984. *Households: Comparative and historical studies of the domestic group*. Berkeley: University of California Press.

Williams, S. W. 1981. Realism, Marxism and human geography. *Antipode* 13:31–38.

Wolin, S. S. 1981. Max Weber: Legitimation, method, and the politics of theory. *Political Theory* 9:401–424.

Wolinsky, F. D. 1981. Expecting sick-role legitimation and getting it. *Journal of Health and Social Behaviour* 22:229–242.

Wollheim, R. 1970. Sociological explanation of the arts: Some distinctions. In *The sociology of art and literature*, ed. M. Albrecht, J. Barnett, and M. Griff, 574–581. New York: Praeger.

World Bank. 1989a. *Ghana: Structural adjustment for growth*. Washington: The World Bank.

———. 1989b. *Women in development: Issues for economic and sector analysis*. Policy, planning, and research working papers. Women in Development, Population and Human Resources Department, WPS 269. Washington: The World Bank.

———. 1991. Research priorities for the 1990s. *World Bank Policy Research Bulletin* 2(1):1–20.

The WPA Guide to 1930s Colorado. 1987. Lawrence: University Press of Kansas.

Wright, E. O. 1983. Giddens's critique of Marxism. *New Left Review* 138:11–35.

Young, K., C. Wolkowitz, and R. McCallagh, eds., 1981. *Of marriage and the market*. London: CSE Books.

Zelinsky, W. 1992. *The cultural geography of the United States*. Englewood Cliffs, NJ: Prentice Hall.

Ziegler, A. P., Jr. 1980. *Historic preservation in small towns: A manual of practice*. Nashville: American Association for State and Local History.

Index

About the Contributors

CHERUB ANTWI-NSIAH is a visiting Assistant Professor in the Department of Geography and also a consultant for the Office of Women in International Development at the University of Illinois at Urbana-Champaign. Her research and teaching interests include third world development; women and the environment; women's access to education and property; the interactions between gender, class, descent systems and location; and the interface between patriarchy and capitalism and its effect on women.

JEREMY D. BROWNING is an Instructor in the Department of Geography at the University of Illinois at Urbana-Champaign. He has published in *Tijdschrift voor Econ. en Sec. Geog.* His research interests include social and economic urban revitalization, race relations, and research methodologies.

MICHAEL J. DEAR is Professor of Geography at the University of Southern California. He has published widely in the fields of social welfare and social theory. His most recent book, with Jennifer Wolch, is *Malign Neglect: Homelessness in an American City* (1993). He is founding editor of the journal *Society and Space*.

JOHN EYLES is Professor of Geography and Research Professor in Environmental Health at McMaster University, Hamilton, Canada. He has authored or edited eight books including *Qualitative Methods in Human Geography* (1988) and *The Social Effects of Health Policy* (1990). His research interests range from health policy issues to the negotiation of everyday life.

JAMES O. HUFF is Professor of Geography at the University of Colorado at Boulder. He also has an appointment in the Institute of Behavioral Science, Population Program. This volume is an outgrowth of his work in behavioral geography focusing on residential segregation and residential mobility. His current interests also include an NSF-funded project on the modeling of industry dynamics as the outcome of context dependent decision-making processes.

ELIZA K. ELLIS HUSBAND is Assistant Professor of Urban and Regional Planning at the University of Illinois at Urbana-Champaign. Her current work focuses on contestation between minority cultural traditions and Anglo-American policy and planning practice. She is the author of a soon-to-be published book on the historical geography of U.S. capital punishment.

JOHN A. JAKLE is Professor and head of the Department of Geography at the University of Illinois at Urbana-Champaign. Books authored and coauthored include *The American Small Town: Twentieth-Century Place Images*, *Common Houses in America's Small Towns: The Atlantic Seaboard to the Mississippi Valley*, and *Derelict Landscapes: The Washing of America's Built Environment*. His interests range widely across historical, social, and urban geography.

JOHN PAUL JONES, III, is Associate Professor in the Department of Geography at the University of Kentucky. His research in social and economic geography has appeared in the *Annals, Association of American Geographers, Antipode, Economic Geography, Environment and Planning A, Geoforum, Urban Geography*, and other journals. Most recently, he has served as co-editor of two interdisciplinary volumes in social theory, *Postmodern Contentions: Epochs, Politics, and Space* (1993), and *Objectivity and its Others* (1994).

ADAM I. MOOS served as Director of Rent Stabilization for the city of West Hollywood from 1984–1986. He entered the film business in 1987 and has since worked as a Producer and Production Manager of theatrical and IMAX feature films.

JEFFERSON S. ROGERS is a Graduate Teaching Associate in the Department of Geography at the University of Illinois at Urbana-Champaign and a Graduate Research Assistant at the U.S. Army Corps of Engineers Research Laboratories. His research interests include community economic development, the geography of tourism, and the geography of the lodging industry.

LYNN A. STAEHELI is an Assistant Professor in the Department of Geography at the University of Colorado at Boulder. She is also affiliated with the Research Program on Political and Economic Change at the Institute of Behavioral Science there. Research and teaching interests include gender and race relations in urban politics and the ways in which restructuring affects community and political activism.

JOSHUA VAN LIEU is a recent graduate of the Department of Geography, University of Kentucky. His research has focused on social theory and its application to the built urban environment.

BARNEY WARF is Associate Professor of Geography at Kent State University. He has published widely in geography journals. His research interests include both conventional urban and economic geography as well as contemporary social theory. Currently, his work centers around the areas of the service sector, telecommunications, military spending, and postmodernist discourses.

DAVID WILSON is Associate Professor of Geography at the University of Illinois at Urbana-Champaign. His research has focused on urban social theory and the built urban environment. His articles have appeared in the *International Journal of Urban and Regional Research*, *Society and Space*, *Urban Geography*, *Economic Geography*, *Journal of Planning Literature*, *Tidschrift*, *The Professional Geographer*, and elsewhere. He is co-author, with John Jakle, of *Derelict Landscapes: The Wasting of America's Built Environment*.